Meditating Entrepreneurs

CREATING SUCCESS FROM THE STILLNESS WITHIN

HAL GOLDSTEIN

Meditating Press
Fairfield, IA

Visit meditatinge.com/goodies for an ever-growing list of bonuses.

ISBN-13: 978-0-9652187-4-0 (Paperback edition)
ISBN-13: 978-0-9652187-5-7 (Ebook edition)

Book design: George Foster

Photography: Jim Davis, Werner Elmker, *Fairfield Ledger*

Lyrics and music of *Happy Cow* - © 2010 Arthur Lee Land

Audiobook production: Jeffrey Hedquist

Grateful acknowledgment is made to the following for
the use of previously published material:

Fred Gratzon, *The Lazy Way to Success: How to do Nothing and Accomplish Everything*, © 2006 by Soma Press

Ron Bovard, *Windows for the Soul, Revised & Updated*, © 2006 by Wardell Publications, Inc.

Francis Thicke, *A New Vision for Iowa Food and Agriculture*, © 2010 by Sustainability Research Institute, Inc.

Janet Bray Attwood and Chris Attwood, *The Passion Test: The Effortless Path to Discovering your Destiny*, © 2006 by Enlighten Alliances, LLC

Published by Meditating Press
110 N. Court St.
Fairfield, IA 52556
meditatingpress.com
641-472-9595

To my wife Rita, my partner, confidant, and true love

Table of Contents

PART FIVE Selling Knowledge

PART SIX Saving the Planet

INTRODUCTION

*Empowering stories of TM meditators who moved to
rural Iowa for enlightenment and world peace and
created extraordinary businesses from nothing*

I am sitting peacefully in my office, Christmas Eve day 2018, just off the Fairfield, Iowa town square in a remarkable entrepreneurial community.

Thirty-four years ago, my wife Rita and I moved here from the San Francisco Bay area. We came to join several thousand others to practice the Transcendental Meditation® (TM®) technique in large groups for our personal development and to create an influence of peace in the world. Despite these lofty aspirations, we had to find a way to survive.

I wrote this book to share discoveries from those of us who created successful businesses starting from nothing in pre-internet rural Iowa. Our journeys demonstrate that inner peace and outer abundance, self-awareness and material success, can go hand in hand.

I want you to see from reading our stories that anything is possible.

I want you to know that self-awareness, self-development, and living your passion are synergistic, not antithetical, to creating material success.

Simply by reading story after story, I want your mindset to shift from "I can't, and I don't know how" to "I can, and I'll find the way."

It is the book I wish I could have read when I began my company.

Whether you are an entrepreneur or plan to be one, are interested in what it takes to be successful, or want a good read about an extraordinary community, this book will teach and inspire you.

Moving to Iowa

In 1979, Maharishi Mahesh Yogi, the founder of the Transcendental Meditation program at a TM retreat at Amherst, Massachusetts asked us to, "Meditate together at Maharishi International University (MIU) in Fairfield, Iowa and create world peace." He went on to tell us, "You'll be rewarded 10,000 times over spiritually and materially."

Maharishi often spoke as if there were no limitations to life. He based his teaching on the understanding and experience of meditation. He explained that when we practice the TM technique, we experience "pure consciousness," an unbounded reservoir of energy, intelligence, and happiness — the field of all possibilities. Then in our daily life, we can manifest any of those possibilities.

Thousands of meditators like myself experienced greater mental clarity, better health, and more happiness from our daily TM practice. The idea of accelerating our personal development while participating in something that might have far-reaching benefits for the world appealed to us. However, most of us were in our 20s and 30s, many starting families. How would we support ourselves in rural Iowa? We didn't farm, and there were only so many volunteer, room-and-board positions at MIU.

At the time, I had an excellent position as a software engineer at Hewlett Packard (HP) in California's sunny and mild Silicon Valley. A short drive took me to the ocean, San Francisco, or Yosemite. Did I really want to move to the land of corn growing and pig farming, hot summers and cold winters, and a five-hour drive to a major Midwestern city?

Over the subsequent years, many of us abandoned the traditional paths that our lives were taking, trusted our intuition, and moved to Fairfield.

In Fairfield, we started hundreds of small businesses. We did so even though many of us had been anti-establishment hippies who knew nothing about business. Some businesses failed. Others succeeded but stayed small. Still others ended up being sold for hundreds of millions of dollars.

We pioneered inexpensive long-distance phone service, infomercials, and testing for genetically engineered food. My publishing business in 1985 started with writing about small computers, and later about today's smartphones.

Other entrepreneurs restored stained glass, took marathon finish-line photos, brokered oil and gas, designed book covers, taught yoga teachers, supplied products to chimney sweeps, created *People Magazine's* best ice cream of the year, sold incense, made a top birdwatching website, developed a no-money-down real estate course, ran an organic dairy farm, started a home health service, built an assisted living center, produced non-dairy avocado ice cream, sold lingerie, invented waterjet cutting for marble artwork, manufactured essential oil diffusers, provided back-end services for financial planners, created a book marketing company that later sold for $380 million, opened a local used bookstore and café, invented sky ceilings, pioneered solar energy in Iowa, produced radio commercials, and so much more.

Teaching "The Successful Entrepreneur"

I've always loved to teach, and I thought young undergraduates would benefit from hearing about the successes and challenges of those of us who moved to Fairfield and started businesses. I wrote the following to my first February 2012 students at Maharishi University of Management (MUM), formerly Maharishi International University.

> This course will likely change your life.
>
> During these weeks, wonderful, successful people give their time freely. They do so to share what they've learned about starting and running a business. Many will speak of the role that the Transcendental Meditation program played in their success.
>
> I promise, if you are proactive, assimilating the ideas that resonate, the class will stay with you.

I've now taught the course for seven years and hosted over 75 talks. Students tell me the class has changed their lives. I am writing this book to change yours.

Read each of the 15 stories. Absorb how the entrepreneurs think. Notice how inner fulfillment and outer abundance work together.

What we had in common

The guest speakers and I surprised the students by how different we were. Some of us were introverts, and others were extroverts. Some were cautious, and some threw caution to the wind. Despite these differences, we all shared the qualities of enthusiasm, persistence, generosity, service, vision, keeping promises, clear thinking, and the ability to adapt to and take advantage of change.

We also shared the daily practice of the TM technique in which we quieted our minds and experienced pure. Maharishi described pure consciousness as "the source of thought" and "the home of all knowledge."

In the 1970s, the TM organization mostly consisted of college students and recent grads. Despite our youth and inexperience, we ran self-sustaining *TM* Centers. In addition to instructing individual students in the TM technique, we organized conferences and spoke to large audiences. We contacted the U.S. president, governors, members of Congress, chief executive officers, and other leaders to tell them about the Transcendental Meditation technique at a time when meditation was considered strange.

Many of us leveraged the confidence and experience we gained from teaching the TM program to start businesses in Fairfield.

Meditation has become mainstream

Maharishi began teaching the Transcendental Meditation technique in 1959. Since then, many millions throughout the world have learned it. Today, meditation is no longer considered strange. Doctors, psychologists, business people, athletes, and cultural icons recommend it.

Even with all of meditation's popularity, confusion remains. People think that all meditation is the same. Many believe that their mind is too active to meditate, and that they don't have the time or discipline for daily practice.

The Transcendental Meditation technique is unique among the various types of meditation. Even ten-year-olds learn it easily and look forward to their daily practice. The TM technique is not concentration and does not involve focusing the mind. It is not contemplation and does not involve thinking deep thoughts. Rather, the Transcendental

Meditation technique is a simple, natural, effortless process. A thoroughly-trained, certified TM teacher provides personal instruction over four consecutive days.

Hundreds of peer-reviewed scientific studies have verified that people who practice the TM technique enjoy less stress, better health, more clarity, and greater happiness. Brain pattern studies show a unique synchronicity during and after TM practice.

The Beatles learned the TM technique from Maharishi in the late 1960s, which generated a lot of publicity. To this day, Paul McCartney and Ringo Starr perform at benefit concerts that raise money for inner-city children to learn the TM technique through the David Lynch Foundation.

Director David Lynch's foundation sponsors Transcendental Meditation-based programs for underserved youth, veterans, at-risk women's groups, Native Americans, homeless shelters, and prisons. Other popular meditating entertainers who appear at David Lynch Foundation events include Jerry Seinfeld, Katy Perry, Tom Hanks, Katie Couric, and Hugh Jackman.

Senator Tom Harkin, comedian Jim Carrey, former Japanese prime minister Dr. Yukio Hatoyama, and Congressman Tim Ryan practice the TM technique and have given Maharishi University of Management commencement speeches. Other well-known TM meditators include hedge fund billionaire Ray Dalio, Tim Ferris, George Lucas, Clint Eastwood, Russell Brand, George Stephanopoulos, Sheryl Crow, Arianna Huffington, Michael J. Fox, Stevie Wonder, Joe Namath, Mike Love, Dr. Oz, Ellen DeGeneres, the late Kurt Vonnegut, Arthur Ashe, and Buckminster Fuller.

After learning the TM technique, Oprah Winfrey had all her staff learn. She visited Fairfield for an hour-long TV special about the town, the TM program, and the K-12 Maharishi School.

To find a qualified TM instructor in your area, visit www.tm.org. You can also find more information about the TM technique in Appendix B.

All the profits from this book will be donated to TM-related organizations.

How I wrote this book

I tell each Fairfield meditating entrepreneur invited to my class, "You have about an hour to share with students the most important lessons you learned on your entrepreneurial journey." Every year, about a dozen entrepreneurs speak. Each talk seems to build upon the previous one; each one more inspiring, compelling, and wise than the last; each one making it seem more possible for students to start and run businesses.

All who have heard the speakers feel that the stories and practical wisdom deserve a wider audience. That's why I decided to write this book, which I based on the transcriptions from recorded video of the class.

The informal setting of the class meant plenty of give and take with the students. Speakers jumped from one part of their story to another with lots of wisdom interspersed. In each chapter, I translate the informal and sometimes meandering spoken word into a tighter, more linear, written expression while trying not to lose the essence of the entrepreneur's voice or message.

To be true to each entrepreneur's voice, enthusiasm, and way of thinking, I wrote the book in first person as if I were the entrepreneur. I found getting inside and retelling the story from the entrepreneur's perspective inspiring and absorbing.

Each chapter begins with a brief third-person introduction. Three sections follow, each more universal in scope than the previous.

Journey — the story of how the entrepreneur began
and evolved the business

Wisdom — lessons learned along the way

Spirit — the essence of the entrepreneur's success and wisdom

Each chapter ends with Twelve Tweets — short summaries of the key ideas, and Ponder — important questions for the reader to consider.

When done, I sent a draft to each entrepreneur and incorporated feedback before a final edit. A big thank you to the featured entrepreneurs for sharing their wonderful, inspiring stories and allowing me to hijack their voice. Apologies ahead of time to entrepreneurs and readers for any inaccuracies, lack of clarity, and inadequate representation of the entrepreneur's voice.

Each story differs and stands alone. When all the stories are read together, common themes emerge, knowledge increases, and inspiration grows.

While the entrepreneurs and their enterprises continue, their stories in the book stop in late 2018.

What this book is and is not

While I consider this book most practical, it does not teach marketing, accounting, or operations skills from an MBA perspective. Rather, through the stories and wisdom of entrepreneurs, this book demonstrates what it takes to be successful.

Although the experience, understanding, and purpose of the Transcendental Meditation technique play a central role in this book, the book is not about TM or how to practice it. It is about what it takes to start and run a successful business — and the role the TM technique can play in it.

How the book is organized

Fifteen of over 200 possible stories about Fairfield entrepreneurs appear in this volume of *Meditating Entrepreneurs*. My selection criteria were arbitrary and based on who had spoken to my class twice, the quality of the transcripts, and my inclination when it was time to choose the next story. It's not possible to rank the 200 stories. In my classes, different talks resonated with different students. You'll likely have the same experience as you read the book's 15 stories.

FOLLOWING THEIR BLISS

I begin with Fred Gratzon and Janet Attwood in Section 1: "Following their bliss." On the surface, they have little in common. The consummate entrepreneur, Fred served his Great Midwestern ice cream at a White House lawn picnic to Ronald and Nancy Reagan and to Congress members. Later Fred founded a telecommunications company that went public. Janet, author of the best-selling *The Passion Test*, runs an organization that has helped hundreds of thousands of people find their life purpose. Fred and Janet see having fun and finding their passion as primary. They take expansive views of what is possible, and they bring lightness and joy to their work. They achieved success by inspiring others with their vision and play.

SERVING THE COMMUNITY

The next section, "Serving the community," looks at the unique town of Fairfield, Iowa. In "The Entrepreneurial Mayor" chapter, Ed Malloy describes how he helped unify a traditional agricultural community with its new non-traditional TM meditating citizenry by having both sides plan the town's future together. His leadership helped transform a quiet, rural, Iowa town of 10,000 into an entrepreneurial, artistic, multi-cultural, sustainable, and entertainment Mecca. Betsy Howland arrived in Fairfield at a time when there was no place in town for TM meditators to congregate. Betsy describes how she and her three daughters used the power of intention to create a community gathering spot called Revelations that features healthy homemade meals and used books.

TURNING ART INTO BUSINESSES

The creative energy of the TM community drew many artists to Fairfield. In "Turning art into businesses," you'll read about how George Foster, Ron Bovard, and Jim Davis applied their talents to create some of Fairfield's most successful companies. George shares how he transformed himself from starving artist to a leading independent book cover designer through service, single-mindedness, and simplicity. Well-known for his gallery exhibits, artist Ron Bovard became fascinated with stained glass and with the Renaissance model of a community of artists. Combining those interests, Ron founded Bovard Studio to design, repair, and install stained glass throughout the United States. Jim Davis started taking photographs when he was young. His company uses photography to memorialize the personal triumphs of marathon runners and high school and college graduates. He found partners who moved the company forward while he continued with the photography he loved.

MAKING BUSINESSES WORK

"Making businesses work" is about the behind-the-scenes infrastructure necessary for entrepreneurial success. Steven Winn, Monica Hadley, and Peter Huggins have each been able to take great ideas and operationalize them. Unlike many of their operations-oriented peers, they understood their importance to out-of-the-box, big-picture-thinking entrepreneurs. They leveraged their worth to form partnerships in various entrepreneurial ventures Steven made, lost, and made millions of dollars again by partnering with marketing geniuses and grounding them with efficient, effective business fundamentals. Monica has partnerships in five businesses and two non-profits. She recognizes entrepreneurial talent and great ideas and then provides the structure to make the businesses and non-profits work. Peter got his start as a "fixer," rescuing an operation weighed down by fraud and difficult people. He applied his secret sauce philosophy of "people come first" to bring success to everything he undertook.

SELLING KNOWLEDGE

Eva Norlyk Smith and I created businesses by "Selling knowledge." Eva uses the internet to provide training for Yoga Teachers. She leans heavily on her professional writing ability and discusses the value of developing a superpower skill. Through my magazine publishing company, I helped HP, Microsoft, and Apple mobile computers users make full use of their devices. I discuss the power of integrity and of uplifting others.

SAVING THE PLANET

Finally, visionaries Francis Thicke and Amy and Troy Van Beek are dedicated to "Saving the planet" through sustainable practices. Soil scientist Francis Thicke explains how he turned his organic dairy farm into a 736-acre experimental lab from which others can learn. The Van Beeks operate one of the largest solar energy companies in Iowa. Amy, a second-generation Fairfield meditating entrepreneur and an artist, brings her visual talents to marketing and building construction. Troy, a former Navy Seal, leads through his inspirational vision of eliminating war through the creation of abundant, inexpensive, renewable energy.

Concluding sections

The final chapter, "Conclusion — Inner Peace, Outer Abundance" pulls together what the 15 entrepreneurs taught us, what they had in common, and ten specific ways to develop "entrepreneurial muscles."

Appendix A provides more information about the Fairfield meditating entrepreneurs who are featured in and referred to in this book.

Appendix B is all about the Transcendental Meditation technique and related programs. In this section, you learn what the TM technique is, how it differs from other forms of meditation, and how to learn it. The appendix details information about Maharishi University of Management and about the programs of the David Lynch Foundation for inner city schools and PTSD sufferers. Appendix C concludes with a glossary of TM terminology.

In addition to the links referenced throughout the book, Appendix D provides an ever-growing list of written, audio, and video bonuses, which can be found at www.meditatinge.com/goodies.

PART ONE

Following Their Bliss

Fred Gratzon

Janet Attwood

Fred Gratzon
THE LAZY ENTREPRENEUR

Through the years, I've admired Fred Gratzon for his generosity, humor, out-of-the-box thinking, and meteoric success. Keep an open mind as you take in Fred's unique philosophy of success. You will read of Fred's incredible journey, from serving Ronald and Nancy Reagan his company's ice cream on the White House lawn to launching a publicly traded telecommunication company from a spare bedroom. You'll read several banker stories that defy logic, and you'll learn Fred's unique, counter-intuitive "Lazy Way" philosophy. (Hint: Fred is a big fan of Tom Sawyer and how he got friends to whitewash Aunt Polly's fence.)

After leaving his business adventures, Fred wrote *The Lazy Way to Success* and *The Mentally Quiet Athlete*. I have used some of Fred's expressions and descriptions from *The Lazy Way* in this chapter. He is now working on a musical about *The Lazy Way*. Fred serves as a trustee of Maharishi University of Management.

At first, I thought Fred was just having fun, praising laziness and dissing hard work. I worked hard and didn't appreciate lazy employees. Then, the light dawned. My work was only hard when I internalized challenges, deadlines, and money problems. Success came not from misery but from the play of solving problems with the team and making a product customers loved.

Enjoy Fred's sense of fun as he describes starting from nothing and creating two companies worth millions of dollars.

JOURNEY: From America's best ice cream to public telecom company

THANK YOU, MAHARISHI AND *TM*

I've never been able to hold down a job — I normally get fired or run away screaming. The longest job I had lasted two months as a lifeguard, and all I did was sit. I even got fired from a civil service job, which almost requires an act of Congress to lose.

I am anti-authoritarian and lazy with no marketable skills. I have a short attention span and despise routine work. In short, I am unemployable.

I never wanted to trade my freedom or time to make money. Fortunately, Maharishi and TM came along. I fell in love with the Transcendental Meditation technique and teaching it to others. It is all I wanted to do, and that's what I did in the 70s.

In 1979, Maharishi invited people to move to Fairfield, Iowa. I didn't want to go since I thought teaching people Transcendental Meditation was the greatest thing on earth and, in Fairfield, with so many other TM teachers there, I wouldn't be able to compete.

But Maharishi made moving to Fairfield and being a part of an expanding community of TM meditators seem irresistible, so I went. There, I became an entrepreneur to avoid getting a job.

BEST ICE CREAM IN AMERICA

The Fairfield white-sugar economy

I soon realized if I didn't want to starve, I needed to start a business. Upon moving to Fairfield in 1979, I noticed that white sugar was the basis of many early businesses. Someone made brownies; another made chocolate chip cookies; someone else made cakes; and everyone seemed to be selling a dessert to the guy next to him.

I'm from the East Coast where they sell great ice cream. The local ice cream was terrible. In the midst of this white-sugar economy, I thought, *I'll make ice cream!*

The first question you might ask: "Fred, do you know how to make ice cream?"

I didn't have a clue. I had no money, no business experience, and didn't know how to make ice cream. But I was starting an ice cream company.

I planned to make it using a small ice cream maker, a freezer, and a refrigerator, and market it as homemade. I would sell it to people in town. Then someone explained that a normal freezer isn't cold enough — ice crystals would form in the ice cream giving it a coarse taste.

In my research, I heard of a man in Texas who sold used ice-cream-making equipment. I called and explained my idea. He said he had the big freezers, the little batch freezers, and kettles — everything I needed to set up a small parlor and sell commercial grade ice cream.

I asked him, "How much is it going to cost?"

He replied, "I'll sell it with everything you need for 7,000 dollars."

I moped around for a couple hours, my dream of an ice cream company melting on the spot. If I had 7,000 dollars, I wouldn't need to start a business.

Then I thought, *I'll get investors!* I hand-wrote my first business plan on a yellow legal pad. It stated that if you invested in my ice cream company, you'd get a percentage of the profits and a lifetime supply of ice cream.

Finding investors

First, I approached a sophisticated, well-established, venerable, solid, conservative financial institution to invest in my ice cream company. I asked my mother.

"Mom, will you invest in my ice cream company?"

My mom is probably like your mom. She answered, "My son, my glorious son, everything you do is great. Of course, I'll invest in your ice cream company." And she agreed to send me a check for $2,000.

$2,000 down, five to go. Who's next? Dad! "Dad, will you invest in my ice cream company?"

My father is probably like your father. He said, "Are you nuts? You've already suckered your mother for $2,000. We're done! Find someone else."

I worked my friends. It took a few weeks, but I raised $7,500 dollars. With a loan for another $2,500, I had $10,000.

My first act as Chief Executive Officer of The Great Midwestern Ice Cream Company was to send the Texas man a check for $7,000. Did I know this Texas man, what I was buying, or how to set up and operate the machine once it arrived? Not a scintilla of an idea. I didn't know a thing.

Two weeks later, a moving van arrived, filled to the brim with shiny stainless steel stuff — motors, freezers, boxes, wires, lights, mixers. The two movers asked, "Where do you want this sir?" I had no idea. It's not like you can just plug the ice cream machine into the wall. This thing was heavy-duty industrial, with three-phase electricity, and what the heck is three-phase electricity?

We built the Fairfield community by helping each other. I had a friend who knew plumbing and electricity. Along with about 4,000 calls to the Texas man regarding hooking this thing into that, and what's this pipe for, it took about two weeks to set everything up.

November 8, 1979 was a red-letter day — that evening I made my first ice cream. It was spectacular, the best ice cream ever made by a human being. If you tasted it, you would have been on your knees thanking God for the experience.

Expanding to Iowa City

I started an ice cream company at the beginning of a cold, brutal, icy Iowa winter.

As much as the community loved its desserts, who thinks of ice cream in the winter? Nobody! I had no customers. My suppliers were asking for C.O.D., and I had no C(ash). After two months, I was losing my shirt. At the same time, I was obsessed with one thought: *Expand!*

Friends went, "Are you nuts? Maybe it's your diet of vanilla ice cream and maraschino cherries. You have no customers!"

Where would I expand? The answer: Iowa City with 25,000 students at the University of Iowa.

The night before heading up to Iowa City, somewhere I'd never been, I tried to figure out how much money I needed. No research. There was no internet, and I wasn't smart enough to get a book or call someone up.

More sophisticated this time, I typed instead of handwriting the business plan. Seven pages. Granted there was only one paragraph per page, but I ran out of things to say. I guessed at a number for the bank loan. I borrowed someone's car and drove up to Iowa City at the end of December. It was cold and awful and the snow was up to my eyebrows.

I walked up to the receptionist at Iowa State Bank and said, "I am here to borrow $23,900."

"What's it for, sir?"

"I want to build an ice cream parlor here in Iowa City."

She said, "You should see the commercial loan officer, but he won't be back until tomorrow."

I said, "I just drove 60 miles in the snow, and I've got to talk to somebody."

"Maybe the Senior Vice President will speak with you."

She took me into his office. And there sat an old guy with those half-reading glasses on the end of his nose.

It took him about three seconds to read my business plan. He looked over his desk. "Son, you've got no experience. Your business shows no operating profit. You have no collateral. You have no equity."

I flunked every reason why a bank gives people loans. It felt like bullets right to the heart, and I was on the verge of tears. He added, "Besides, for what you want to do, $23,900 is not nearly enough."

I really wanted to build an ice cream store in Iowa City, and this guy shot me out of the water. I was thinking, *There are more fish in the sea, more banks in Iowa City* — as if another bank would tell me something different.

With limited time in Iowa City, I cut to the chase. "Are you interested?"

He thought for a second and he said, "Yeah, I'm very interested." He didn't lend me $23,900. He lent me $35,000.

It took $55,000 to build the Iowa City store. The extra $20,000 came from plumbers, electricians, carpenters, and restaurant supply houses. I ran up a debt with these guys.

"Fred, where is the money?" I would tap dance wildly and say to these contractors, "Give me another month, and I can pay a little bit. In the meantime, can I give you some ice cream?"

"Okay, yeah, you can have another month." It was good ice cream.

Years later, I became friends with the bank's senior vice president. I said, "Dick, why did you lend me the money?"

He said, "Because of your enthusiasm. Besides, it was my birthday, and you were bringing me ice cream."

Isn't that cool?

People Magazine's "Best Ice Cream in America"

Five years later, in 1984, *People Magazine* sponsored a competition to find the best ice cream in America.

I wasn't aware of the competition. Fortunately, a Kansas City writer did her homework well. She called the librarian at the University of Missouri to ask if there was any good local ice cream. A recent graduate from the University of Iowa, the librarian said, "Forget Columbia. Check out the Great Midwestern Ice Cream Company in Iowa City."

The writer called me without introducing herself. She asked how far we distributed our ice cream. I told her that sometimes someone buys an ice cream cone and walks around the block. Then she explained the contest and said, "But I don't know if I can include you because you are not in my region."

I told her, "If you don't include us, you'll end up with the second-best ice cream in America."

She called her editor, who said our ice cream could enter. I FedExed ice cream to her using dry ice in a Styrofoam box. We easily won the Kansas City contest.

We and 30 other regional winners sent ice cream to the Time-Life building in New York. A group of movie stars, athletes, and food critics judged. *People Magazine* declared us the best ice cream in America.

The floodgates opened. The world's hungry appeared at our doorstep. Celebrities and politicians came and formed long lines. It was great.

I learned that public relations is smoke and mirrors. I took the *People Magazine* article and showed it to other media outlets, milking it for all it was worth. It snowballed. *Fortune, Forbes, Newsweek, The New York Times, The Wall Street Journal,* and many other magazines and newspapers wrote us up. *The Today Show, Good Morning America, CBS Morning News, NBC Evening News,* and countless other TV and radio shows interviewed me.

Reporters would ask me what made our ice cream so good. Haagen Daas and Ben & Jerry's — the fancy French style ice creams — both use egg yolks as an emulsifier. I never liked the yolk's sulfury taste, the way it overshadowed the delicate flavors of vanilla and fruit. Using a natural emulsifier, our ice cream was as rich, dense, and gorgeous as the other premium ice creams, but had a cleaner, fresher dairy taste.

I told the press that ice cream comes from cows, not chickens, and Iowa has the best cows in the world.

All the publicity also got me invited to the White House. Twice.

Serving Ronald Reagan and Michael Jordan

The assistant coach of the U.S. Olympic basketball Dream Team that included Michael Jordan and Patrick Ewing tasted the ice cream and asked me to serve it to them. First Lady, Nancy Reagan, tried the ice cream and insisted it be served at White House functions.

The White House invited us to serve the ice cream at the President's annual picnic for members of Congress and their families. On the south lawn in front of the White House, there were tents, the Marine Band, and fireworks. I invited my friends, TM teachers in Washington

DC, to help serve the ice cream to the senators and congressmen. I wore my suit and tie and worked the crowd.

Someone told me that the President would walk right in front if you stood there. We trailed Nancy Reagan to the buffet line. The President went first, then Nancy Reagan, followed by my wife Shelley and me.

My wife and I had been married two months. I had now taken my wife to the White House and met the President, a hard act to follow.

Getting fired from the company I founded

In 1988, I got fired. I can't keep a job, even when it's my company!

We were the first packaged ice cream to be sold at Bloomingdales. United Airlines served our ice cream to its first-class customers. We had eight franchise stores and won awards for packaging, truck design, and franchise store design. We got lots of publicity and all the Iowa primary presidential candidates came to the store to get their pictures taken.

However, the ice cream company was under-capitalized. As good as the ice cream was, to expand and compete with Ben & Jerry's and Haagan Das in major supermarkets, we needed money. So, to get a million dollars of investment capital, I gave up majority ownership and signed a non-compete agreement.

Then I got fired. Pushed out.

I had been married for just over a year and had a one-month-old son. Now, I was without income. I had made major financial decisions based on a salary that I thought would never go away. Savings had gone for a down-payment on a house and now mortgage payments were due. We had purchased furniture and other necessities on loan. But, I couldn't go back into the ice cream business because of the non-compete.

Further, I was embarrassed. I had built a factory in Fairfield, invited my friends to move to town and had given them jobs. I was friends with the governors of Iowa, Michigan, and Illinois, and had been invited twice to the White House. I hung out with the Olympic basketball team. I got my picture in *Forbes* and was on *The Today Show*.

Getting fired from the company I started was heartbreaking. I was bitter and hurt. I thought, *I'm the one who fixed the toilets when they overflowed at the Iowa City store. The guys who manipulated me out of my business hadn't done that.*

Getting a million-dollar investment is a great thing. However, when you get more than dollars, you get the investor's karma. If the money comes from a sleazy place, then you get that sleaze too, and that influences the business.

The bitterness didn't last.

HOW I MADE AND LOST $260 MILLION LAUNCHING A PUBLICLY TRADED TELECOMMUNICATIONS COMPANY

Selling cheap long distance

I didn't know what to do or how to support my family. I was moping on the sofa, when someone told me about a way I could get long distance phone call discounts for people through AT&T and sell them at a profit. In 1988, calling New York or California from Iowa could cost 50 cents a minute. By brokering discounted long-distance minutes, I could help people save money and make a living at the same time.

Knowing nothing about telecommunications, but desperate, I committed $180,000 that I didn't have to AT&T. If I sold enough long distance minutes in three months, I wouldn't have to pay the commitment.

I went to my friends in town — will you be on my long-distance service? People knew and liked me and were embarrassed by my humiliation. Out of sympathy, they signed up left and right for inexpensive long-distance calling.

That business, which I named Telegroup, became the largest employer in our county. It grew to employ 1,100 people worldwide, had an additional 1,200 independent sales reps, and serviced 250,000 customers in more countries than any other telecommunication company.

Yet, we almost didn't make it.

Can you grow too fast?

We were out of money again, having already maxed out the bank's extended credit from the previous month.

We were adding customers much faster than projected. An ongoing cash flow crisis ensued, since our suppliers demanded payment before we could collect from our customers. Plus, we needed more employees to handle the growth, which meant more training, more desks, more computers, more phone lines. We burned through cash.

Our primary vendor was threatening to cut us off. We needed $500,000. Art, from the bank, told my colleagues, "No way. No more money." We didn't have the weeks and months necessary to court new investors.

I called Art. He told me the bank couldn't loan us more money until we could substantiate our position. Unfortunately, our accounting system was a mess and months away from being upgraded.

I told Art, "It isn't only the accounting system. Everything is strained to the breaking point — people, office space, phone systems, computer network, parking. Since our database software can't handle the load, we've divided customers into two separate databases, a nightmare for customer service. We started the company on a shoestring, and those early choices are killing us. Even if we had known the business would take off, we didn't have the money back then to do things differently. We're working on a comprehensive solution, but it takes time."

"Fred," he sighed, "Are you making money?"

"I don't know," I replied honestly. "With the accounting system a mess, we can't tell for sure."

I pondered the tragic irony that my business would fail because it was too successful.

And then the universe must have hiccuped; God must have shot an air ball. I don't know what caused it, but this slicked-down, big time, urban banker said something completely uncharacteristic of the linear, logical, analytical, left-hemispheric world of his profession. "Fred," Art asked, "does it *feel* like you're making money?"

In my experience, mercantile-dom worships the left-brain hemisphere with such fervor that any expressions from the spatial, emotional, intuitive right-brain hemisphere are demeaned, discredited, and dismissed as having no value. That is a problem for me since the right hemisphere is where I have set up shop. My left one is, to be charitable, not very alert. No amount of schooling, vitamins, or flagellation, self-imposed or administered, has been able to wake it up.

My drowsy intellect notwithstanding, I recognize a hanging curveball in my wheelhouse when I see one. I whacked that pitch into the left center field bleachers.

"Well, it feels like we are making money," I replied, my moist eyes glistening with fresh, heart-felt tears.

Again, there was a long pause. I heard Art exhaling resignedly. "I need some numbers," he said. "So just send me something. Anything! Even if it is on the back of an envelope."

I thanked him profusely, sent him some numbers, and promised we would never put him in such an untenable position again.

Three weeks passed. We were out of money again. We needed $750,000 to continue. My colleagues called Art, who just screamed at them. I called Art. "No, no, no, no, a thousand times no! I told you it was the last time. I can NOT go to the loan committee again. And I won't."

"I know you can't," I said, despair flooding my body. "We don't know where to turn, and you are our last hope. Do you have any advice for us? Can you at least point us in the right direction?"

There was a long stretch of silence. I heard computer keys being clicked.

When he finally came back on the phone, his mood had mollified. "Why don't you borrow it from yourself?"

I said, "None of us have that kind of money."

"I mean from your business. I just checked. Your average daily cash balance never dips below $775,000. Since that is what you need, why don't you just borrow it from yourself?"

"How?" I asked naively.

"By managing your cash more tightly," he responded.

Appearing hopelessly stupid — a sure way of scaring off what little confidence Art had in me, I asked, "I don't know what an average daily cash balance is or what it means to manage cash more tightly."

He said, "You just have to manage your cash more tightly," with a hint-hint-nudge-nudge emphasis on his words.

"But we've already written checks against that money. It's just that those checks haven't cleared yet."

"But if you manage your cash more tightly, you'd have the money you need," he said impatiently.

"Are you suggesting we kite checks?" I asked in astonishment.

"Absolutely not. I'm simply suggesting that you manage your cash more tightly," enunciating the last five words slowly and deliberately.

From my limited point of view, I would be bouncing checks. From the bank's perspective, used to dealing with large institutions that carefully manage their cash flow for maximum efficiency, it was business as usual.

I asked a clarifying question. "Let's say, hypothetically, while managing our cash more tightly, we accidentally slip up and a check clears sooner than we planned, and we end up writing a check that exceeds our cash balance by say—"

"By, say, $250,000," Art interrupted. About to say $25, I was blindsided.

"Okay, let's say we bounce a check for $250,000 more than we have in our account, will you cover it?" I asked.

"Yes," he responded.

"But we'd have to pay interest on it, right?" I assumed.

"No," Art said.

"We'd have to pay some kind of penalty, right?"

"You'd have to pay an overdraft fee," he explained patiently.

"How much is that?" I asked girding myself against what was sure to be an astronomical figure that would make managing one's cash more tightly both too risky and impractical, given our slipshod accounting system.

"Thirty-five dollars," Art said.

"Thirty-five dollars!" I shrieked. "We bounce a check for $250,000, and we have to pay $35?"

"That's right."

My brain swooned with the implications. "How many times, hypothetically speaking of course, could we bounce a check of this magnitude before the bank got irritated with us?"

"Let me put it this way," Art answered, "I wouldn't make a regular habit of it."

Art, incensed with us for wanting to come through the front door with another loan, now enthusiastically waved us down the alley and through the back door. To this day, I shake my head in disbelief. If it weren't for the integrated hemispheric functioning of Art's brain (and heart), we'd have died ingloriously in mid-sprint.

His heaven-sent strategy of managing cash tightly gave us enough money, time, and flexibility to continue operations and get our financial house in order. Obtaining a mezzanine investment of 20 million dollars meant that we would not need further loans before eventually taking the company public.

I think my guileless approach in discussing the business convinced Art to give us more chances. I never tried to hide our many warts. I suspect my frankness was refreshingly rare given all the spin and hand-waving he received from other business people.

$338 million in sales and going public

In our ninth year, with annual sales of $338 million, we had become a sophisticated international long-distance player. In 1995, *Inc. Magazine* had Telegroup as second in their list of the 500 fastest growing companies in America. On July 9, 1997, we took Telegroup public.

Telegroup Announces Initial Public Offering

Fairfield, Iowa — Telegroup, Inc. (NASDAQ: TGRP) today announced its initial public offering of 4,000,000 shares of common stock at a public offering price of $10.00

per share. All of the shares were issued and sold by the Company. Smith Barney Inc. was the lead-manager of the underwriting group, and Alex. Brown & Sons and Cowen & Company served as co-managers.

Telegroup, Inc. (the "Company") is a leading global alternative provider of international telecommunications services and offers a broad range of discounted international and enhanced telecommunications services to over 200,000 small- and medium-sized business and residential customers in more than 170 countries. Telegroup has achieved its significant international market penetration by developing what it believes to be one of the most comprehensive global sales, marketing and customer services organizations in the telecommunications industry.

Stepping Down and Collapse

Telegroup, the largest employer in home base Jefferson County, had a huge team of programmers in Iowa City and major customer service centers in Germany, France, and Australia.

In July of 1998, heeding Maharishi's personal advice, I retired as Chairman. I stayed on the board and retained an executive position and office. One month after my retirement, the board made an awful acquisition. Our stock price plummeted. My net worth at that time was $260 million, but what goes up comes down. By 2000, thanks to Telegroup's decision and a credit squeeze, the company collapsed.

Fortunately, my wife, having gone through the Great Midwestern Ice Cream experience, had squirreled away my salary during the Telegroup years. Although I viewed my salary as chump change, my wife had faithfully saved enough for us to live comfortably moving forward.

Two Books and a Musical

Years later, after stepping down as CEO of Telegroup, I was quizzed by Craig Pearson, Executive Vice President of Maharishi University of

Management: "How hard do you have to work to be successful?"

My answer shocked him: "It takes no work at all. Hard work is a fraud."

After hearing my answer, which I discuss later in this chapter, he convinced me to write a book, which became *The Lazy Way to Success — How to do Nothing and Accomplish Everything.* Using a related theme, I later wrote *The Mentally Quiet Athlete.* I am now at play turning *The Lazy Way to Success* into a musical.

WISDOM: Commit. Collaborate. Play.

FIND YOUR CALLING

We all have a purpose in life and are generously endowed with the talent to fulfill it. Our calling provides the greatest possibility for growth, success, happiness, and contribution to the world.

How do we figure out our calling? Joseph Campbell, scholar of world mythology, gave us succinct advice: "Follow your bliss!"

Look to where you naturally excel, where things go easily, where you feel the most passion, where you get the breaks. If you notice even the slightest glimmer of passion, there's smoke. So, pour on the gasoline! You know you are on the right track when the activity gives you pleasure, when it feels natural, comfortable and right, and when it provides meaning and a sense of mission.

I had two companies that each ended a decade after starting them. Some might view that as failure. I see it as success.

Even if a business doesn't achieve its vision, its real value is in the ultimate calling — personal evolution. I look at business as a playground, a way of growing personally. As a 1960s hippie, I once viewed business as superficial and a waste of time. Once involved in business, I saw business as an art project, a creative undertaking. A businessman must integrate product development, finance, marketing, legalities, management, planning, fundraising, and human resources, all while turning a profit. That's the ultimate creative endeavor.

I was able to evolve only so much in my nine years at Great Midwestern. A hundred times bigger, Telegroup offered huge and wonderful lessons. The reason we walk this planet is not to get rich or manage 20 franchise stores or a big factory. It is to become enlightened. Everything else is just an illusion.

Commitment creates miracles

It can be scary to have a vision, but it is also exhilarating. I would stand on one side of a chasm knowing I had to leap across to continue growing the endeavor. I saw the risks — lost money, failure, wasted time, and embarrassment — but I also saw the bliss, the quantum leap in fulfillment.

In my businesses, I took the leap when the love was there, and I followed my bliss. Landing on the other side: miracles! Within days, even hours, nature rushed in and endowed the endeavor with marvelous good fortune.

Most people back off. They either quit altogether or stay in limbo, dilettanting, dabbling, and going nowhere. They later say, "I could have been great if only . . ."

Commitment comes from following your bliss and leads to nature's support. Commitment is just nature's price of admission as she weeds out the weenies and prunes the pretenders.

With commitment comes good luck and with good luck comes more bliss and with more bliss comes more commitment. The whole cycle continues until there is complete support from nature. I have gotten to a point where I find good luck an absolutely dependable, reliable feature in daily life.

At the start, how do I create that inner fire necessary for commitment?

I start with a vision that inspires me and addresses one or more of my passions. No sweat, no effort, no strain, no pain, no pressure, no aggravation, no commute, no bosses, no deadlines, no distractions, no work. Just relaxing with a quiet desire. For days I play with my imagination making a million starts and restarts, adjusting, tweaking and refining the goal. I enjoy the dreams and don't get impatient or try to force anything.

The closer I get to creating the vision of what I want to accomplish, the more the juices flow. When those juices reach a critical mass, the next step is automatic. I can't wait to put the pieces together.

Apparent barriers to entry such as money, knowledge, experience, or formidable competition do not deter me. When the vision inspires, the activity required to fulfill the goals becomes irresistible.

Form a team and have fun

Now comes the coolest part. In every case, I have found that my vision attracts people with the necessary skills who want to join the fun. When you add creative, talented people to the mix, the project becomes even more fun and alluring, which attracts more talent, which makes it more fun, which attracts more people.

Then, while doing a lot of cheerleading, my "job" reverts to relaxing and dreaming of ways to make it even bigger and better. I noticed early on the fun of collaboration at Great Midwestern Ice Cream. From that experience, I decided I always wanted to be on a team with creative people. I don't know finance, don't know law, don't know technology, and have no marketable skills. My secret — find smart people, put them on the team, and churn them like crazy.

Collaboration at fast-growth Telegroup was glorious. My partner, Cliff Reese, had perfect college boards. He's that kind of smart. I'm not. But we complemented each other. With a spirit of love and trust, we evolved solutions greater than what either us could have come up with independently.

My friend, Lawrence Sheaff, surprised me by agreeing to illustrate my book, *The Lazy Way to Success*. I knew only of Lawrence's formal and classical designs from his work with Maharishi, creating graphics for books and conferences for TM organizations worldwide. I wanted something edgy and weird, where the reader could open any page and be treated to an illustration or cartoon.

We pitched each other ideas and soon one of us came up with an idea that stimulated the other. Lawrence might say, "Yeah, yeah, yeah, and the cartoon figure can do this." Sparks flew, and we roared with laughter. It was so much fun.

Team building is about fun, love, and trust. Always do right by each other. Never allow backstabbing and criticizing. With positive, collective, and creative energy, it can become explosive, like rocket fuel. Any small crack between people on the feeling level must be attended to immediately.

If it starts to crack, then the whole thing falls apart. When it involves lots of money, people can easily get corrupted by greed and power. When cracks happened at the feeling level at both Great Midwestern and Telegroup, it got worse and worse.

Those cracks contrasted with the joy and energy that took place in the collaboration building.

Lead by turning work into play

For punishment, Aunt Polly had Tom Sawyer whitewash a fence. Tom's friends came to watch and tease him. Tom ignored the taunts and with enthusiasm began whitewashing the fence. Tom conveyed his good fortune so convincingly, his friends wanted to be a part. They paid Tom apples, toy soldiers, and other booty for a turn at the fence.

Tom got the job done many times better than Aunt Polly would have settled for. He made a glorious profit without lifting a finger, making the task seem irresistible. That's inspired leadership.

At Telegroup, I tried to make it a wonderful environment on every level. If you talk to former Telegroup employees, they will say it was the best job they ever had and wish they could be there again. Good leaders create a fun-filled, creative, environment of freedom and responsibility. That environment allows people to express themselves, be passionate, and grow personally. And in such an atmosphere individual talent takes flight.

A person's passion for a project produces the results. It is not an authority figure barking orders but a leader following the golden rule. I never wanted to be bossed and didn't boss anyone else. I created an opportunity and said, "Here's the job. You want to do it? Fine. Have fun."

Good leaders create an inspired vision and sell that vision with enthusiasm. Leaders celebrate achievement and create heroes, cheering joyously and unabashedly. How much fun you have accomplishing it together matters more than the actual project. It comes down to enthusiasm. The more passionate you are, the more irresistible your project will be.

Sincere concern for the customer is the secret of sales. The secret of being a great boss is the same — make sure employees know that you are there for them, not the other way around.

High productivity and harmonious social interaction begin with a strong sense of self. When people are nervous and afraid, they don't think clearly or intelligently. The best leader makes people feel good about themselves. If you ask someone to dig a ditch six feet long, and he digs one foot, you praise him for the one foot. Period.

There is no limit to how lavish your appreciation can be if it is sincere. Phony praise never cuts it.

Money comes from doing what you love

We have no control over how much money comes from our activity. No matter how much we think we need money, a money-only focus retards our progress and drains our power, and any money that comes in is pedestrian and incomplete. When we are true to ourselves and do what we love, money flows naturally.

There's no real difference between having lots of money and not having it. And yes, it's easy to pay bills when you have it.

At Telegroup's peak, my net worth was 260 million dollars. Telegroup's failing bummed me, but not terribly so. Obscenely rich or not rich, I noticed that inside I was the same guy. Any apparent difference was an illusion. Yesterday, I wore a gold shirt and, today, a blue shirt with holes. The shirt changed, but I stayed the same.

Illusion or not, I've been without money and with lots of money. I prefer lots of money!

You need only so much to live comfortably. How many houses and pairs of cashmere socks do you need? The reason to make a lot of money is to do wonderful things with it; such joy and blessings come from giving it away.

SPIRIT: Have fun — hard work is a fraud

MOTHER NATURE IS ONE LAZY MAMA

Displeased, Dad bellowed. "Someone has to hold a gun to your head for you to work. Then, when you have no other choice, you work harder trying to make the job easier than if you just did the work. You'll never get ahead with that attitude!"

Throughout the incredible success of Great Midwestern and Telegroup, I never for a second changed that attitude. My workaholic colleagues to this day accuse me of being lazy, always looking for ways to avoid work, always wanting to have fun.

I readily and proudly confess my guilt.

The very attributes my dad and other like-minded souls condemned as character flaws have proven to be the rocket fuel to achieving stratospheric success. Further, these so-called "lazy, fanciful, and unrealistic qualities" are absolutely essential for the advancement of civilization, the generation of vast sums of wealth, and fulfillment in life.

When we throw a ball up in the air, it doesn't zigzag all over the place in a random pattern. The ball always follows the easiest, shortest, straightest path up and the easiest, shortest, straightest path down.

It turns out that physicists express this principle of "least action" describing the motion of celestial bodies, electro-magnetism, the propagation of light beams, and quantum theory. Everything in the entire universe joyfully follows the principle of least action.

The conclusion is obvious: Mother Nature is one lazy mama.

By abstaining from work, advanced black belts in laziness enjoy the pleasures of work avoidance, accomplish great things, and amass great fortunes. They succeed as does nature, always looking for the easiest, fastest, and most effortless way.

I learned this lesson of effortlessness in the early 70s when I was fortunate to work on Maharishi's international staff at an old hotel in the foothills of the Austrian Alps doing whatever needed to be done.

At the hotel, the TM organization planned to design and print materials for use in Africa and Europe. Luxurious at the turn of the century, the hotel was falling down by 1970. The German Gestapo had used it as headquarters, and the Russians liberated it by running their horses through the hallways.

The room we wanted as the design studio had a grimy black floor. A closer examination revealed a parquet floor with fancy interwoven woods that would be gorgeous when sanded and finished. Unfortunately, in the middle of the floor, lying on its side, was a big, black, rusty, ugly, six-by-three by three-foot safe. We had to get rid of it to refinish the floor.

Seven of us, all macho young men, tried to move it. We pushed, pulled, and lifted, grunting, sweating, cussing, sweating some more, and straining. As if bolted to the floor, the safe did not move an inch.

Frustrated, someone finally said, "Let's go to lunch. We can always put a sheet over it with flowers."

I came back from lunch and saw another guy who was not a part of the original fiasco. He was on the floor next to the safe with screwdriver and hammer, tapping and checking it out. I asked him what he was doing.

He said, "Moving the safe."

I told him, "Seven guys couldn't move it, so we're going to put a tablecloth with flowers on it."

He said, "We can move the safe."

"How? It's stuck."

He said, "We'll think of a way."

I watched him tap with a hammer, and I got intrigued. I went downstairs, hoping something would inspire me. I collected some boards, old piping, and other stuff, and carried it upstairs and dumped it on the floor.

While experimenting, we hammered the tip of a screwdriver under the safe, slid a piece of pipe on the screwdriver handle, and put a two-by-four under the pipe to serve as a fulcrum. We pulled the pipe down and levered the safe up the tiniest bit, enough to slide a few pieces of paper underneath.

That tiny bit allowed us to push the tip of the screwdriver under further and lever the pipe a second time, lifting the safe high enough to replace the papers with a magazine. We adjusted the lever and fulcrum angle once more and added a second magazine. Eventually, we were able to slide a pipe underneath. We repeated the process at the other end. Then, like two grandmothers pushing a baby carriage in the park, we rolled the safe on those pipes out of the room, replacing a pipe in the front when one fell out the back.

Two people using their brains accomplished what seven people using force could not. We did not avoid the job; we just avoided the work, finding an effortless solution.

That single incident was a turning point for me. From then on, I knew anything in life could be accomplished. It is simply a matter of finding the right angle. Whether moving a safe or dealing with people, products, money, situations, thought, or emotions, the basis of success is doing less, not more work.

Hard work is a fraud

There is nothing wrong with hard work and long hours if you don't mind sacrificing your health, your family life, and your personal growth and spiritual evolution. And if you are willing to settle for pedestrian achievement.

Hard work is a fraud. Having to work hard to be successful is pure bunk, and anyone who tells you that you must work hard is an idiot. Hard work had zero to do with my success.

The secret of success is finding magical ways of avoiding work. How did David defeat Goliath? Working hard would have meant fighting Goliath hand to hand, getting dirty, sweaty, bloody, and dead! Rather, with a mere flick of his wrist, David defeated Goliath and was home before lunch.

Think of progress in society: it's driven by lazy people trying to find ways of avoiding work. People, fed up with the old ways of doing something, advance the world by knowing there must be an easier, faster, or cheaper way involving less work.

These folks are lazy. The guy who domesticated the horse was tired of walking. The guy who invented sails was tired of rowing. The guy who created the elevator didn't want to walk up the stairs.

I couldn't bear the shame if I said I had to work hard. That would demonstrate I hadn't found an intelligent way to accomplish a task. Yet, other people don't share my squeamishness. They boast how hard they work, as if inefficiency and ineffectiveness are things to be proud of. No sane person would do something the hard way if an easier, more effective solution were available.

If you want the success of Wall Street investment bankers, then you need to replace the 16-hour-a-day mindset with new math. The old math tells us that if you can achieve something in one hour, you will achieve two somethings in two hours. If your limit of desire is 16 somethings, then you have found the correct, mindless formula.

What if you want a million somethings? Then you need a new math. The pure, simple, and elegant truth is that success is inversely proportional to hard work. As effort and hard work become less, success becomes more.

Conversely, hard work impedes success and leads to effort and fatigue. The world is full of hard workers, and few are successful. We must use our brains to work less and eventually avoid work altogether.

People claim that their hard work pays off. I don't doubt that their activity produces wonderful results. I dispute that hard work had anything to do with it.

What successful people call hard work is not work and, for that matter, not hard. It would be less misleading, more inspiring, and more truthful for these same people to exclaim how their love for what they did brought them to their goals.

What about the entrepreneur who works 16 hours a day? Any entrepreneur will tell you that building a business from scratch is exhilarating, profoundly absorbing, and intoxicating. Each small step of progress produces a euphoric feeling that seduces you into accomplishing the next step. This irresistible joy of coming closer to a dream results in the long hours, not some masochistic discipline.

Have fun — more play means more success

As play increases so does success. Play allows the mind to flow without restrictions — to explore, to experiment, to question, to take risks, to be adventurous, to create, to innovate, and to accomplish — without fear of rejection or disapproval. Thus, a business that regards fun as unprofessional, improper, or trivial causes rot.

Fun fuels growth. Disapproval causes cancer. Having fun is the fastest way to the goal because fun is the goal (or at least one of them). So, have fun! Play with everything. Play with things, play with ideas, play with machines, play with co-workers, play with customers, play with words, play with food, play with fabric, play with paint, play with academics, play with money, play with music, play with science, play with technology, play with computers, play with kids, play with friends, and play with Grandma.

Above all, play with what you are doing right now. If it isn't fun, you're wasting your chances for success.

To be successful and great at something, you must love doing it. It must cause your blood to race, challenge your creativity, and be absorbing, passion-inspiring, and joyful. It must be so compelling that you would do it without money.

When you love what you do, it's not work. The more you love it, the more you commit to it, and the more nature reveals her secrets. Money becomes an abundant by-product.

Meditate and find solutions within

Anyone who appreciates only the surface value of life will be doomed to frustration, failure, and, worst of all, hard work. Toiling on the surface requires energy. It creates strain.

Tapping into the subtle produces powerful solutions. Nuances in words communicate most powerfully. Subtle expression of ideas and emotions makes great art. Technology evolves, not by getting cruder, but by harnessing the power of very small particles.

Knowledge is key to success. Yet, the more we learn, the more we realize what we don't know. That means an entrepreneur must rely on his inner knowing, his intuition, the subtlest level of thinking and feeling.

During the TM practice, we experience thinking that is subtler and then more subtle still. Finally, by experiencing the source of thought and the source of all subtlety, we gain on all levels.

If it weren't for my daily TM practice, I don't know how I would have survived. It's where I went when I got overwhelmed. An entrepreneur experiences days of abject terror — bills, payroll, personnel challenges, and this guy over there who did that; there are always issues. In my case, it was most unpleasant being fired from the company that I founded.

Again and again, I've found that after settling deep in my TM practice I was able to find solutions to my problems and good fortune.

Fred Gratzon's twelve tweets

1. To be great at something, you must love doing it. It must cause your blood to race, challenge your creativity, absorb you completely, stoke your passion, and bring you joy.

2. We all have a purpose in life and the talent to fulfill it. Following that calling provides the best chance for growth, success, happiness, and contribution. To find your calling, look for activities that give pleasure, feel natural, seem right, and provide meaning.

3. Lazy people avoiding work have always advanced the world with easier, faster, and cheaper solutions. Someone tired of walking domesticated the horse. Someone tired of rowing invented sailing. Someone tired of going up stairs created the elevator.

4. What successful people call hard work is not work and not hard. It would be less misleading, more inspiring, and more truthful for these same people to exclaim how their love for what they did brought them to their goals.

5. As play increases so does success. Play allows the mind to flow, explore, experiment, question, take risks, be adventurous, create, innovate, and accomplish. A business that regards fun as unprofessional, improper, or trivial causes rot.

6. Most people quit or stay in limbo dilettanting, dabbling, and going nowhere. Commitment is nature's price of admission as she weeds out the weenies and prunes the pretenders.

7. Focusing on money retards our progress and drains our power. Any money that comes in from the money-focus is pedestrian and incomplete. When we are true to ourselves and do what we love, money flows naturally.

8. Always do right by each other. Any small crack between people on the feeling level must be attended to immediately.

9. Good leaders create a fun-filled, creative, environment of freedom and responsibility that allows people to be themselves, express their passion, and grow. In such an atmosphere, individual talent takes flight.

10. Good leaders create an inspired vision and enthusiastically sell it. Then they celebrate achievement and create heroes, cheering joyously and unabashedly. The fun of accomplishing the goal together matters more than the actual project.

11. Getting a million-dollar investment is great. However, the investor's karma comes with the dollars. If the money comes from a sleazy place, then you get that sleaze too, and that influences the business.

12. An entrepreneur experiences days of abject terror — bills, payroll, sexual harassment issues, this guy over there who did that; there are always issues. Repeatedly, I've found that practicing the TM technique has brought me solutions and good fortune.

Ponder

1. Fred says he's not smart. Do you believe him? What does he mean?

2. Fred said he and Cliff, who is off-the-charts smart, complemented each other. Based on your reading of this chapter, how did they complement each other?

3. What do you think of Fred holding Tom Sawyer as a role model? What does Tom model for Fred?

4. Do you think Fred is lazy? Is he just exaggerating? What does he mean when he calls himself lazy and unemployable?

5. In what ways is hard work a fraud?

6. Fred says luck comes from commitment, from leaping across the chasm. Can you think of examples in your own life?

7. Fred said "I saw having $260 million and having much less as an illusion." What does he mean by illusion? Does that mean money doesn't matter?

Fred serving ice cream in front of Great Midwestern in Iowa City

MUM Trustee, Fred, and wife Shelley with 2014 graduation speaker Jim Carrey

Shelley and Fred Gratzon shaking hands with Nancy and Ronald Reagan

Reagans holding branded tea shirts with Gratzons

Fred with Bill Clinton after Telegroup went public

Fred on left with meditating Beach Boys in 1971

Janet Attwood
DISCOVERING YOUR LIFE PURPOSE

Janet Bray Attwood is a transformational leader and co-author of the *New York Times* bestsellers, *The Passion Test: The Effortless Path to Discovering Your Life Purpose* and *Your Hidden Riches: Unleashing the Power of Ritual to Create a Life of Meaning and Purpose.*

Hundreds of thousands of people have taken Janet's Passion Test. Janet and her partner, Chris Attwood, have trained 3,000 certified Passion Test facilitators in over 65 countries.

Speaking throughout the world about discovering passion and purpose, Janet has shared the stage with His Holiness the 14th Dalai Lama, Dr. Stephen Covey, Richard Branson, Nobel Peace Prize winner F.W. de Klerk, Jack Canfield, Zappo's CEO Tony Hsieh, Reverend Michael Beckwith, and many others. She is also a founding member of the Transformational Leadership Council.

For her ongoing work with homeless women and youth in lockdown detention centers, Janet received the highest award for volunteer service in the U.S.: the President's Volunteer Service Award.

I've known Janet and Chris for 40 years. Caring, giving, loving people with open hearts and open minds, they live what they teach. I used talks from both Janet and Chris to form this chapter.

Find more about the Passion Test at www.thepassiontest.com.

JOURNEY: Creating "The Passion Test" by living its teaching

IN THE BEGINNING

At age eight, I would lie in bed waiting for my family to fall asleep so I could sneak out. Beneath the corner streetlight, my world became a brightly lit stage, and I was a beautiful, world-famous actress. I imagined performing in front of thousands of ardent admirers. Into the quiet early morning, I sang and danced with total abandon, feeling free and alive.

I begged my parents to let me attend the Pasadena Playhouse, but they couldn't afford it. At 10, my dad finally agreed to send me. I told my father, "I'd love to go, but I'm older than Shirley Temple was, and it's just too late." By the time I turned 18, I had stopped dreaming and started living a rather uninspired version of "real life." What I had loved to do, hoped to do, even wanted to do was long forgotten.

At 18, I left home and audited courses at San Jose State, partying and doing drugs with the money my father sent me to attend college.

One day, I said to my boyfriend, Walt, "Know what I think?"

Walt responded, "You don't think – you don't even have a brain!"

Devastated, I called my brother, John, in Los Angeles. My brother listened to my sobs and said, "Janet, it's going to be okay. I just learned something you will love."

Four days later, he knocked at my door. He had driven eight hours to rescue his little sister from her drug-filled world. We packed my belongings and drove to Santa Barbara to find a place to live. On the way to Santa Barbara, John told me he had started practicing the Transcendental Meditation technique. Soon after, I also began learning TM, which has been one of the most important gifts of my life.

I wanted to attend Maharishi's TM teacher training course in Majorca, Spain. I found that I could apply to work on staff and earn credit. On my application, I told a lie — I said I was a professional cook. They told me to come as soon as I could. Arriving in Majorca, to my horror,

I discovered that they had hired me to be the head chef for over 500 people at the hotel where Maharishi stayed.

Fortunately, I'm a quick study. I faked it, stopped burning things, and became a good cook. Inspired by Maharishi's teaching and way of living, for years I traveled around Europe with Maharishi as the Co-director of Kitchens and, for a short while, Director of Housing.

Stalking Debra Poneman

At home in California, whenever I needed a job I scanned the classifieds. I would check out the pay and the difficulty of the work. At the same time, I loved the Palo Alto *TM* Center, meditating, giving lectures, teaching the TM technique, and hanging out with friends.

At one point, I was the sole TM teacher. Due to lack of finances, I slept on the meditation center floor. Every morning at 6:00 AM, I would jump a fence and shower at the apartment pool across the street. I was in my 30s, and although I loved teaching meditation, I was tired of being poor.

The meditators who came to my lectures worked in Silicon Valley, many making lots of money. One day, several friends approached me. "We want you to work with us. You're perfect. You love to talk to people. You like making money and having fun, and this job is fun. You'll be recruiting disk drive engineers."

The elite, twelve-person company hired me. Almost everyone was a friend. They knew me as a great networker, communicator, a real dynamo of energy who could get anything done. A bell rang whenever someone made a placement, and it rang many times each day.

Unfortunately, it never rang for me. I watched placement after placement, everyone congratulating everyone else, new cars and houses bought, wonderful vacations taken — while I just sat at my desk waiting for the clock to strike five.

As it turned out, I had no engineer-like, left-brain capability and couldn't communicate with my clients. I'm about as right-brain creative as you can get. Each day I left work humiliated, angry, embarrassed, depressed, and broke. I felt like such a loser.

One afternoon, I was remembering my mom's words. She always said, "You are here for greatness."

Greatness, I thought. *I feel anything but great. I'm not only failing; I'm letting my friends down.* That evening arriving at the meditation center, I saw a poster advertising a seminar in San Francisco called, "Yes to Success."

I knew I had to take it and called into work sick.

The seminar leader was a young woman, a meditator named Debra Poneman. What impressed me was that Debra lived her passion. It showed in every word and gesture. Debra seemed truly happy. She uplifted everyone with her knowledge and radiant love.

She spoke about being in integrity, doing what you love, and listening to your inner voice. Debra asked, "What do you care about? What turns you on?"

Debra loved what she did and did it brilliantly. She was making money and traveling the world. As she spoke, I thought, *I want to uplift others, doing what she's doing. I'm going to ask her to mentor me.*

I waited for the perfect moment. It didn't come. Then she said, "Could someone take me to the airport?" I quickly raised my hand. On the drive to the airport, the right time still didn't come. As we waited for her plane, Debra stared straight into my eyes and said, "What is your dream, Janet?"

Staring right back at her, I said, "I'm glad you asked! I was just thinking today that you should either hire me or move over because I am going to be your next competition." The plane was ready for boarding. Without commenting, Debra gave me a hug, turned, and walked off. I stood there horrified that I had just blown the most important moment in my life.

The next day I returned to work, knowing my days as an uninspired drone would end soon. My one thought: *How can I convince Debra to hire me?* What if I flew to each of her next classes, to New York, Boston, Washington, DC, Fairfield, Iowa, and Los Angeles? Debra would see me sitting in the first row and know I meant business.

Somehow, I knew I would go. That night I passionately declared to a friend at the Transcendental Meditation center that I had discovered my purpose on this planet. I told her of my plan to attend all of Debra's classes.

The following evening as we were ready to get up from our TM practice, I felt pieces of paper falling on my head. I opened my eyes to discover my friend with whom I had shared my purpose showering me with $100 bills. She laughed and said, "Merry Christmas. Go live your dream."

I went to each of Debra's seminars not saying a word. Debra would wave, stare, or glare at me at the different locations. Finally, at the last seminar in Los Angeles, she came up to me. "Okay, if I can't get rid of you, then I better make use of you. You're hired!"

Today, Debra is one of my best friends, and I am living my dream of being a speaker and transformational leader.

The birth of The Passion Test

During each seminar, Debra mentioned that the most influential, financially successful individuals in the U.S. shared one thing: they all lived their "top five passions."

The light went on. If I could figure out my top five passions, that would be the first step to my success. I made a list of the 15 top things I wanted to do, be, and have in my life. From the 15, I selected the top five:

1. I am a brilliant, successful transformational speaker, uplifting humanity all over the world.

2. I travel the world first class.

3. I am treated like a queen wherever I go.

4. I give and receive love in every part of my life.

5. I work with an enlightened team.

All five came to be.

And so, the Passion Test was born while failing terribly at my job.

Ever since I wrote out my first list of passions, I had been refining the Passion Test, retaking it myself, and giving it to friends. Ten years later, I gave the Passion Test to 500 people at a conference in La Jolla, California. After I finished presenting, I received a prolonged ovation.

That acknowledgment inspired me to write the initial ebook version of *The Passion Test*.

So, what is the Passion Test?

The Passion Test book and business help people answer, "Why am I here?" The only test people never fail, the Passion Test is a series of exercises where people get crystal clear about what they want in life, so they can change the way they live.

Corporate girl

Before becoming a transformational leader and author, I was a corporate girl. Through the years, I would follow my dreams, get sidetracked, pursue my dreams, and get sidetracked again. I served as the kitchens and housing director in Europe, recruited engineers, worked for Debra, and sold ads while putting together environmental features in USA Today.

After moving to Fairfield in the mid-80s, I managed the telemarketing division for Books Are Fun, the third-largest book buyer in the U.S. One of the first telemarketers and a top salesperson, at one time I had 40 telemarketers working under me. Reader's Digest eventually bought the company for $360 million.

None of these positions were mistakes. The skills I learned from each job have served me well.

Working with Mark Victor Hansen, Jack Canfield, Robert Allen, and other top transformational speakers

In 2000, my good friend and meditating entrepreneur, Marci Schimoff, a *New York Times* bestselling author, asked me if I would like to help at a Mark Victor Hansen seminar in Cedar Rapids. During the seminar, a hotel alarm went off. The manager herded the 250 people from the workshop into the hallway. We stood beneath the stairs to prepare for a possible tornado. For the next hour, Mark Victor Hansen spoke with and reassured each person.

He asked me, "What's your dream?"

I replied, "Be a transformational speaker."

Mark said, "Jack Canfield and I are offering speaker training in four months. I'll send you a ticket."

To my surprise, a few months later I received a ticket in the mail. At the conference, as Marketing Director of Books are Fun, I was able to spend time with Jack, Mark, and other interesting people.

Afterward, I had the idea of having well-known authors doing signings at our Books are Fun book fairs. I called Mark. I asked him to come to our book fairs and sign books. I told him that I would take good care of him and make sure we sold a ton of *Chicken Soup for the Soul* books. Mark did 10 book fairs.

One evening while eating dinner with Mark, I saw how burned-out he was. I told him that I would teach the TM technique to him and any of his staff. Shortly after, I flew out to California at my expense and taught a grateful Mark.

After I became his teacher, the dynamic between us changed. A few months later, in the fall of 2000, Mark and bestselling author and seminar leader, Robert Allen, invited me to Newport Beach to join a 40-person mastermind group of the top marketers in the US. Mark and Bob brought these amazing marketing minds together for a weekend with the challenge, "If your loved one's life depended on it, how would you pre-sell a million books?" From the event, Mark and Bob created a series of books and DVDs.

At the end of the Marketing Mastermind weekend, Bob Allen approached me. "Janet, we'd like you to partner with us over the next year. We want you to head up your choice of the projects that we identified over the weekend."

I picked "The Enlightened Millionaire Program," a year-long mentoring program. They wanted a business plan in three days.

Not my forté, I contacted my ex-husband, Chris Attwood. He and I had remained good friends after our divorce. With Chris's MBA and analytical mind, our skills perfectly complement each other.

I laid out the scenario for Chris. He loved the idea of me working with Mark and Bob but was too busy to write a plan in three days. However, he agreed to draft an outline for my next meeting in Chicago with Mark and Bob.

After reading Chris's outline, I begged him to join me at the meeting in Chicago, just to make sure all the tough questions Mark and Bob might ask me were answered brilliantly. It was during that meeting when Bob Allen asked what Chris's role was. I kicked Chris under the table and said matter of factly, "Chris is my business partner."

Bob Allen, who had written the bestseller, *Nothing Down*, practices what he preaches. Mark and Bob did not fund us. We had to start our new business from scratch.

Mark and Bob suggested we organize a public seminar. We could advertise that they would call in for a few minutes.

Sixty people showed up at the Fairfield, Iowa library. One person signed up for our $1,000, yearlong mentoring program. The $1,000 just covered the cost for the posters and ads. After that presentation, heartbroken that we had only signed up one person, we spoke with Bob Allen for an hour. He told us that at seminars there are always people who definitely will or won't sign up. We needed to connect with the hearts and minds of the people on the fence.

Forty-five people came to our next meeting, and 15 signed up for The Enlightened Millionaire Program. We now had $15,000 as our startup capital. A year later, the program brought in a million dollars from over 800 people from around the U.S. Through the program, we made unbelievable connections in the industry.

Bob said of us: "You guys are awesome and a joy to work with. When I think of you, I think of integrity, love, passion, persistence, steadiness. I count both of you as my friends for life."

We learned a ton partnering with Mark and Bob with the launch of their book, *The One Minute Millionaire*, and its follow up programs. We met T. Harv Eker while working with Mark and Bob. After finishing our project with them, Harv asked us to help him create joint ventures to promote his courses.

At his first event in California, he had 1,300 people, half of whom came from the joint ventures we created. Over the next couple of years we brought thousands of people to Harv's courses.

One time, Jack Canfield and I were both speaking at a Harv Eker conference. I had been writing *The Passion Test ebook* and wanted Jack's testimonial in it. I called Jack in his hotel room. "Jack, I've got this amazing test to discover your passions. It will only take me a few minutes to guide you through it."

Jack said, "I would love to, but I'm just leaving for the airport, and my taxi's here."

I replied, "Perfect. I'll come along in the taxi and give it to you on the way to the airport."

He laughed, "Okay, you crazy redhead. Come on."

On the way to the airport, I explained how the Passion Test worked. In a few minutes, he listed his top 15 passions. With over 100 million *Chicken Soup for the Soul* books sold worldwide, obviously the guy thought big and knew where he wanted to go.

I wasn't surprised to see that Jack had actualized his top five passions. It surprised Jack that number six, be part of a spiritual leaders' network, was nowhere in his life. As we said goodbye, he told me he would get started on number six right away.

Six months later at his home in Santa Barbara, he hosted 30 of the top transformational leaders and the Transformational Leadership Council was born. Chris and I became founding members of the Council, a growing group of over 100 speakers, authors, and trainers from around the world.

Suddenly, our networking contacts expanded dramatically.

My Partnership with Chris

Chris and I continue our incredible partnership to this day. In our extraordinary journey, we have experienced the power of following our passions.

I'm so thankful for our partnership; I couldn't have done it alone. Chris and I co-authored *The Passion Test*, and together we built the Passion Test business. Besides being my business partner, Chris is my best friend and I am godmother to his three children.

Chris will tell you that I'm an idea generator and an outrageous out-of-the-box thinker. When sharing my ideas with others, at best they might nod. But Chris gets my ideas and can turn the best of them into something functional. Chris says that people misunderstand me because I am the one making the new path. He can help people understand where the path leads.

Chris is left brain, analytical. I am right brain, creative. What he's great at, I am not and vice versa. We respect and lean on each other's brilliance. That's why our partnership works.

For example, I wrote the original *The Passion Test* as an ebook. When Chris agreed to write the print version with me, the book became even more profound. His qualities of clarity, patience, and deep spirituality come through with everything he does.

I own the Passion Test business now. Chris is working on the Beyul Project, which provides training and sacred physical and online space. Chris still consults and travels with me to places like China and Japan. We continue to do lots together because our partnership just works.

Interviewing holy men in the Himalayas and almost dying

By 2003, it was time for me to once again take the Passion Test. I asked myself, "If I could do anything anywhere in the world — something that would turn me on — what would that be?"

A new answer came up: "I want to travel the world and interview the enlightened." Spontaneously, I had a huge grin on my face.

Being near Maharishi was a fabulous honor and profound. However, Maharishi had been in seclusion starting in 2000. With my intention clear, I trekked to the source of the holy river Ganges high in the Himalayan mountains. I met more than 60 "saints," individuals revered for their wisdom and enlightenment, and there I had some of the most profound insights of my life.

I also got so sick I couldn't leave bed for a week. I almost killed myself falling off a mountain. I nearly froze to death in the Himalayas, got kicked by a donkey, and had to travel by myself in India, something I swore I'd never do.

Aligned with my deep passion, the dramatic ups and downs didn't throw me. That trek was one of the best and most amazing experiences of my entire life. I interviewed beautiful, saintly men and women, each with a gift to share. At the same time, it became clear that no one approached the depth of wisdom and Beingness of Maharishi.

I ended my travels in 2005 when Chris and I rewrote *The Passion Test*. My visits with the holy men and women greatly influenced the writing.

Launching *The Passion Test* book

Liz and Ric Thompson, participants in The Enlightened Millionaire program, were planning an online magazine, *Healthy, Wealthy and Wise*. They had an email list of 75,000 but needed great cover stories to make the magazine successful.

They approached Chris and me. "You are great at building relationships and have a large network of well-known leaders. We would like you to create the magazine's cover stories."

At the time, we wanted to get the word out about my ebook version of *The Passion Test*. So, we agreed to write the cover stories in exchange for being able to mail to their list twice a month. We used the email list to publicize our monthly "Discover Your Passion" conference calls. Often, we had high profile guests. On average 3,000 people registered with half showing up.

We emailed people reminders about the calls and gave them assignments to do in preparation. We included a guide for the call and suggested that they buy a copy of the 93-page ebook version of *The Passion Test* for $4.50. We sold 5,000 copies.

We financed the rewrite of *The Passion Test* through ebook revenue and from helping Harv Eker bring his training program to the U.S.

Since we weren't able to secure the agent we wanted, Chris and I decided to self-publish the print version. Self-publishing at the time was less accepted and more cumbersome than today.

In January 2005, we started planning the launch of *The Passion Test* book. Following advice, we decided on two launches rather than one.

We had spent years networking with inspirational leaders. We helped them out, always saying yes to whatever they needed. We gave them exposure in *Healthy, Wealthy, and Wise* stories and with our Discover Your Passion teleconference. We asked our ever-growing network of luminaries and fans to support our two launches. Everyone just said, "Of course."

With over 200 partners in our first launch in May, we went to number two on both Amazon and Barnes & Noble best seller lists. We wanted to be number one. We got busy for our second launch in September. We added new partners at a time when it was unusual to get so many in the transformational world to promote a book.

It is easier to get to number one on Barnes & Noble than Amazon. So, in our second launch, we directed visitors to our web page to buy our book only at Barnes & Noble.

The book became number one in an hour and a half.

Then, we removed the Barnes & Noble link and sent all the traffic to Amazon. After a day, it became a number one Amazon bestseller as well. With so many partners promoting us, we stayed there for over a week.

New York publishers reason that if someone on their own can sell 10,000 copies in six months, they should be able to sell between 100,000 to a million copies of the book. Unfortunately, that's not necessarily true.

When they saw that we sold 25,000 copies of the book in less than a year, they thought, *This is gold.* With the help of our new agent, seven publishing houses bid on our book. Starry-eyed, we had offers each worth hundreds of thousands of dollars. We chose the one that paid the most rather than the one with which we most resonated. In addition to receiving a big check, we reasoned that a substantial cash advance showed a real commitment from the publisher.

In retrospect, we believe we would have done better trusting our feelings and choosing the publishing team most competent and most congruent with our values.

To this day, *The Passion Test* continues to be well-ranked and recommended on Amazon. We don't actively market it, but our Passion Test facilitators continue to drive sales of the book.

The Business of The Passion Test

Hundreds of thousands of people have become clear about what they want in life due to the Passion Test.

After Chris and I published the book, people started asking us to speak. At talks we always mentioned a Harris Poll survey that found only 20% of working Americans are passionate about what they do. We told the audience that we wanted to turn that passion statistic upside down.

We soon realized we couldn't turn the stat around by ourselves. We needed to teach people to do what I did. So, Chris and I developed a four-day certification program to teach people how to give the Passion Test.

Initially, 70 people signed up. Those 70 formed the beginning of what we call our cosmic army. As of 2018, we have around 3,000 Passion Test trainers in over 65 countries.

Now my big thing is teaching master trainers to train trainers of the Passion Test program. I want to create rock stars. As the elder of this movement, I want other Energizer Bunnies to go out and teach what I taught.

The Passion Test business has developed live events, books, training classes, and online seminars each bringing in revenue. We also use our extensive mailing list to promote products that we believe in. We receive affiliate revenue from those sales. Similarly, affiliates promote our products. Currently, the bulk of our income comes from the on-line $97 three-hour passion test and the $3,500 four-day Passion Test Certification program.

We are all over the world, with lots of interest in Japan, China, Thailand and other Asian countries. Most years I speak at the International Yoga Festival in Rishikesh, India, where I renamed "The Passion Test," "Yoga of the Mind."

Chris, our close friend, Marci Shimoff, and I have authored six books with a total of 118 weeks on *New York Times* bestseller lists. From that experience, we teach The Enlightened Bestseller Mastermind Program which focuses on the author's marketing platform.

Chris and I also collaborated with *Your Hidden Riches*, a book about how the power of ritual contributes to a life of meaning and purpose. This book has also become a *New York Times* bestseller.

What matters most to me is seeing people wake up. The foundation of what Chris and I present comes from Maharishi. Chris and I integrate information about the TM technique into all our talks and all our books. My clarity to do what I wanted in my life came from practicing the TM technique. As Maharishi explained, humanity will survive and thrive by raising the consciousness of the planet.

WISDOM: Always choose in favor of your passions

ENLIGHTENED ALLIANCES — THE FOUNDATION OF OUR SUCCESS

Our success comes from creating and nourishing what we call "enlightened alliances." Enlightened alliances are more than just making a deal, more than business relationships, joint ventures, or strategic alliances. In an enlightened alliance, we under-promise and over-deliver. We genuinely care about our partners, the outcome, and the overall impact of our efforts. As a result, many of our alliance partners have remained friends for over 20 years.

The perfect alliance partner is that person or organization for whom we are uniquely qualified to fulfill their most critical need, and in fulfilling it we also fill our most critical need.

I have always had my antenna up for people who inspire me and who are doing what I want to do — speak, teach, present, and offer programs. If I didn't have the money to pay for their offerings, I looked for a way to be useful and volunteered. I cooked for Maharishi's TM teacher training classes, drove Debra to the airport, and volunteered at Mark Victor Hansen's seminar.

Chris and I cultured the habit of service. We used our skills, talent, and knowledge to support people we admired. In doing so, we put ourselves in a position to benefit from their wisdom and platform.

It is not tit-for-tat thinking, not "I'm going to do something for you, and you will do something for me." We approached people we admired, felt aligned with, and could learn from. We forgot about ourselves and focused on them. We would identify their critical need, what they cared most deeply about at the time. We often helped even though they might not have been able to help us. Whether they assisted us or someone else did, the act of serving and giving always seemed to come back around.

So many people come to us and say, "We'd like to partner, and we're doing this." They express little interest in our priorities or time constraints. We are more favorably inclined toward the person who says "You have a book coming out in the fall. I've got a big Facebook following and a contact that could prove helpful."

If they've tried to understand what's going on with us and can offer something to support us, then there's a law of reciprocity. When you help someone with something that's important to them, they're going to want to help you.

Chris and I got clear on the things we did well that others found difficult and we nurtured those talents. For example, we are really good at creating and building relationships. Repeatedly, in our alliances we combined the ability to network with our willingness to serve and desire to learn.

The critical need for *Healthy, Wealthy, and Wise* was creating great content for its readers. Our critical need was a platform to publicize the Passion Test. The online magazine ended up with great stories, and we had a 75,000-person mailing list platform. Further, we formed enlightened alliances with subjects of our cover stories, providing them publicity. Later, we used their goodwill to help launch our book.

With Mark Victor Hansen and Bob Allen and *The One Minute Millionaire*, we provided boots on the ground for the book launch and for the followup programs. We were rewarded with a wealth of knowledge and experience from Mark and Bob's mentorship.

Applying the Passion Test principles to my life

I created the initial version of the Passion Test while at a job I hated. After taking the test, I began saying yes to what I cared about without concern for what others thought. With each yes, I reclaimed my power and grew in self-love. By choosing the things that brought me the greatest joy, I became more joyful. I can't imagine a life without fun, and living my passions is fun.

If you're not loving what you are doing, you need to look inside. The Passion Test helps you get clear about what you want. And when you are clear about what you choose to show up in your life, it shows up, but only to the extent that you're clear.

When I first took the Passion Test, my passions were different than they are now. As people start to live their passions, passions change. From taking the Passion Test repeatedly over time, my desire to interview holy people emerged. The important thing is to be innocent and open each time you take the test.

The Passion Test takes practice and repetition. Gradually, students let go of self-imposed limitations and begin thinking in new ways. Breakthroughs occur, limitations disappear, and clarity emerges by asking the Passion Test questions again and again. In seminars, I ask the class, "What do you care about?" "Is it fun?" When they realize that they can have what they want, the light goes on all over the room.

In an all-possibility world, if you can dream a thing, you can have it. The possibility starts to take over when you repeatedly state intentions and always choose in favor of them.

When I first wrote down my passions, I didn't see them as possible. As I wrote *The Passion Test* ebook, I realized I was playing it safe, only writing down passions I thought I could have or accomplish.

I told myself. "Janet, be the teacher that lives the teaching. Be real. Speak truth when standing in front of people." I asked myself again, "If I could have, do, or be anything, what would I want to have, do, and be?"

The more I allow myself to be vulnerable, transparent, authentic, and open, the deeper I connect with myself. As a bonus, others usually get something out of it.

The universe doesn't play tricks. We won't have the deep desire to do something that we're not capable of achieving. We just need to change our thinking and let go of limitations.

When we are clear about our purpose in life, we can more easily help others find their purpose. Discovering what others care about and then supporting them nourishes our relationships. If everyone lived a passionate, loving life, the world would be kind and sweet.

Everything that we do at the Passion Test comes from our maxim, "Inspiring transformation through love." Love goes a long way. We love our students as much as we are capable. In our programs, rather than having people share what they don't do right, we put attention on their greatness.

25 Tips for clarifying and actualizing your passions

CLARIFYING YOUR PASSIONS

1. Create a list of at least 10 unique passions from different areas of your life: relationships, health, education, career, spirituality, lifestyle, location, and so on.

2. Complete the statement: "When my life is ideal, I am…" What would be the best of the best of the best?

3. It's an inside-out job, so get clear inside. You don't have to push or shove or manipulate the world. Change your thinking inside to manifest what you want outside.

4. Make the passions short, succinct, and positive.

5. Write only one passion per statement.

6. Use passionate words that sing to you like "fabulous," "excellent," "outrageous," "flamboyant."

7. Use positive rather than negative statements. Everything is energy.

8. Stay in your heart. Finish the test in five to ten minutes so you don't over think.

9. Take the position that since it's only a thought and a piece of paper, why not write down what you would really love to do or be?

10. If you're stuck, think about what you don't want and turn it around. Write your vision of what you want for yourself. So, if you've been physically abused, "I'm in a beautiful, supportive relationship."

11. Don't count the process as a passion. Instead of, "I work out seven days a week," write, "I'm beautiful and in shape."

12. Don't be on your way, be there.

13. Use an elimination process to come up with your top five passions.

14. Create markers (milestones) for your passions. If your passion is to be a world-class Olympic skier, a marker might be standing on stage receiving a gold medal.

15. When done, read it over. Ask yourself, "Did I play it safe? Did I write down only those things that I know could happen? Did I allow myself to be, do, and have as big as I want?" Give yourself permission to have what you love.

ACTUALIZING YOUR PASSIONS

16. Get clear on the what, and the how will begin to appear.

17. Stay open. Be present. Let go of concepts of how life should be. Embrace life as it is. Adjust your passions to changing situations and circumstances.

18. You are aligned with your passions if it doesn't bother you when others find them uncomfortable, undesirable, or distasteful.

19. Always see the blessings in what seems to be adverse circumstances.

20. Be courageous and follow your unique path.

21. Be around people that support you.

22. Passion is a journey, not a destination. Whenever you are faced with a decision or opportunity, choose in favor of your top five passions. If you always decided in favor of them, imagine what your life would be like.

23. Stay patient and committed. Realize that living your passions is seldom a straight path and often brings challenges.

24. When you love the doing, results take care of themselves.

25. Life is to enjoy and to expand happiness. If it feels otherwise, you are off your path. Ask yourself, what you need to change to favor your passions.

The Passion Test formula: Intention, Attention, No Tension

Together we co-create our universe. If you want to be a manifesting magnet, you must decide what you want, stay focused, and let go. We express this fundamental Passion Test teaching in a formula: Intention, Attention, No Tension. Follow this recipe, and allow the unbounded laws of the universe to create what you want in life.

Intention

Intention is getting clear on what you choose to create. This first step requires taking the time to stop and step out of your busy life. When you are clear, what you choose to show up shows up.

Attention

If you are like most people, you don't realize how powerful you are.

Whatever you input shows up in your life. False beliefs keep you from living your life purpose: "I'm not good enough, I'm not smart enough, my circumstances prevent me, blah, blah, blah..." Those ideas block you and create grooves, neural pathways in your brain. Garbage in, garbage out.

Become a conscious creator. If you want more passion, fulfillment, and joy in your life, then give your attention to that. Remind yourself every day what you are passionate about.

Move through the doors that open and don't grumble about the doors that don't. Everything is cosmically set up for you, if you just allow for it and keep moving forward. When you notice that your attention is on something negative, just say, "Cancel." Replace that thought with something you choose to create.

Because of the neural pathways already created, fearful thoughts may continue for a while. Just keep canceling negativity and replacing it with the picture of what you want. With a little time, new neural pathways will be created, and your experience will change.

No Tension

This last step, No Tension, letting go, is where the magic resides — where people, places, and things just show up to support you living your passion. Once you know what you want to create, strike like lightning in all directions. Take massive action. Then, once you've done everything you know to do, let go. Surrender. Chill.

Letting go completely and trusting the universe can be the greatest challenge. It's like walking in the dark with total blind faith, not knowing where the next safe footing is, afraid that the unknown will unveil more than you can take. I've learned that the key to living a happy, fulfilled life is becoming completely comfortable with not knowing what comes next.

As an example from my life, after traveling to Yes to Success seminars, Debra Poneman finally hired me. She asked me to house-sit at her home headquarters in Los Angeles while she embarked on a speaking tour and said I could study her success tapes while she was gone. When she returned, I would start my work. I was in seventh heaven!

I said goodbye to my friends at the recruiting firm, packed my bags, and filled my vintage red Toyota with gas. I headed to Los Angeles, radio blaring, singing at the top of my lungs, ecstatic that I was on my way to start my dream career.

Two miles into my journey, my red Toyota sputtered. Steam rose from inside the hood. I pulled over. My trusty car took one big last breath, let out the most god-awful sound, and died.

When the initial shock wore off, I decided to take a train to Los Angeles. After paying the tow truck, buying the train ticket, and taking a long taxi ride to Debra's apartment in Santa Monica, I arrived at Debra's door with $13 to my name. Terrified that Debra wouldn't hire me to teach success principles if she knew I was broke, I said nothing. I kept a sunny smile until she finally waved good-bye.

Then, I scooped myself a massive serving of Debra's chocolate ice cream. Lying down on the couch, I fell into a drunken chocolate sleep. I awoke knowing my only option. I grabbed the keys to Debra's blue Chevy (she'd said I could borrow it for emergencies — this was an emergency) and headed down the Pacific Coast Highway.

Arriving at the great saint Paramahansa Yogananda's Self-Realization Fellowship Lake Shrine in Pacific Palisades, I immediately felt a deep sense of calm come over me. I walked past the beautiful buildings to the majestic and serene gardens that graced this special place.

Reaching into my purse, I pulled out my treasured, crisp one-dollar bills and stuffed all $13 into a little wooden donation box located in the garden. I sat down on a nearby wooden bench and had an intimate talk with God, pouring out my heart. I told Him what was going on with me and that I could use a little of His support.

When I drove back to Debra's, the self-recrimination began: Are you crazy? How could you give away the last money you have in the world?

At Debra's, as I began rationing the food left in the fridge, the phone rang. Frances, my ex-husband's father, whom I loved and hadn't heard from in over a year invited me to lunch. At least I'd have a full belly.

Animated, Frances told me about Herbalife, a natural weight-loss program. He put four bottles of the stuff on the table. "This is something which you could make a lot of money from in your spare time." He knew that I had an outgoing personality and loved to share things that benefited others.

I told him, "The opportunity sounds great. When I have extra money, I'll order some."

Frances said, "I have 500 dollars' worth of the stuff in my car. You can have these four bottles and the 500 dollars' worth as well. Pay me back after you sell them and make some money."

As he handed over the four bottles, our very overweight waitress walked up to the table and said to me, "What's that?" I told her everything I could remember that Frances had just said to me about these wonderful, effective, all-natural products.

"I'll take everything you have!" she said. She whipped out a $100 bill from her apron, grabbed the bottles, and walked away.

When I had given up and let go completely, the powerful force that guides and directs our lives took over. Out of the blue, I was provided with the means that allowed me to go on and begin a career that has brought me so much fulfillment.

What you love and God's will are the same. Let go, and be open to what shows up.

10 steps to becoming a transformational leader

On my website, I say:

"If you have a burning desire to make a difference in this world, if you long to be on a global stage inspiring others, if you love to learn and connect with people, and if you want to earn a great income from doing what you love, then find out more about my new International Rockstar Master Trainer Program."

On the website and at workshops and conferences, I share the things I wish someone had told me when I started.

1. Take the Passion Test, create a vision board, and write your 100th

birthday speech to get crystal clear on the legacy you want to create.

2. Find a great mentor. Everything changed when Mark Victor Hansen and Robert Allen became our mentors.

3. Create a book or a product. My *New York Times* bestselling book, *The Passion Test*, formed the foundation for my speaking engagements, workshops, interviews, and videos.

4. Focus on your mindset. As Henry Ford said, "Whether you think you can or think you can't — you're right." Keep challenging yourself. Stay positive. Be unstoppable. Make your dreams a reality.

5. Join a mastermind group. You need people who believe in you, hold you accountable, and encourage you to move towards your dreams. We put everyone in our programs in a mastermind group.

6. Meditate. I can't emphasize this enough. My daily practice of the Transcendental Meditation technique saved my life.

7. Let go of your ego. You are not the general manager of the universe. The more you see yourself as an instrument, the more successful you will be in uplifting others.

8. When communicating your message with others, focus on the transformational promise and not much on how the change will happen.

9. Lead with love. I became a top salesperson at Books are Fun because I cared more about the clients than the sale. After seeing that I cared, they were more open to the sale.

10. The more grateful you are, the more abundant your life will be. Be the humble, wide-eyed child saying, "Thank you." If you are ungrateful and shut down, you aren't open to gifts that are always present. When stuck, ask yourself, "What smile, what precious moment came my way today?"

SPIRIT: Be true to yourself

Although Chris and I stumbled with each step on our path, we did one thing consistently: nothing stopped us from following our passions. Even when it made no sense, we followed our passions. We got clear about what we loved and cared about most, and made decisions based upon that. We had no idea that Liz and Rick would show up, or that they had an email list.

The universe doesn't play tricks. It's not a mistake that you love what you love. So, when you feel a resonance with a person or task or some piece that will further realize your passions, pay attention.

The Passion Test process is about helping people get clarity about what they love and care about, so they can continually make choices that favor those things. Ask yourself "Will this choice help me be more connected to what I love, or will it take me farther away?" If it takes you farther away, then no matter how much sense it makes, it's the wrong decision.

Most importantly, remain true to yourself and to that deepest part of your heart. Passions are the pipelines to your soul. Consistently favor your passions, and you fulfill your purpose in life.

Passions are like a trail of breadcrumbs. One day you wake up and say "Oh my God, this is why I am here. I am fulfilling my purpose."

Janet Attwood's twelve tweets

Choose in favor of your passions

1. When you are clear about what you choose to show up in your life, it shows up, but only to the extent that you're clear.

2. Passions are the pipelines to the soul, so remain true to the deepest part of your heart. Consistently favor your passions, and you will fulfill your purpose in life. Passions are like a trail of breadcrumbs. One day you wake up and say, "Oh my God, this is why I am here."

3. Once you know what you want to create, strike like lightning in all directions. Take massive action. Then, once you've done everything you know to do, let go. Surrender. Chill.

4. Move through the doors that open and don't grumble about the doors that don't. Everything is cosmically set up for you if you just allow and keep moving forward.

5. Join a mastermind group — people with whom you regularly meet who believe in you, hold you accountable, and encourage you to move towards your dreams.

6. You know you're standing in your power when you don't want anything, when you're not comparing yourself to other people, when you're happy to be who you are.

7. In an all-possibility world, if you can dream a thing, you can have it. The possibility starts to take over when you repeatedly state your intentions and always choose in favor of them.

8. It's an inside-out job, so get clear inside. You don't have to push or shove or manipulate the world. Change your thinking inside to manifest what you want outside.

Serve

9. When you are clear about your purpose in life, you can more easily help others find their purpose. Nourish your relationships by discovering what they care about and supporting them.

10. Culture the habit of service. Use your skills, talent, and knowledge to support people you admire. In doing so, you put yourselves in a position to benefit from their wisdom and platform.

11. Lead with love. I became a top salesperson because I cared more about the clients than the sale. After seeing that I cared, they were more open to making a purchase.

12. Be clear on the things you do well that others find difficult. Nurture those talents and use them to serve others.

Clockwise from top right: Janet Attwood with Maharishi (to her left, John Gray, author of *Men Are From Mars, Women Are From Venus*); Janet presenting in Denmark; Janet with Debra Poneman; Janet enjoying life; Janet with the Dalai Lama; Janet with T. Harv Eker

Ponder

1. Janet says always choose in favor of your passions. Do you agree? What are your top five passions? Are you willing to choose in favor of them, even if common sense and other people tell you otherwise?

2. Janet threw caution to the wind as she followed Debra around, gave away her last $13, trekked through the Himalayas, and jumped in a taxi with Jack Canfield. What was the effect of Janet's high level of commitment? Are you willing to go all in?

3. When Janet saw an opportunity, she didn't use not having money as an excuse. She looked for a way to be useful and volunteered. She ran a kitchen to be near Maharishi and self-funded a business to be mentored by Mark Victor Hansen and Robert Allen. Are there people you can learn from that you are willing to help?

4. Chris and Janet call their "enlightened alliances" the foundation for success. Are there potential partners for whom you can fill a critical need and, by doing so, you fill your own critical need? Would you be will to put your needs on the back burner to serve them?

PART TWO
Serving the Community
Ed Malloy

Betsy Howland

Ed Malloy
THE ENTREPRENEURIAL MAYOR OF FAIRFIELD

Ed Malloy was born in Glen Cove, NY, one of eight children. He received his BA from Ricker College in 1974.

Ed and his wife, Vicki, moved to Fairfield in 1980. He joined the oil brokerage firm, Danaher Oil, in 1983 and became president and a partner in 1994.

After founding the Fairfield Entrepreneurs Association and serving two terms on the city council, Ed successfully ran for Fairfield mayor in 2001. In 2010, he became a trustee of Maharishi University of Management.

Ed's generosity, service-orientation, people-skills, and entrepreneurial affinity helped transform Fairfield into the wonderful place those featured in this book call home.

JOURNEY: From oil broker to mayor
FINDING OUR NICHE AS MIDWEST OIL BROKERS

In 1980, I moved to Fairfield and joined a community of meditators committed to creating an influence of peace and harmony in the U.S. Thanks to the move, I've had a life full of fantastic occurrences.

Upon arriving in Fairfield, fellow meditators and I discovered a small, 150-year-old, traditional, agricultural and manufacturing-based community with an established academic environment. Most of us did not have the skills or passion to farm or manufacture, nor did we want to volunteer at the university. We had to reinvent ourselves, and many of us did so as entrepreneurs. In the process, we reinvented Fairfield.

Fairfield is a four- to five-hour drive from Chicago, St. Louis, Kansas City, Omaha and Minneapolis. We communicated with the outside world by mail, phone and telex. We collaborated and networked. Ideas churned, and we formed hundreds of small businesses in our rural Iowa town, population 10,000.

In 1981, Jim Danaher founded Danaher Oil, and I joined the company in 1983. Our company's team looked for a brokerage opportunity in a stable Midwest industry that we could run from Fairfield. Brokers put buyers and sellers together within a particular market and then help with price negotiations. Most people are familiar with real estate brokers.

We searched for a niche market that we could dominate. During our research, we found 10 oil refineries connected to a dozen pipelines that serviced the 10-state Midwest area. With study, we became experts in the day-to-day trading of fuel — understanding the infrastructure and knowing the individual buyers and sellers.

Having been instrumental in Danaher Oil's growth, I became partner and president in 1994.

Danaher Oil brokers gasoline, diesel fuel, and jet fuel in the Midwest — fuel produced in refineries distributed through pipelines and ready for market. We broker on the open-spot market. There, fuel is sold for cash at current market prices for delivery within a month. Each transaction of millions of gallons of fuel travels from oil refineries through pipelines into storage areas, and then from storage areas to trucks to gas stations.

The center of the U.S. oil industry is in Houston with major presences in New York, Denver, and other major cities. Approaching companies in those cities from Fairfield, Iowa, was challenging, especially since we didn't have proximity to meet clients personally. We began introducing ourselves by phone. We shared our knowledge and service orientation, inviting business.

Many brokers just want to make the sale. Our approach is different. Before the purchase, we educate our customers so they feel good about the transaction. We show them why current conditions make it a good time to do the trade. Slowly, with this approach, we built sufficient market share to establish ourselves.

For over 30 years, we've continued to educate customers as part of the sales process. In doing so, we've developed a reputation as a premier brokerage firm.

With the advent of the internet, operating out of Fairfield has become an advantage. People can now telecommute and connect to major financial markets anywhere in the world. Customers are envious of the quality of life in our small town, a great place to raise a family.

Change in oil prices doesn't affect us because our commissions are paid based on volume, not price. Today, fuel demand remains as high as ever, even though we will make the transition to clean energy. I am often asked how I reconcile my work in the oil industry with my passion for creating a sustainable community. As mayor, I worked hard to put Fairfield on the path to sustainability. As a businessman, I know that political forces and the liquid fuel-based transportation infrastructure mean the transition will take between 10 and 30 years. Solar and wind energy are already a viable and readily available resource to replace coal.

From the start we had a clear intention. We decided to create a niche brokerage business based on integrity, expertise, and service. Our subsequent success came from the strength and clarity of our vision.

Becoming mayor

My desire to serve came from observing my parents. My mother's work as chairwoman for multiple church committees inspired me to give back to my community. My father's 42 years as a police officer taught me the value of integrity when serving the public.

In Fairfield in 1991, standing in a downtown restaurant buffet line, someone joked, "Hey, Malloy, I hear you're running for city council."

Startled, I turned. Several tables of people looked at me as if asking, "Well, are you going to run?"

The integration of new arrivals from around the world into the Fairfield community had not gone smoothly. People moved to Fairfield with bold ideas and different cultural values. The local population resisted. They were unclear about the direction for Fairfield. They didn't know how long the influx of new people or even if Maharishi University of Management would last. With so much uncertainty and doubt, tension grew.

When I turned around in the restaurant, I felt that my friends wanted representation, someone who could build a bridge to the local community, someone to sort out the discomfort.

So, I decided to run for city council. Once elected, citizens knew me as the representative of the meditating community. In my second four-year term, I broadened my constituency, championing the concerns and good ideas from everyone.

As one of seven city council members, I built trust. Yet, we still weren't making progress as a community. A stifling energy prevented the full expression of possibilities for Fairfield.

I knew that if feelings within the community shifted, Fairfield could be more productive with a better quality of life and could serve as a model for small cities all over the country. The community just had to come together and collaborate on a common vision.

For such a vision to occur, we needed a change of leadership. I had been a successful Fairfield entrepreneur and on the city council for eight years. Perhaps more than any meditator or Fairfield native, I knew what needed to happen. But could I bring the community together in a meaningful, graceful way? Eventually, I decided to run for mayor.

Having multiple things to do energizes me. By 2001, I had created a situation in my business where I could block out time to do more.

The existing mayor had been in office for 28 years with little opposition. During the election, I operated under the radar, registering meditators and making sure they voted. I also met individually with local people who saw the need for change.

I won by less than 200 votes.

The short election cycle of a mayor means that if the mayor embarrasses or alienates the community, he can be out in two years. Some locals said, "It's just two years, let's see what happens."

When I took office, the relationship between the community of meditators, the university, and local residents was not cohesive. I wanted to bridge the gap and bring people together by having them plan together and create a common vision.

In business or government, creating and actualizing a vision requires collaboration. To start, I appointed a commission of 24 people — half meditators and half Fairfield natives. We met to develop a strategic plan for the community and set a 10-year agenda.

What did we want Fairfield to become?

Taking our time, we brought in The Institute for Decision Making of the University of Northern Iowa to facilitate objective and open discussion. Neutral and professional facilitation of the process was key. The consultant worked with us to clarify goals in language that we all could agree on.

We bounced around a lot of ideas. We started with a vision statement that we divided into five goal areas. It took us 14 months for everyone to feel comfortable with a final plan.

The May 2003 vision statement reads:

> Fairfield in 2012 will be a shining success story in Iowa, featuring a revived and vibrant dow ntown, a dynamic

growing economy, and a leading center for culture and the arts. Fairfield will showcase the unique blending of its rich heritage and small town qualities with the diversity, cultural richness, and economic opportunities of a thriving city.

Fairfield...the best of all worlds

Anyone familiar with Fairfield today will think, *That's Fairfield.* It was not the case in 2002, when there was no Fairfield Arts and Convention Center, Jefferson County loop trail, or vibrant downtown square.

The five goal areas we identified were economic expansion, beautification, recreation and culture, education, and helping the needy and elderly. We divided those goals into 70 specific projects.

We took the draft of our plan to public meetings. We showed the plan to community organizations, suggesting where their goals synced with the city's plan. We asked if they would help us accomplish the projects. We got buy-in from 80 organizations.

It's bold to put together a 10-year plan and assume that you will be there at the end. The process worked because it was a broad community plan, with the different church and cultural groups owning the objectives. The fact that we wanted to make Fairfield a showcase for the country made the plan even more appealing.

Fairfield accomplishments since 2003

Effective local government is not about ideology, but about good management and progress. A city government provides police, a fire department, a library, zoning, and recreation, as well as intangibles that encourage progress and livability. These activities require fiscal responsibility from well-managed tax dollars. With good stewardship, Fairfield has enjoyed many achievements since it started working on the plan in 2002.

When on the city council, I served as a member of the Service Agency, which oversaw the law center. The state inspector was pressuring Fairfield to build a new jail, and our city and county law enforcement needed better facilities. I worked to pass Fairfield's first local option sales tax to fund the new Law Center, and it passed on the first ballot.

Passing a tax law may not sound like something to be proud of, but after we paid those bonds for the Law Center, we used the sales tax funds to invest in our community in ways that couldn't have been done before. After I became mayor, the tax funded initiatives like the Fairfield Arts and Convention Center, Downtown Streetscape, Loop Trail, 1st Fridays Art Walk, City Beautification, and many cultural and community events.

The Fairfield Arts and Convention Center

We made the Fairfield Arts and Convention Center a priority, opening it in 2007. The-state-of-the-art Stephen Sondheim Center for the Performing Arts has an expo hall, flexible meeting spaces, art gallery, and a commercial kitchen. It is one of the most comprehensive art centers in Iowa. Audiences drive in from a wide circle of neighboring communities to enjoy music, comedy, theater, and dance. This facility is used to showcase local talent and hosts a myriad of business meetings and conferences. It has been a strong galvanizing gathering place for the whole community.

Jefferson County Trail system

Our strategic plan made the 16-mile trail — already under construction by volunteers — a priority, helping with grant writing and other resources. The full trail opened in 2011, connecting some of the most beautiful natural areas in the city.

Fairfield First Fridays Art Walk

Inaugurated in 2003, Fairfield First Fridays Art Walk became a signature event for Fairfield as a center of arts with four permanent galleries on the town square. The event won the state's Tourism Event of the Year in 2005 and continues to this day.

FAIRfest

This three-day, outdoor music festival features nationally famous musicians and local artists. By its fifth year in 2017, FAIRfest had featured over 100 performances by musicians from all over the country.

The town square keeps its character

When Walmart came in the 1980s, local clothing and hardware stores could not survive. With the city's leadership, the city, state, and downtown building owners (including this book's author) partnered to help bring the town square's storefronts and the streetscape back to its original vibrancy and character. Fairfield has preserved and transformed the character of its square with herb stores, art galleries, restaurants, jewelry stores, and specialty clothing. With a $500,000 Community Development Block Grant from the State of Iowa the city partnered on $1 million of improvements to downtown facades.

Solar-powered Fairfield Library

Traffic for the solar-powered library rivals cities three times our size. Our library is the center for many of the lifelong learning opportunities Fairfield residents have.

Outdoor pool and indoor recreation center

In 2016, the city constructed a new outdoor pool to replace the aging one. The following year, we completed a brand new indoor recreation center with a walking track, three gym floors and workout space. The new facility was the first indoor public gym built in Fairfield in over 60 years and was named for the lead donors: the Cambridge SportsPlex.

Tourism

With the help of a grant, we started the Fairfield Visitors and Tourism Bureau. In 2006, with funding from a new hotel-motel tax, we opened the Fairfield Convention and Visitors Bureau. The town square, the university, the meditation domes, and the art and music festivals attract tourists from around the Midwest and from the rest of the country. Fairfield's downtown features multiple ethnic dining options, coffee houses, and boutique shops that are thriving because of the tourism attraction efforts.

Fairfield Airport

I personally lobbied the head of the FAA in Washington, DC, to support our airport with a $10-million-dollar discretionary allocation from the federal budget. With the money, we completed the Fairfield Airport runway expansion and new terminal.

Recognition

Since 2002, Fairfield has received much recognition. For example:

- In 2003, Washington DC nonprofit, The National Association of Towns and Townships, named Fairfield the most entrepreneurial city in America with a population under 10,000.

- The Center for Community Vitality of Iowa State University named Fairfield the most entrepreneurial city in Iowa in 2004.

- Out of 900 cities in Iowa, Fairfield was named one of the "Iowa Great Places" in 2006 along with five other cities. With that selection, community pride was palpable. Remaining tensions dissolved. Everyone began to understand that diversity was our strength.

- The Fairfield story has been written up in several rural economic development studies.

- *Mother Earth News* named Fairfield to its list of Best Places to Live You Have Never Heard Of.

- Oprah Winfrey ran an hour TV special on Fairfield, "America's Most Unusual Town."

- *The Smithsonian* magazine selected Fairfield as seventh in the 20 best small towns to visit.

- Buzzfeed.com declared Fairfield second in a list of "The 11 Coolest Small Cities to Take a Road Trip To."

- In 2013, Fairfield was featured on two national TV shows — one hosted by William Shatner about entrepreneurship and another on musical talent.
- Fairfield was certified as one of the "Iowa Blue Zones" (a health and wellness initiative).
- In 2018, Expedia.com named Fairfield one of the "50 Best Places to Escape to."

10-year Go Green sustainability plan

Our 2002 strategic plan included several objectives about Fairfield becoming a sustainability knowledge center.

In 2008, with the collapse of the financial system and soaring energy prices, I saw an opportunity for the community to come together and collaborate on a sustainability plan. In that time of crisis, an energy-independent and financially self-sufficient Fairfield had broad appeal.

Businesses and individuals already practiced sustainability principles such as renewable energy, energy conservation, and good land stewardship. Fairfield could be a laboratory and role model to the nation for what a small community can accomplish. The ongoing success of the original 2003 Fairfield 10-year plan gave me the political capital to say, "Let's do this again around sustainability."

Fairfield became one of the first small cities in the country to take a comprehensive approach towards energy conservation, renewable energy, and changing the culture around local resources towards sustainability. We identified 40 sustainability objectives clustered around jobs, culture, and infrastructure.

Right from the start, we saw progress. We increased recycling participation by 70% with systems changes. We ran an 18-month energy conservation program, setting a goal of reducing energy consumption by 4%. Energy audits were conducted on large manufacturers, the city buildings, and several hundred homes. Solar systems were installed.

After 18 months, we more than doubled our original goal, reducing energy consumption by 8.5%. Alliant Energy selected Fairfield as one of three Iowa communities to be the first beneficiaries of its Hometown Rewards efficiency program.

In 2009, a journalist heard that we had designed our own plan and requested a copy. His story, entitled "The 15 Greenest Mayors in America," included mayors from San Francisco, Chicago, New York, Atlanta, Miami, and me from Fairfield.

The journalist told me, "I need a photo, a picture of you doing something green." I didn't have such a photo, and it was the middle of winter. I sent him a picture taken in 2007 during the Iowa Caucus campaign of me speaking with candidate Obama. (I told Obama that you won't find a community anywhere in the U.S. more unique and with so much to share as Fairfield, Iowa.)

As of 2018, we have executed most of the plan. We put half a million dollars towards retrofitting buildings for energy efficiency. We received funding for the Maharishi University of Management (MUM) Sustainable Living Center and for the Fairfield Eco-village.

MUM created the first degree program in Sustainable Living in the country. Classes are held in the net-zero energy Sustainable Living Center.

North of campus, meditators created the 15-acre Fairfield Abundance EcoVillage designed to be socially and environmentally responsible. They apply cutting-edge sustainable technology to meet water, energy, and waste treatment needs.

Fairfield is fortunate to have two locally grown solar energy companies. One of those companies, Ideal Energy, was started by two MUM grads (one a former Navy Seal). Troy and Amy Van Beek formed a company for solar projects, and the city works with them encouraging development. Fairfield commercial buildings that are powered by solar panels include Sky Factory, with 50KW of panels, the community radio station, and a town square building owned by the author of this book. The other company, Solaray, also employs MUM graduates and is one of the leading companies in the Midwest. By 2018, over four megawatts of solar energy powered Fairfield homes and businesses.

Other programs include the quiet zone — eliminating horn noise as trains pass through Fairfield, solar installations on city buildings, housing expansion projects, and the wastewater treatment plant currently under construction.

Trustee of Maharishi University of Management

In 2010, I was honored to become a trustee of the university. The university has been a part of Fairfield for 45 years and the impact it has had on the overall community is significant. As a community leader, I wanted to invest myself in the continuing success of MUM.

As a trustee, I want to see the university grow and be recognized for the incredible unique educational experience it is. What happens at MUM is precious, and many people would love to be here.

We want MUM to be self-sustaining. I am working to create a large endowment for scholarships and the faculty.

The future of Fairfield

The people of Fairfield do so many things that I think of Fairfield as The City of 1,000 Passions. Through personal commitment, leadership, networking, and collaboration, those passions take form in art, business, music, retail, literature, architecture, media, and ecology.

From 1980 to 1998, Fairfield entrepreneurs created over 400 businesses, about 150 of which remain in 2018. In 1989, I started the Fairfield Entrepreneurs Association to insure that entrepreneurs and start-up companies could access the expertise they needed to grow their business. Today, Fairfield is a mature entrepreneurial environment thanks to networking, resources, and infrastructure coupled with bold ideas and risk tolerance.

Visitors often look at the many different things we have and ask, "How do you start? Where do you find people willing to make those kinds of commitments?" I share that everyone has the resources within them, and TM practice develops inner potential.

We've invested in many things that attract people. With many great employers, we now need more housing so that we can grow.

I think a larger university and a larger population base will mean dramatic growth in all that Fairfield offers. Fairfield's population has grown by 9.4% since 2010 and new entrepreneurs are springing up from the next generation.

WISDOM: Begin knowing the goal is already accomplished

YOU CAN DO IT

When speaking to MUM students, I always tell them that they will be successful. I say the same to you. If you have doubts or lack of confidence about achieving what you want, start by getting rid of those doubts. Just let them go.

Start with your core passions. They form the basis of what you can achieve, whether it be in business, art, or service. Then act on your passions. Be willing to lead so you can make a difference for yourself, your community, and the world.

Think about the outcome. What do you want to create? How will it look and feel? Keep adding and refining. Clearly see the vision. Write out your vision and be able to articulate it. Then know that it will be accomplished.

Practicing Transcendental Meditation helps. With meditation, intuition and nuanced thinking become part of the conception and envisioning process. Effective visioning and planning come from passion, confidence, self-knowledge, and intuition.

The businessperson and the city planner face similar challenges starting something new — capitalization, expansion, customer support, marketing, networking. Confidence that the vision can be accomplished empowers all involved. You can be bold if you have the inner certainty that it is already done. Achieving the vision becomes just a matter of time and working out the details.

Goal setting is key. Goals should be both strategic and realistic.

To feel a sense of achievement and encouragement, be realistic about your goals. Learn the discipline of challenging your ideas as you create specific goals and plans. Set the level of achievement bar high enough to bring satisfaction, but realistic enough for success.

If you manufacture something, and you feel that you can sell 5,000 in the first 18 months, deconstruct the number. What steps must you take to get to 5,000? If you see the goal as unrealistic, and 500 makes more sense than 5,000, shoot for 500. If you do better than 500, then you'll set your next goals more accurately.

Last year, Danaher Oil brokered 187 million barrels of product. We couldn't set that type of a goal in 1985. There wasn't a path. We got to that level by continually moving our benchmarks.

Align with others

You need to align yourself with others to manifest your passion and vision. Networking allows you to bounce ideas around, get feedback, and shape your goals.

Finding mentors shortcuts your work. Rather than agonizing over a decision, one 15-minute conversation with a mentor can point you in the right direction. A mentor can also provide you with referrals, references, and ways to shorten the learning curve.

In business, nothing is more important than relationships — relationships with your co-workers, your partners, your customers. We all have similar hopes, aspirations, insecurities. It's all about building trust and friendship with those you do business with.

You must be able to sell yourself to be successful in business or in public service. Selling yourself means selling your service, your personality, your thinking, your dealings with others, your integrity. You may have a terrific product or service. Yet, if you can't genuinely share, communicate, and establish a level of trust with a customer, you won't be successful.

It takes practice to overcome resistance to promoting yourself and your service. Having a style and technique helps. Most important is to be comfortable and non-judgmental with yourself.

Leadership

Leadership is based on authenticity, honesty, and believing in the goodness of people. By going within, I find what inspires me, how to empower others, and the direction to lead.

I love the diverse nature of Fairfield, starting with the families who have been here for generations. Their respectful acceptance of new residents since MUM's 1974 arrival has been a process and, in the end, a successful American story.

As mayor, I am responsible for bringing people together to make Fairfield a great community. I work to find common ground and then appoint commissions with people from all backgrounds to build consensus and get things done. Working together in good faith on shared goals brings positive outcome.

I am committed to being a positive, articulate, energetic, and passionate representative of the city. Everything I'm involved in within the community is important to me. Whether conducting city business or expressing a new vision, I use my commitment, energy, and attitude to empower individuals and organizations.

When I talk about Fairfield, I talk about one community, not differences. I am proud of Fairfield's heritage, proud of the university, proud of the culture and arts, proud of the businesses, proud of the diversity. I am most proud of the cooperation between the city council, administration, department heads, and private partners — all motivated by the greater good of the community.

I represent what I believe strongly and passionately. Accordingly, I supported Obama early in the 2008 Iowa caucuses. At the same time, especially as mayor, I don't want anyone to feel demeaned by my ideas and positions. I respect what others feel and believe. I always try to find the merits within any position and look for common ground to be able to connect.

I've gained self-confidence, self-knowledge, and comfort from my daily TM practice. After meditation, my focus increases, my picture expands, and I am better able to see the reality of a situation.

SPIRIT: Bring in light to dispel darkness

Upon taking office, many of us felt deeply about the rift in Fairfield. Someone would say, "You can't have him involved because he is a "Ru" (guru/meditator)." Next door, someone else would be saying, "He can't join us because he is a townie." Today, it's a non-issue, anyone can be part of anything. Groups and organizations work together.

When I began, I did not want discussions about getting along better. We had done that, and it didn't get us anywhere. It would have been looking in the darkness for the cause of darkness.

The 10-year strategic plan was a way of bringing in the light to dispel the darkness. Starting with common values and shared aspirations, the entire Fairfield community cooperated. Accomplishing our goals put us in sync. More than Fairfield's wonderful reputation, I'm most proud of its citizens working together to create our special community culture

The path of reconciliation was having the community work together for the future. We used basic human skills to understand each other. We discovered and shared each other's passions, collaborated, and enjoyed the fruits of our efforts.

With mutual respect and shared pride as part of the culture, the fertile Fairfield ground is set for even greater success. I believe in public service, and I am confident that what we have created in Fairfield can be modeled in other small towns across Iowa and the country. I ran unsuccessfully in 2018 in a primary race for the Iowa State Senate. I hope I will get another opportunity to use my skills and vision to lead and contribute to the success of others.

Ed Malloy's twelve tweets

Passion and vision

1. Start with your core passions. Act on them and be willing to lead from there to make the world a better place.

2. Refine your vision by writing it out and articulating it so it is 100% clear.

3. Know inside that your vision is already accomplished. Then you can be bold since it's only a matter of time for the vision to appear in the world.

4. Set goals high enough for satisfaction, yet realistic enough so you can feel a sense of achievement and encouragement.

5. To manifest your passion and vision, you must align yourself with others.

Leadership

6. The key is to build trust and friendship with all those with whom you do business. Nothing is more important than your relationships with co-workers, partners, and customers.

7. You must be able to sell yourself to be successful in any endeavor.

8. Find mentors. They help with making decisions, referrals, references, and shortening the learning curve.

9. You must be comfortable and non-judgmental with yourself. Then, by going deep within, you will be able to communicate effectively, build relationships, and know where to lead.

10. Respect what others feel and believe. Don't demean anyone. Find the merits in the other's position and connect by finding common elements.

11. Empower individuals and organizations with your commitment, energy, and attitude. Look inside yourself to find what inspires you. Use it to empower others.

12. Reconciliation takes place by working together for the future. Start with common values, shared aspirations, and mutual understanding. Enjoy each other's passions and celebrate the fruits of everyone's efforts.

Ponder

1. Can entrepreneurial principles really be applied to non-profits and government? Won't bureaucracy and lack of profit motivation get in the way?

2. Ed says let go of doubt and know that you will succeed. Is that easier said than done? How can you be confident of success with an unknowable future?

3. Ed was successful as mayor because he did not focus on existing discontentment. Rather, he led people to work together and create a future fulfilling to everyone. How practical is this approach with dissatisfied customers or employees?

4. Can you think of an example in your life when you solved a problem by bringing in a second element rather than focusing on the problem?

Fairfield City Council meeting, Mayor Ed Malloy center

Welcome to Fairfield sign greets visitors

Jefferson County Courthouse, view from a Rene Holmberg drone

Francis Thicke and friends perform during the December Artwalk inside the Fairfield Arts and Convention Center

People enjoy a leisurely summer evening Artwalk

Fairfield audience inside the Fairfield Arts and Convention Center watching Oprah's show about Fairfield, "America's most Unusual Town"

Fairfield Central Park gazebo in winter

Above: MUM Student Union. In front, the Vedic Observatory is an ancient Vedic technology that has the effect of expanding awareness, while focusing the mind on the mathematical order and precision that regulates the universe.

Left: MUM meditation dome along side Tower of Invincibility

Below: Inside MUM meditation dome

Inside the ICON gallery during Artwalk

Everybody's Whole Foods annual holiday train exhibition

Meditating entrepreneur Stacey Kitakis Hurlin, a Greek American living in Iowa, has brought back some of Greece's finest handcrafted textiles which she shows at Artwalks to help support the Greek economy and 70,000 Syrian refuges.

Octoberfest Artwalk, Francis Thicke with horn, Ed Malloy clapping

MUM Sustainable Living Center classroom in background was opened in 2012 as a teaching building for the world. Solar, wind, geothermal creates more energy than it uses. The energy is stored in the front building.

Dick DeAngelis (center) is producing eight-part documentary on the history of Fairfield. Photo is of actors and production team for run-away slave scene. Werner Elmker, photographer of Fairfield photos, in upper left.

Since 1996 over 3,000 international students from 100 Countries have participated in the Maharishi University of Management Computer Professionals Master's Degree program.

Saturday Fairfield Farmer's Market

Part of 15.9 mile Fairfield Loop Trail through and around the city.

Spring flowers in front of the Fairfield Arts and Convention Center

Betsy Howland
BOOKS, FOOD, AND COMMUNITY

Fairfield is a warm and welcoming place to live, and Betsy Howland has contributed to making it so. When Betsy arrived in Fairfield, she found it hard to meet people. She would see people on campus at the meditation dome, but the dome is a place for silence, not socializing.

Betsy recognized the need in Fairfield for a gathering place. In 1995, Betsy and her daughters Julie, Joan, and Jennifer started the popular Revelations Café and Book Store.

Previously, Betsy lived in upstate New York, where she was a foster parent for 17 children. Finding her entrepreneurial spirit early, she and her husband owned a Montgomery Ward franchise and added a department store. In addition, Betsy sold Mary Kay cosmetic products, ran a commercial cleaning service, presided as co-president of the PTA, chaired the local cancer society, served on the Montgomery Ward corporate board, and for several summers ran a small saw mill.

While running Revelations, she took charge of the Fairfield First Fridays Art Walk for several years. She was also instrumental in launching the Fairfield Maze of Murals project.

JOURNEY: Creating community with Revelations Bookstore and Café

THREE DAUGHTERS, TWO IDEAS, ONE GARAGE

My daughters, Julie, Joan, and Jennifer, and I envisioned a place where people could feel comfortable, relax, meet friends, and feel a part of the Fairfield community. My youngest daughter, Jennifer, had the idea of recycling books. We put our ideas together and started Revelations.

Out of goodness and a sense of community, the owners of Everybody's Whole Foods, John and Coralee Dey and Paul Praither let us use the large garage behind their store. We had only to clean it out. The previous occupant, a Toyota dealer, had used the garage as a paint shop.

Tires, old coolers, lawn mowers, old furniture, dough machines — almost anything you could imagine — packed the garage from floor to ceiling. Everything seemed too big to move and there was no place to move it to. For two weeks my daughters and I worked to clear everything out at an excruciatingly slow pace.

During this time, Jennifer overheard a conversation: "They don't have a chance. They know nothing about running a bookstore."

Depressed, Jennifer said, "We can't do this, Mom."

"Yes, we can," I replied. "We just need to take the first step. We don't have to know the whole process."

I then told my daughters to take the day off and rest. After they left, I took on one square foot of a corner of that garage, removed everything, and painted the walls and floor. When the girls returned, I pointed to the spot and said, "This is the beginning of Revelations."

Revelations became four square feet, then seven, then ten. We just kept moving stuff and claiming new territory. We acquired 200 books from garage sales and our own collections. On each shelf, we placed three books face out to create the appearance of abundance.

We started slowly, but we weren't discouraged. My daughters and I would celebrate even on days when only two books sold. To this day we're still improving, expanding, and remodeling.

The Revelations building

As cars whizzed by the former Toyota paint shop garage, we envisioned a beautiful bookstore on a quiet street, filled with light, accessible and inviting to all.

One daughter surprised us and took a job at a new Italian restaurant. The location was central but quiet, right off the town square. It had a beautiful wooden floor and tall windows that flooded the inside with light. As I ate at its grand opening, I imagined selling our books in that building. It would be perfect.

Ten weeks later, the restaurant went bankrupt. The owner wanted to sell us the restaurant, but we just bought the building and eventually ended up using it as a restaurant. We discussed what to do with the kitchen. My daughters said, "Rent it out." They wanted a bookstore, not a restaurant.

But we were in business for the customer. A few weeks in, we purchased an espresso machine so customers could have coffee while looking at books. Then a customer requested a sandwich with the coffee. We made two chicken, two tuna, and two cheese sandwiches and didn't sell one. Still, we kept making them, and each night for weeks we would eat sandwiches for dinner. Eventually, the sandwiches began to sell.

One day a lady said, "I wish I had soup to go with my sandwich." So, I made a little crock of cream of broccoli. Next, it was cream of tomato. For a good while the girls and I had soup for dinner every night.

Over time, the soup and sandwiches sold, as did the books. Today, we make two huge pots of homemade soup and over 100 sandwiches a day.

It took us a year to peek inside the pizza oven that had been imported from Italy. We had no idea what to do with it. The original restaurant owner told us that his son was visiting Fairfield for two weeks. Did we want the son to make pizza? Yes, we did. Watching him carefully, we realized that not only could we make pizza, we could improve it. He used frozen dough; we made homemade. He used canned sauce; we made it from scratch.

That's how we did everything, moving slowly forward, step by step, focusing on what the customer wanted.

How do you eat an elephant? One bite at a time.

Mother is at home

Our vision of creating community always included providing space for different activities, whatever the interest. We now use our upstairs and the lower level as a gathering place for seminars, workshops, business meetings, parties, political organizing, anniversaries, and book signings. Many come from out of town and give classes. For example, we just had a pet psychic come to Fairfield who taught pet owners how to communicate with their pets.

A woman teaching classes in our upstairs seminar area told me that Revelations felt like "mother is at home." I liked that. It's true: Revelations nourishes the body with food, the mind with books, and the soul with art and music.

Revelations has a life of its own, and we feel we are just along for the ride.

Art Walk and Maze of Murals

I've been involved with many community-nourishing, art-related projects that showcase Fairfield artists' talents. These activities help develop and enliven downtown Fairfield where Revelations resides.

As Executive Director of the Fairfield First Fridays Art Walk for two years, I managed the monthly downtown events that took place in rain or shine, in sweltering or freezing weather. Each Art Walk featured a theme, with the art galleries open to the public, and included music, film, food, children's activities, and outside vendors. Hundreds of Fairfielders along with visitors from throughout the Midwest still attend the monthly Art Walk, which continues today.

I also helped launch the Fairfield Maze of Murals project. Artists demonstrate their talents on downtown walls, making well-used alleyways more attractive.

WISDOM: Lead like Mom — be firm, consistent, loving

START SMALL

Revelations and my other entrepreneurial ventures taught me to start small. Take care of the customer, and the customer will show you the natural path to expansion.

As an entrepreneur, you don't have to know everything when you start. At the beginning of Revelations, we knew nothing about how to run a bookstore. We just took the first step — a location and some books on shelves. Everything we needed to learn, we discovered along the way. Now, using the internet, it's even easier to learn how to do almost anything. Information about getting a license, incorporating, and obtaining a tax ID is just a Google search away.

I believe our job at Revelations is to serve the community. What does it need? What does it want? I listen, and then do what I enjoy and makes sense.

Part of serving the community is being true to ourselves. For example, no matter how many customers requested it, for years we wouldn't open on Sundays. Finally, this last November and December 2018, we yielded to requests from customers, the Fairfield Chamber, and downtown merchants. Our Sunday business was OK, but the experience reaffirmed our initial decision. We found ourselves working six and seven days a week, and we just didn't have the energy to treat our customers the way we wanted to, so no more Sundays.

Hiring: "We take strays"

Some years ago, I raised over 20 children, including 17 foster kids. At Revelations, we have had as many as 20 employees, mostly young people. As with foster kids, at Revelations I take chances on young people. I've had employees with health, legal, and drug problems.

Many rules for parenting and managing are similar: be firm, mean what you say, be consistent, and be loving. At Revelations I praise employees when they do good work, but I'm strict. I know what I want, and I know how I want it done.

If a job isn't working for a new hire, I don't just push them aside. I am aware of how my words can affect not only an employee's livelihood but their feelings and self-esteem. At the store, we will keep moving someone around to different positions until they click and feel comfortable. Someone hired to cook might turn out to be a great waitress.

I hire people on a temporary, part-time basis to see if we can find a match. Some people just don't fit. I'm honest. I tell them I'm sorry. "I like these things, but these other things seem difficult for you. It just doesn't feel right. Why don't you look for something you are more suited for?" I usually let them continue to work for us until they find a better fit elsewhere.

We encourage employees to further their education. I had one fellow with a serious drug problem. He would be in and out of jail, in and out of rehab. Every time he went to rehab we'd keep the job open and take him back with open arms. Now, sober for some time and ever so grateful, he got his GED and enrolled in college. Seeing him become such an incredible young man made it worthwhile.

Cultivating repeat customers while learning to say no

Revelations attracts visitors from across the state thanks to our large and varied book collection, our fresh, wood-fired pizza, and our unique "arty and spiritual" atmosphere. That said, it's our regular customers that make our business work, especially in a town of 10,000. Even if I don't know their names, I know where the regulars sit and what they order.

People are always asking me for favors at Revelations. It is hard to say no, because I want to satisfy everyone. For example, one person asks if he can use a café table to sell his artwork. Another customer requests hot water for her own tea bag. Yet another brings a birthday cake for a party, even with "no outside food" signage and knowing that we make an assortment of cakes. I have to turn them down.

Some people get upset when I say no. They storm out, saying they will never return. I feel terrible, but if I make an exception for one person, I would have to say yes to everyone, and that would be a catastrophe. I do my best to be gracious when denying their requests, explaining that we must make a profit to keep the doors open.

Whether it is foster kids, employees, or customers, the same rules apply: be firm, consistent, and loving.

Revelations creates community

In my mind, a business must have meaning and purpose and fulfill some desire of the owner. Whatever you do should make you feel satisfied and happy. Don't do something that makes you miserable, even if you think it a great idea, even if someone you value wants you to do it. If you aren't happy doing something, change what you are doing.

For more than 20 years, all of our hearts have stayed with Revelations, even though now it is just my daughter, Joan, and I who run Revelations. Jennifer, my youngest daughter — the one whose idea it was to start selling used books — spent the last eight years becoming certified as a five-element acupuncturist. My other daughter, Julie, and her husband, Dale, launched a service that replicates fine art.

Revelations offers visitors a homey, casual, leisurely atmosphere. It is not like going to a regular restaurant where you go in, order, and leave. We never rush anyone out. People feel comfortable just sitting around and chatting.

Writers write books and poetry at Revelations. People meet and fall in love. Old friends re-bond. We've even hosted several weddings and receptions.

Our vision has always been about community.

Stay in the moment

My best advice for dealing with the chaos of running a business is to stay in the moment. Otherwise, everything can be a challenge. There are always issues to deal with: licenses, insurance, a leaking roof, a dead furnace. Often, entry-level young employees leave.

What's here right now is all that I know. No matter how overwhelming a challenge appears, it can be handled by breaking it down into small, bite-sized tasks.

Integrity, gratitude, and dealing with negative people

People recognize integrity when they see it. Throughout my career, bankers have loaned me money even with a weak asset position. Once we give our word, we honor and stand behind it. In a small town like Fairfield, everybody knows everybody, and everybody knows if you lack integrity.

When I wake up, I appreciate all that's good in my life. Doing so brings me happiness and gives me the power to get things done.

I ask, "What's going to charm me today?" I might think, "Valentine's Day is over. I'll put the St. Patrick's Day window in." If the work feels like it's getting to be too much, and I lose my patience or passion, I will simply stop. I'll get to it another time. The window remains half done because I go by what feels right in the moment.

Occasionally, we'll encounter a customer who complains, saying something like, "That was the worst pizza I've ever had." We think maybe their taste buds are off that day, so we give them a credit slip and say, "Sorry, see you next time."

I can't control how people think, how they respond, or what they say. If people attack our practices or plans, I don't buy into it. I listen to them and thank them for their input, but I don't give it energy. If they are negative, I rarely agree because I know what is right for me. At the same time, I refrain from telling others what's right for them.

An overheard conversation didn't deter Revelations at its inception. If it's our vision, if it is what we want, we just keep going.

SPIRIT: Create your world through thought
MANIFESTING A SWIMMING POOL BY INTENTION

When I was young, I watched the original version of the movie, *Cheaper by the Dozen*, a comedy about the tribulations of the parents of 12 children. I recall thinking how fantastic it would be to have all those kids.

Later, I had three children, adopted three, and took in six foster and homeless kids. Having 12 children in the house was every bit as fun as the movie — and just as crazy.

We needed a bigger house, so we bought an old farm house in the country. I thought it would be wonderful to have a swimming pool for the kids. My husband, the kids, and I designated a spot in the yard for the pool, even though we had no idea how to manage it financially.

We had such a clear vision for the pool that whoever cut the lawn had to wear a bathing suit when mowing over that part. We never walked over the pool location unless we wore a swimsuit.

Later that summer, someone knocked on my door and said, "I hear you want a swimming pool."

I said, "That's right, but it has to be an in-ground pool." As it turned out, a few miles away someone was giving away an in-ground pool with a stainless steel liner.

We still needed money to dig a hole, move the pool, and fill it with water, but our clear intention prevailed. A neighbor with a contracting business knew we were helping kids and wanted to assist. It would have been many hundreds of dollars to hire someone to come with a bulldozer and backhoe and dig the big hole. Our neighbor dug the hole, charged me only $50, and allowed me to pay in $5 weekly installments. The kids enjoyed the pool for years.

When my daughters and I moved to Fairfield, my husband was to join us later but never did. Our interests and life-styles had grown apart, and we ended up separating. When he became sick, my daughters and I took turns going back and caring for him.

Your thoughts create the future

Thoughts are powerful. By being intentional about your thinking, you can create the future. A thought put a man on the moon. The energy to start and run Revelations came from the thought of recycling books and our vision of creating community.

Look back a few months. How did your thinking create your current circumstances?

Everyone creates their world by default or by deliberate intention. Those that live by default get up each morning, put on clothes, walk, eat, drink, perform daily activities, and go to bed. Like a driver without a destination, without clear intention, these people can end up anywhere or nowhere.

Alternatively, we can create our world through deliberate intention. We put our attention on the goal, know why we want it to happen, and do what's necessary to achieve it.

For years, I wanted a Harley Davidson motorcycle. I'd get excited imagining the Harley ride, the engine's roar, the blast of wind on my helmet, the sun — and then I'd think about how much a Harley costs. Creation stopped in its tracks.

I finally realized that by focusing on the negative, I was sabotaging myself. Instead, I formed a clear intention in my mind. I decided that I would have the Harley whatever it took, even if I had to empty my piggy bank or get dealer financing. The clarity was liberating.

With that decision, motorcycles seemed to come from all directions. At the time, waiting lists for Harleys were up to three years. I traveled to a Harley dealer in Quincy, Illinois and told him I didn't want to wait. I wanted a Springer Soft-Tail, and I wanted it now.

"That's amazing," the sales guy said. "I have one that came in a half-hour ago, still in the crate. Only 104 were made for the Super Bowl and this limited edition is one of two that wasn't used. You can have it today."

In the end, I decided not to buy it because my friends would never have let me take a collector's edition out of the crate. However, I did buy a Suzuki Intruder, similar to the Harley, at half the price. I loved it. I invested the difference in Harley stock, and the Harley stock paid for my next three vehicles.

I changed my thinking and had my ride.

I've noticed that "practical" people often don't move ahead. Their minds focus on the inevitable obstacles, and nothing happens.

At Revelations, we envisioned a beautiful alternative to our garage location. Although we did not know how it would happen, we were clear and precise about what we wanted. A moment of pure positive thought began the manifestation process.

My twice-daily TM practice not only relieves the stress from my work at Revelations, it strengthens my thinking and intentionality. From my quiet mind, creative solutions emerge. Thanks to TM, my thinking is clear, precise, and powerful, and I am able to create what I want in life.

Change your story, change your life

If someone's ill, they talk of poor health. Someone with problems tells everyone about their problems.

Why put your energy there? What you put your attention on becomes your reality. If you don't like how things are, tell a different story. Change your life by changing your thinking.

Many years ago, my daughter totaled my car. Then shortly after, the transmission went out in our van. I had no money to repair the vehicles. I required transportation for my work traveling to art fairs around the country. I borrowed a friend's van, didn't realize it used a lot of oil, and destroyed the motor. That was three vehicles in less than two months!

It was all I talked about.

Then we found large snakes slithering around in our basement. It seemed everything bad that could happen did happen. I realized what I was doing: I was playing a part in my misery, creating a downward spiral by constantly talking about what was going wrong.

I stopped. I waited for something good to happen so I could try something different. A friend came over to repair my bathroom sink, and that was all I talked about — how wonderful for someone to do that. Once I changed my thinking, the downward spiral ended. I stopped creating negativity, and things got better and better.

In business, you can create a negative spiral by continually thinking and talking about problems. Focus on successes and vision, and you will create a better outcome.

To succeed in business, you must be in the moment and deal with what's in front of you. I'm not saying to be blind to possibilities, but why dwell on non-existent problems created by the mind?

Once, I wanted to spend Christmas with my parents, so I decided to drive all night — 1,100 miles — to New York. With a wind-chill of 50 below and blizzard conditions predicted the entire way, I thought, *I must be out of my mind.*

I drove with a death grip on the wheel. I was terrified. Then I realized, *There's no snow now, so why am I upset?* By staying in the moment and not making trouble by thinking about problems that didn't exist, I made it to New York easily.

Similarly, in business, I do what needs to be done now. My mind may see all sorts of problems, but I ask myself, "Is there a problem right now?" If there is, I'll do something about it. If there isn't, I don't create more problems.

Your inner guidance system

Everyone has an inner guidance system. It never fails. It never fools you. It's always right.

The guidance signals can be gut feelings, a "knowingness" in the heart, or even a physical experience like an intense headache.

Close your eyes and try this experiment: think of a question and take the first answer that comes. See what your body says about the answer. How does it feel? The mind will try to override it, but if you listen, the body knows.

I had a friend who had a tough decision to make regarding diet. I told her to sit quietly with her eyes closed and think about the diet she was asked to be on and how it made her feel. Instantly, she got a horrible sensation in her body and felt choking. I changed the subject and then had her be quiet again. I asked about an alternative diet. She immediately responded, "Yes that one, there's no doubt. I feel settled and peaceful."

Whenever you have to make a decision, you can find the answer by settling down and listening. Ask the question one way and then the other way. Wait for the reaction. It may seem like it will be hard to recognize, but it won't be. There will be some strong bodily signal like a tightness in the throat or a feeling in the stomach. The subconscious mind knows and expresses itself in the body. If there is no real reaction, then it is OK either way.

For 20 years at Revelations, we have used our inner guidance system to make decisions.

Betsy Howland's twelve tweets

Create your world through thought

1. Everyone creates their world either by default or deliberate intention. If you live by default and function on automatic, you could end up anywhere. Instead, create with deliberate intention. Put your attention on the goal, know the "why," and do what's necessary.

2. Picture clearly and precisely what you want. A moment of pure positive thought begins the manifestation process.

3. If you don't like how things are, change the story you are telling. In business, you can create a negative spiral by continually thinking and talking about problems. To create a better outcome, focus on successes and your vision.

4. When I wake up, I appreciate all that's good in my life. I think, What's going to charm me today? That attitude brings me happiness and gives me the energy to get things done.

5. Everyone has an inner guidance system. Guidance signals can be gut feelings, knowingness in the heart, or even a physical experience like a headache. If you listen to your body, it is always right. The mind tries to override it, but if you listen, the body knows.

6. I've noticed that "practical" people often don't move ahead. Their minds focus on the inevitable obstacles, and nothing happens.

Act with intention

7. The way to deal with the everyday chaos of running a business is to stay in the moment. I do what needs to be done now. My mind may see all sorts of problems, but is there a problem right now? If there is, I do something about it. If not, I don't create more problems.

8. Whether it is children, employees, or customers, similar rules apply: be firm, be consistent, be loving.

9. Start small. Take care of the customer, and the customer will show the natural path to expansion. No matter how overwhelming the challenge, break it into small, bite-sized tasks. Just take the first step. You don't have to understand the whole process.

10. I'm aware how my words not only affects an employee's livelihood but their feelings and self-esteem.

11. Your business should have meaning and purpose and make you feel satisfied and happy. Don't do something that makes you miserable, even it is a great idea and even if someone you value wants you to do it. If you aren't happy doing something, change what you are doing.

12. Celebrate success, even if at the beginning it doesn't seem like much.

Ponder

1. Betsy emphasizes both living in the now and having clear goals. Is that a contradiction? Why or why not?

2. Betsy's vision and passion was to create community. What is your vision and passion for your business and for your life?

3. Betsy discusses deliberate intention and creating from thought. She gives examples of the swimming pool for her kids and the Revelations building. Do you believe you can create from your thoughts? Do you have examples?

4. What do you think of Betsy's notion of a fail-proof inner guidance system? Have you ever used it? To what effect?

5. Betsy gave several examples about how her negative thinking perpetuated her problems. She didn't get the Harley and she kept destroying vehicles. Is it your experience that your story creates reality or that reality creates your story?

Betsy Howland with part of her collection of used books

Lunch at Revelations

Winter night Artwalk outside Revelations

PART THREE

Turning Art Into Business

George Foster
Ron Bovard
Jim Davis

George Foster
THE ART OF BOOK COVER DESIGN

George Foster is a leading independent book cover designer. Over the years, his cover designs have helped sell millions of copies of over 100 bestsellers, including three from the Chicken Soup for the Soul series and three by Pope Francis. He has earned more than 300 awards, and his clients include leading publishers, such as Simon & Schuster and St. Martin's Press, as well as scores of independent, first-time self-publishers.

George also lectures on cover design. Numerous print and online publishing resources recommend George and feature his work.

Cover design is not his only talent. Fairfield music fans enjoy George's singing, bass guitar, and quirky humor when playing blues with Skunk River Medicine Show, worldbeat with Bambu, or jazz with 3=One.

In 1985, I asked my friend, George, if he could lay out our newsletter. Given my limited budget and propensity for making last-minute changes, I could never have produced our first labor-intensive issue without George's heroic, going-the-extra-mile efforts. Through 2011, he created all of my company's almost 200 newsletter and magazine covers.

And, of course, George created the cover for this book. His portfolio can be found at his website, www.fostercovers.com.

JOURNEY: Starving artist to leading book cover designer

EARNING A LIVING AS AN ARTIST

I received my first award and payment for my art at five years old, winning five silver dollars for a Halloween-themed watercolor.

Twenty-one years later, in 1979, after completing a B.A. in illustration from Columbus College of Art and Design, I moved to Fairfield, Iowa, the center of the Transcendental Meditation universe. Fairfield bubbled with talent and creativity. I couldn't turn around without bumping into an entrepreneur or toss a stone without hitting a graphic designer. The problem for me was that experienced designers got the all the freelance and salaried jobs available.

With no graphics work to be found, I painted watercolors and held a one-man show. No one bought anything. At loose ends, I thought, *What am I going to do now?*

Then someone called. "I hear you're a graphic designer?"

I said, "Yes!"

"We want graphics for a video. Can you do that?"

I said, "Yes."

"Have you done it before?"

"Yes!"

Actually, I'd never done that before, but I knew I could deliver what they wanted. The client loved the result and hired me for additional projects. New prospects started calling with more work. I dove into every project, never complaining about late nights or tight deadlines, doing whatever it took, and learning as I went. Clients appreciated the results. Word got around, and the phone continued to ring.

To attract additional clients, each Saturday I showed my tiny portfolio of art school work at a trade fair in the Maharishi International University student union. More people began to hire me. I also bartered, exchanging my design of a newspaper ad for a chiropractor visit or a bag of groceries.

I worked one job at a time, not charging much, staying busy, always giving 100%. Clients called back and told their friends.

Then Hal Goldstein came along in the mid-eighties. He hired me to design his technical, 24-page newsletter, *The Portable Paper*, a catalog called *The Portable Equipment Exchange*, and scores of ads for his products.

My business kept growing. By the early 90s, I had done everything my expanding list of clients could want — direct mail, ads, stationary, brochures, logos, restaurant menus. I also designed book covers including *Chicken Soup for the Woman's Soul*, which to date has sold six million copies. Back then, I considered a book cover just another design project.

Short deadlines taught me to work fast. I started, finished, and delivered multiple projects each day on a six-days-and-nights-a-week schedule.

I said "Yes" to everyone, and my reputation grew.

Going broke — the turning point

Almost from the start, I brokered printing. I knew which jobs the different printers did best, and I knew how to talk with printers so clients would get what they wanted. I made 15% commission from the print bill for 30 minutes of work.

But then, in 1993, a friend and client who for years had given me a third of all my work, died suddenly. He owed me $10,000 for printing. I did not want to ask his widow for the full payment, so we settled on half.

Two weeks later, my next largest client went broke, owing me $25,000 for printing I had ordered for him under my name.

Friends advised me to file for bankruptcy and to sue the client for fraud. Even though I owed considerably more than my net worth, neither path felt right. Instead, I worked out a plan with the printer, paying him monthly over the next five years.

Another friend told me of an entrepreneurial venture in which he made $100,000 in nine months selling coupon book ads to retailers. He thought I'd be perfect for it and offered to coach me.

Desperate, I followed his lead and became a buttoned-down businessman. I opened a Cedar Rapids office and joined the chamber of commerce. I had employees and a phone bank. People did all sorts of things for me as I created the ads for the coupon book.

Instead of making $100,000 the experience cost me $10,000 and six months.

The coupon book misadventure and the other adversities proved a turning point, a stepping stone for eventual success. Although I learned important lessons about myself from the coupon book, it took time to recover from the losses. I went into a spin for more than a year, sort of a long dark night of the soul.

The Fairfield economy was changing. Bigger companies formed and gobbled up smaller entrepreneurs, decreasing my work load. With finances tight, I would quietly wonder, *What should I do?*

Then, one day I rolled out of bed with the answer: book covers. My livelihood wouldn't depend on the small local Fairfield economy. I could go national. I knew that my experience designing marketing material and advertisements would serve me well.

I realized I wasn't a businessman; I was an artist. I didn't need employees or big plans, just my skill and creative talent and the desire to do good work. If I had to be broke, I would at least enjoy my day. If I became wealthy, it would be as a graphic designer. I would be myself and be happy.

I went bohemian. No more neckties, no fancy haircut. Just my two hands doing graphic design.

At the time, I had designed maybe a dozen covers, including three of the earliest *Chicken Soup for the Soul* books. But how to get more business?

I called my good friend, John Kremer, a meditating entrepreneur and book marketing expert. I had designed the original cover for his classic, *1001 Ways to Market Your Books*. He sold me an ad in his newsletter and started recommending me at his seminars. I wrote a chapter about cover design in his next edition. People began to call.

To get additional clients, I ran ads in two more newsletters, began speaking at seminars, and created a brochure for new prospects. Samples sell, so in my free time I redesigned existing covers for free.

I showed publishers my expanded book cover portfolio at trade shows like Book Expo America. Covers with "Designed by George Foster" began appearing in book credits, increasing my credibility and reach.

Initially, I kept my rates low so people would hire me. As demand grew, I increased my fees. Each time I raised my fees, I lost some clients and gained others. I found that charging more attracted authors and publishers who valued an effective cover over a cheap one.

I focused on doing good work and sticking to my niche and began to benefit from the old way of going viral — buzz about me. Since 2005, I have no longer needed to advertise. Now, business comes from word of mouth, repeat customers, and my website. Industry professionals such as consultants, printers, editors, authors, and publishers recommend me. A printer receives an awful book cover and tells his customer, "Don't print that cover. Call George."

Always aiming for a wow from the client, I did eight covers the first year, 15 the next, and then 20, increasing to an annual average between 50 and 60 a year with a top of 80. Aside from a monthly local ad for a long-term client and some pro bono work, I only design book covers.

Here's what I have learned from my experience and the advice I would give anyone: do what you love. Do what gives you energy. Start inside, then look outside. Don't do something just because you think you should or because someone tells you to. Use your passion to fuel your success.

Technology changed my job

In the 1980s, I designed hundreds of ads by hand on a drafting table using pencils, pens, a T-square, tape, cardboard, glue, and translucent tissue for instructions to the printer. I would give typeface specifications and hard copies of text to Ron Flora, a fellow Fairfield meditating entrepreneur. From his large typesetting computer, Ron produced high-quality type on rolls of glossy paper for me to paste onto white artboards. (The term "cut and paste" originated from the process of cutting and pasting type from those rolls.)

In 1984, Apple introduced the Mac and suddenly everyone thought they could design their company logo over lunch. For about a year, I lost business.

Then those same people started calling me again, realizing that design wasn't their thing. Computers don't create design; people do, leaving the good designers still standing.

In November, 1985, Hal gave me a printout of text for the first issue of his newsletter, *The Portable Paper.* I wrote Ron the instructions on the printout pages, specifying margins and fonts. Ron and his wife, Susan, retyped it all into the machine. We stayed up two consecutive nights before we could get all the correct type output and pasted properly onto boards. I prayed for no revisions.

The next day, Hal ran in. "I've got revisions!"

I marked the many changes and gave the pages back to Ron for another all-nighter. Ron went to his machine, created the changes, and output the new revisions in one long column of type. I used an X-Acto knife to remove the old type from the artboard and stick in the new type, fitting it as seamlessly as I could. We often fixed typos one letter at a time by finding the correct letters in the trash.

We finally got the issue finished, revisions and all. (Four nights without sleep can make you hallucinate.) With the issue at the printer, I was off the hook until the next issue which only required one all-nighter.

I didn't buy a computer until 1990. I had been making ovals painstakingly by hand with pens and plastic templates, but the Mac's ability to generate ovals in seconds convinced me to enter the computer age. I leased a Mac, a monitor, and a printer for $20,000. The unhealthy, noisy, desk-filling, 19-inch cathode-ray monitor made my hair stand up on end! I'd take breaks just to get away from it.

I had my new computer, but I didn't know a thing. Hal told me, "I've got a catalog to do."

I said, "Yes, I can do that on a computer, and it will go real fast!" Boy, was I wrong.

During the day, I did all my other client work, the phone calls, and the running around. At night I went back to Hal's catalog, four long all-nighters in a row.

Back then, in Photoshop I would make one small command on the computer and then have to wait 20 minutes, praying it wouldn't crash. After years of such pain, MacOS 10 was a huge relief and computing got much better.

You can sell a book by its cover

I don't create book covers for decoration or fine art. I design covers to sell books. A good cover paints an inviting picture of the book's content so that a reader explores and buys. Done well, a cover blends beauty with targeted communication. There's nothing like an eye-catching, professionally designed cover for selling a book.

Today, in the exploding digital ebook and audiobook market, effective book covers are as important as ever. Online viewers scan screens quickly. Digital covers must make readers pause and be drawn to start looking at reviews and sampling the product.

I prepare by reviewing the manuscript and talking to the author. Nonfiction is straightforward and I generally know my approach right away, but a work of fiction has it's own beating heart inside so I must read the entire thing to find it. From my understanding of the book, I think about who will buy it and why. My covers target those readers. I want to grab their interest. I want them to ask, "What's that about? Tell me more."

The design should be clean and elegant and amplify the message. I never want the design to get in the way — if you confuse, you lose. My covers balance color, shape, and typeface with simplicity and spaciousness. Viewers should find the cover so arresting and cool that they don't want to look away.

A good cover requires know-how and experience. I stay open, because ideas can come from anywhere. I often start at the computer with a blank screen, then play with this idea and that one. I trust my intuitive sense and conscious intent for the cover to lead me as I work, and my excitement builds as the cover takes form. I like to think of it as imbuing consciousness into the design. And when the cover is right, when there is enough consciousness in it, I can practically feel the design vibrate — like the ringing sound of a beautiful bell.

I don't shoot out ideas or show early versions of covers to gain praise. I keep things to myself until they are ready; there's power in keeping a project inside and telling only the people who need to know.

My website sells

I've spent a lot of time refining my fostercovers.com website to educate customers about my service. Years ago, Hal told me, "Just put everything they might want to know on the site, including your fee."

I worried my fee would scare them. Hal pointed out that if I didn't list the price, I would continue spending a lot of time talking to people unwilling or unable to pay. Instead, with the cost clearly specified, I speak only to qualified people who are interested in working with me.

So, I've put everything on the site: my cover portfolio, testimonials, input needed from the customer, a well-defined description of services, and my fee. It's such a time saver. People just call me and say, "Let's go. Let's do it."

Customers' endorsements play a key role on my website and are an essential to growing my business. When customers tell me how much they like a cover, I ask for a testimonial. That way, when I need an endorsement, I have plenty to choose from.

I've rewritten the website fee page many times, always making it more customer-oriented. They're interested in me, but I must make it about the customers. Why should they hire me? What's in it for them? They don't buy because I am good; they buy because I can do something for them.

WISDOM: See every situation, every decision as the whole business

RUNNING MY ONE-MAN BUSINESS

You can't get any smaller than one guy. I do the whole thing — answer phones, bill customers, track receivables, respond to email, attend meetings, market my services. In the early years, it wasn't until evening that I had time to do the design work.

Working at home has its perks — I can go to the computer in a bathrobe and bad hair without consequence. At the same time, working at home requires discipline and a special passion. My business works only if I work. I must continually attract clients, make them happy, get paid, and attend to the details that allow the business grow. I give 100% to each project, focusing on the work, not minding the time. I know when to push and when to let go.

If I were lazy or only out for fast money, I would have missed out on the personal growth that comes from giving my best. I also would not have been in business long.

Making my business work better

I think holistically, paying attention to the details and seeing the entire business in every situation, no matter how small. Every decision connects to and supports everything else.

I also think long term, continually improving my graphic art and my business systems. I work on my craft, always getting better, learning from each project, never thinking, *Oh God, they want that! How will I get through it?* I see each project, no matter how rough, as an opportunity to learn and be smarter the next time. I ask myself: Who am I at the beginning of the job, and who am I at the end?

I identify heroes, people I emulate and can learn from. When stuck, I think, *What would they do?* For example, I study books written by influential graphic designers. Seeing how they make use of an image or technique often jumpstarts my own creativity. For years I've had large, framed posters of Bob Dylan, Jimi Hendrix, and Miles Davis above my desk. Their dedication and originality changed our culture and inspires me to generate my own original ideas.

Hal and I were both clients of Michael Gerber, author of *The E-Myth Revisited: Why Most Small Businesses Don't Work and What to Do About It.* Gerber emphasizes working on the business rather than in it. That means I refine systems until they are turnkey, so I can do what I enjoy rather than fight fires.

I am always tweaking systems. If an office problem happens once, it might be a fluke. If it happens twice, I fix it. I don't want to waste time or give poor service by repeating a fixable problem. For example, I once promised a client to overnight him color proofs. I ran out of ink halfway through, which meant I wasn't able to keep my promise to deliver the proofs. Starting the next day, I always had extra ink cartridges on hand.

Whatever works best, I do again. It's like making a path — see where people walk and pave there. I find the natural flow as it evolves and support that. I never try to force things to be a certain way. For example, before computers I assigned a number and a manila envelope to each open job. Today, using the search capabilities of a Mac, I no longer need envelopes, file cabinets, or even job numbers.

I create paths — routines, simplifications, refinements — for every aspect of my business. I have systems for communicating with new clients, servicing clients, giving quotes, invoicing, paying taxes, buying supplies, developing the website, and using Facebook. That way I can focus most of my time on doing what I love — designing for my clients.

When the Mac gets too slow, I purchase a faster model. I value my time and don't want to spend it staring at a screen. Taking the long view makes the expense a good investment.

I used to answer the phone before the second ring, believing it a good business practice. Maybe it is, but that meant spending much of the day talking to clients and telemarketers. To complete projects I would work at night when the phone stopped ringing. Now, I screen the calls with voicemail, stay focused, and only return calls as necessary. The time saved still amazes me.

I outsource as makes sense. I don't know how to do taxes and don't want to know, so a CPA does that. I created the content and design for my website but hired a professional to make it functional. I'd rather the expert do it right than waste my time struggling.

Finding the prestige-level price niche

I didn't think of money until I got married at age 29. Then I learned that without money a so-called business is really a hobby. If I wanted to succeed, I had to start paying attention to the finances.

In any field, most of the price-level competition is found in the middle of the price spectrum with much less at the big discount and prestige levels. I started my graphic design work at the low end and gradually increased my fees over time.

Each time I raised rates, it felt like a nightmare. I hated telling clients the bad news. Even though I was working six days and nights a week, I feared that no one would hire me and that raising rates went against my mission to serve. The decision felt personal: what am I and my art really worth?

When I finally raised rates, for a little while I had less work and more time. Then it would get crazy again, and I would raise my rates again. I have always made it about value for the customer, whatever I charge.

I've now staked out an expensive, prestige position. Having a high price and high perceived value sells — as long as I deliver a product that matches or exceeds the price.

I learned from Michael Gerber that if you offer a service, you can set yourself apart from the competition by marketing it as a product. (Similarly, you can market a product as a service.) So, rather than billing hourly for my cover-design service, I charge a fixed fee for my cover-design product. Then I work until I satisfy the customer.

Naturally, clients want to know the cost ahead of time. A client may compare hourly rates to find the best deal, but the lowest rate can mean lower quality and frustrating results. My clients are happy with my guaranteed book-cover-design product rather than being charged hourly. Early in my career, a new client told me, "No guilt trips. If you spend too much time on this, I don't want to hear about it. Tell me now what it will cost, and that's what I'll pay."

Customers can budget my fee and forget about it. They don't care if I spend one hour or a hundred hours, as long as they get the high-quality results I promise.

As I've raised my prices, I get far fewer people telling me how to design their covers. They just let me have at it. Funny how that works.

At one point, I more than doubled my fee to $5,000. New clients came, but my workload and revenue decreased. After six months, I lowered the fee to its present level. Someone once told me that prices with "75" in them were golden online numbers. True or not, I advertise $3,750 for a printer-ready book cover (front, spine, and back cover). I lose sometimes, but over the course of a year, I win, and I don't have to track my time.

One time, I spent countless hours showing cover after cover after cover to a client. One late night, I decided: I'm going to kill the pain.

I told the guy, "I am unable to give you what you need. You will be better off finding someone else." That approach works better than saying, "I quit." I never want to burn bridges. I start my jobs with half the design fee upfront. I decided to give him all his money back; It would have felt wrong saying, "I'm not the one, but I'll keep your money."

Follow your passion

I tried being a starving artist once and didn't like it. Yet, I never worried much about money. By listening to my heart and doing what felt right, by staying inspired and following my intuition, things always worked out.

The fact is, if you don't want to be at work on Monday morning, you're in the wrong profession. If what you do excites you, you will never work a day in your life. The people who love Mondays and can't wait to solve problems are the game-changers in their fields.

Following others' advice, I once tried hiring other graphic artists to expand my business. Two things happened. First, I started dreading Mondays. Second, I realized I was a poor manager and a mother hen. I would assign work to someone and expect them to do it right the first time. I would then redo their work to suit my tastes. Training requires repetition, something I wasn't willing to do, so I went back to being a one-man operation and loving Mondays.

I see book cover design as my passion in motion. Ideas never run out, and the ones that thrill me always work best. The creating process is a kick, just a kick.

SPIRIT: Serve with a pure heart
SERVICE GROWS MY BUSINESS

The rock in my life is service. The client always comes first.

My artist's ego was destroyed years ago at art school; I'm not attached to my creation. Making the client happy is what counts, no matter the number of revisions, no matter if it means scrapping what I just created.

The client may tell me, "That's not it at all. What were you thinking?" I reply, "Okay, thank you, no problem. We'll try again." I then retool and restart. New ideas come, ideas not there the week before.

An attitude of service to others has grown my business and grown me as a person. My skills continue to improve through service, and that brings better clients, better reputation, and more satisfying work.

A guiding principle for me is "People don't care how much you know, unless they know how much you care." Care about what? Care about them, their needs, their goals.

Although I spend most of my time at the computer designing, my work is a people business. I want my clients to have a pleasant, enjoyable, uplifting experience. I've seen excellent artists fail in their business because they're difficult to work with. They think they know more than the client, and clients don't have time for that.

I no longer take every job, but I always treat everyone with kindness. I often help people even though I know they won't hire me. If I can't do what someone wants, I try not to say "No." Instead, I communicate what my "Yes" looks like and see if there is a path forward that works for both of us.

A client may ask for something that I don't think will work. I never argue. If they insist on something, and I shut that off, they won't forget. I might win the argument and lose the client. I stay open to the back and forth flow with the client. I say, "Yes," by showing a design that may differ from the author's request but enhances the essence the author really wanted.

When you treat people right, word gets around. If you treat somebody wrong, that gets around too, maybe even faster.

I can serve and still set limits. We all have to draw the line somewhere. I ask myself, "Will it be time well spent?" If necessary, I'll be quick with someone, but always gentle.

In the beginning, I could only afford one pair of pants. During the past 30 years, I have just kept working hard — kept "throwing wood on the fire" as they say — always with an attitude of giving, rather than taking. And my life keeps getting better and better.

Purity

According to Maharishi, purity of heart attracts success. I do everything I can to serve with simplicity, love, and openness, and that approach protects me. "Please" and "Thank you" are basics in my vocabulary. Hal once confided that when he got annoyed with me, it felt like "yelling at Bambi."

By cultivating a giving heart and always providing excellent service, my good fortune has increased through the years. Even when it doesn't bring money, it brings wonderful friends, good health, and happiness. You can't predict the future. You can't make a new customer call you. You can only deserve it. Then they call.

By nature, I see the good. If a deal goes bad, I learn something I didn't know before that will help me in the future. If my back goes out from too much time at the computer, I enjoy the rest.

I took to heart something I learned from watching Hal. In the late 1980s, I was at his office to work on a catalog. People were in line waiting to talk to him, and somebody handed him a piece of paper. It was obviously bad news, but he didn't react right away. Instead, he stared at it for five full seconds. Then he asked himself with all sincerity, "What's good about this?"

I remain undisturbed

TM opened me to unbounded awareness, fullness inside, self-sufficiency, and freedom of the need for outside validation. The TM-Sidhi program integrated that unbounded awareness into my design work and ability to communicate.

As a result, I don't need to show off or be praised. I smile when criticized, which serves me well as a designer. It's not a lack of ego, but a lack of fragility and insecurity. I simply enjoy my work.

Sure, I love to hear I've done a great job, and I treat a client's disappointment seriously. But neither praise nor complaint disturbs my peace of mind.

George Foster's twelve tweets

1. I see every situation, every decision, no matter how small, as the whole business. Every decision connects to everything else.

2. Whatever works best, I do again. Like making a path, I see where people walk and pave there. I find the natural flow and don't force things to be a certain way.

3. I am always refining systems so I can spend most of my time designing for clients, which is what I love. If something takes too much time once, it's a fluke. The second time, I fix it.

4. They don't buy because I'm good, but because I can do something for them.

5. Having a high price and high perceived value sells as long as I deliver a product that matches or exceeds the price.

6. I start inside, then look outside. I don't do something because I should. I listen to my heart. I do what feels right and notice that things always work out.

7. If you don't want to be at work Monday morning, then you are in the wrong profession. If work excites you, you will never work a day in your life.

8. I'm an artist but lost the ego part years ago. I make the client happy no matter the number of revisions, no matter if it means scrapping what I just created.

9. By cultivating an open and giving heart and always providing excellent service, my luck has increased each year.

10. A designer, no matter how excellent, can't make a business fly if he is difficult to work with.

11. Although I spend most of my time at the computer designing, I see my work as a people business. I want my clients to have an enjoyable, uplifting experience.

12. I credit the TM technique for opening me to unbounded awareness, leaving me full inside, self-contained, and free of the need for outside validation. I love clients' praise and take their disappointment seriously. Neither disturbs my peace.

Ponder

1. It served George and his clients well that George always said, 'Yes,' when asked if he could do a graphics job, even when he had no idea how to do it. On the other hand, do you think there might be something wrong or unethical about this approach?

2. When one client died, George didn't ask the widow for full payment. When, soon after, another client went bankrupt, George paid the printer bill. He ended up in bad financial shape for a year and a half. Did George make the right choices? What would you have done?

3. George gave up his passion for watercolor painting. Did he sell himself out? If he were determined, do you think he could he have made it?

4. George says, "Put the client first." He also says that, as an artist, he needs to do his own thing. Is it possible to do your own thing while serving others? Can you think of a time when serving others and doing your own thing came into conflict? How did you resolve it?

"George is covered" photo © 2010 Marandah Jain

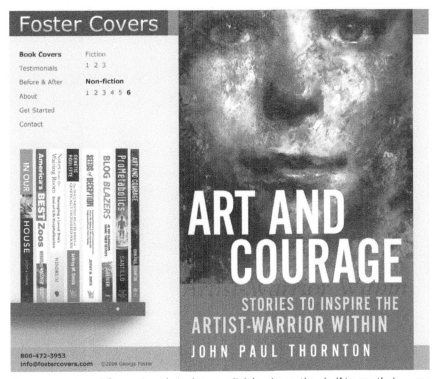

An early version of George's website let you click books on the shelf to see their cover

George's wife, Mary, is an artist whose creative input is essential to the success of each book cover.

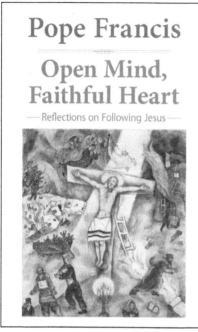
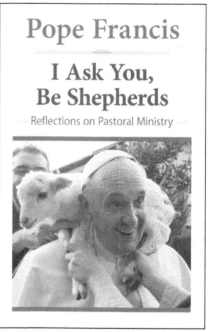

George designed the cover for Pope Francis' first book in English, followed by a series.

You can see some of George's bestselling book covers at fostercovers.com

One of many #1 bestsellers

George with some of the more than 1,300 books that have his cover designs

Ads in newsletters for self-publishers stand out on the page if they show the designer instead of the typical cluster of book covers.

Ron Bovard
HEAVEN ON EARTH WITH STAINED GLASS

Ron Bovard began exhibiting his spiritually uplifting art in museums and galleries in the United States and Europe in 1972.

In 1985, in Fairfield, Iowa, Ron launched Bovard Studio, which creates and restores stained glass windows. By 2000, Bovard Studio had expanded to employ over 70 people, including some of the world's finest, award-winning artists and craftspeople. Each year, the studio takes on over 100 church, courthouse, library, and college projects.

Located in over 40,000 square feet of modern production space, on 20 acres of highway frontage, Bovard Studio can meet any stained glass need. Facilities include a state-of-the-art graphic design department, a glass painting studio, a stained glass production space, stained glass restoration facilities, wood and metal shops, a showroom, and office space.

JOURNEY: Fusing the art, science, and business of stained glass

TWENTY YEARS EXHIBITING MY ART

After college, for 20 years I worked as an independent artist. I often painted hu man beings surrounded by vibrations of consciousness, illustrating the bridge between the terrestrial and the celestial. In 1972, I participated in my first significant group exhibition. That show led to a period of 25, one-man exhibitions in museums and prestigious galleries in New York City and across Europe.

While producing exclusive works, I joined artist guilds and trade organizations, finding the camaraderie and cooperative atmosphere of working alongside other studio artists most rewarding.

Newspapers and magazines positively reviewed my work, and some of my art was published in art books. That notoriety boosted my creative ego but was not that helpful in supporting my loving wife and five children. Although I sold many pieces of art, I had little money to show for my efforts.

Soon enough, I recognized that the gallery system does not favor artists. Although 90% of the art sold in the U.S. is traditional, most art school graduates paint in a contemporary style. Artists compete to have galleries show their work in order to sell art and create a reputation. The galleries display art on consignment, taking 50% to 60% in commission. In addition to the cost of materials, artists often pay for expenses like framing, fliers, and brochures. As a result, artists compete for limited spots and few of them make a reasonable living.

Many artists believe that if they create something, the world will come and buy it. I was more proactive, marketing my work and securing shows and exhibits. Even so, I found it difficult to support a family.

While developing and exhibiting as an artist I supported my family as a social worker. The 35-hour work week with vacation and sick leave gave me time for my art.

Launching Bovard Studio

After 10 years as a social worker, I quit my job. At Maharishi's urging in 1982, I moved to Fairfield, taking a job as the art director for Creative Glassworks.

Creative Glassworks developed and patented a process using abrasive water jet cutting to lasercut difficult materials like marble. The company designed, fabricated, and delivered architectural projects, and I created viable art products with this new technology.

My contagious enthusiasm has always helped me sell my work, so selling Creative Glassworks products came naturally. As the most successful salesperson, the company made me sales manager, which meant I created less art.

Realizing I was no longer doing what I loved, I decided to resume my career as a full-time artist. Fortunately, my compensation at Creative Glassworks included a stock package. I sold the stock in 1985 and opened Bovard Studio in an old Fairfield factory that housed 30 other artists.

Shortly after I left Creative Glassworks, a manufacturer's representative asked me to develop and manufacture a product line of stained glass for the door and window industry. We would distribute these windows through lumberyard chains and home supply stores. For many months I declined, wanting to be a fine art painter who also worked with stained glass.

But, by January of 1986 I had hit rock bottom financially. When this representative called again, I said yes. He needed the product line developed and shipped within 30 days. I told him it would take me at least that much time to raise the capital. He asked me how much I needed. I gave him a number. The next morning, I received a check, and "Bovard Art Glass Studio" was born.

I designed the product line, hired several craftspeople, built jigs, set up a production system, and 30 days later, shipped out several hundred octagon-shaped, stained glass window inserts. Within a year, I set up a production facility, did market research, and ended up with a Lowe's account, making thousands of windows a month.

For successful sales, you must know who you're selling to, and what motivates them to buy your product. I discovered that retailers such as Lowe's and Home Depot carried products based on dollar value per square foot of floor space. With Lowe's in mind, I created a unique display for a half-dozen octagon stained glass window designs that required the floor space for one window.

We innovated in other ways. At Creative Glass Works, I had developed a commercial product line for Marvin Windows using brass. Bovard Studio came out with a gold-plated line of glass windows for Lowe's, since brash tarnishes.

By the end of 1986, we had landed several other window insert accounts, and our production department was in full swing. However, these mass-produced items were artistically uninteresting. Furthermore, no matter what we developed, six months after it hit the shelves, Stanley Door, Peach Tree, or another large window company would come up with the same product for less. Today, brass and gold-plated art glass windows are sold everywhere.

At the same time, we continued to develop our custom art glass division and had completed several smaller commissions, but more importantly we successfully completed our first church window commission. Soon after, we restored and recreated windows lost in a fire for a church in Hamilton, Illinois. Over the next two years our custom business grew and, by the end of 1988, it was clear to me that Bovard Studio's future was in architectural and ecclesiastic windows. I made a decision to concentrate our efforts in that direction.

We gave our commodity product customers our copyrights and suggested Korean manufacturers. Within a few months, we had filled our last production orders.

We are now 100% committed to creating and restoring stained glass for churches, courthouses, libraries, museums, state government buildings, military bases, restaurants, and hotels. Architectural glass is the most fulfilling business I have been involved in, and we have been growing ever since.

Producing great stained glass art

By 2000, our art department consisted of eight glass painters and four designers from Germany, Hungary, Bulgaria, Ukraine, Canada, Jamaica, and U.S. Our fabricators, restoration staff, and installers, like our artists, have rich and varied backgrounds.

I don't hire glass painters. I hire talented artists and teach them how to paint on glass. I can't turn a glass painter into a great artist. I can take a brilliant artist, show them the new medium, and allow them to create brilliant art on glass. Along with a strong portfolio and classical training, the artists we hire must be productive. I can't run a business with an outstanding artist who takes six months for one painting.

Designers must be well-skilled in Photoshop and CAD. The initial rendering of a design takes as much time to create in Photoshop as it used to in watercolor. These days, using Photoshop, we show the customer the design over the internet. The customer can say, "Change this color" or, "Move that over there," and then see the difference immediately.

Our artists are grateful and happy to make a living doing what they love — art. It's fulfilling for the designers, builders, and craftspeople to create a spiritual product that beautifies the world and that will last over a hundred years.

Similar to reverse type, glass artists create whites and bright areas by allowing light to shine through the glass. No matter how skilled a traditional watercolor or canvas artist, the artist finds it challenging and fundamentally different to paint on glass. We solved the training challenge in a way that has had many benefits.

In the late 1990s, we saw the need for ready-made glass medallions with traditional hand-painted motifs that could be incorporated into stained glass windows. We developed prototypes that featured religious and secular painted designs. We showed them to a trusted glass supplier.

We explained that the growing number of professional and hobby-craft artisans would be interested in authentic, hand-painted, stained glass medallions. Further, since few people paint on glass, studios would be willing to purchase the medallions for their stained glass window installations.

The supplier gave us a purchase order. I prefer doing business that way, first selling the concept, and then developing the product line. Today, most art glass distributors carry our elegant, hand-painted, glass products. They sell the medallions to stained glass retail supply stores all throughout North America, Europe, Japan, Africa, and South America.

Not strong money-makers, I use medallion production for training. When I hire a talented artist, I have them paint hundreds of medallions. From this simple low-end work, creating a product that we know we will sell, they learn how to paint on glass. The medallion business also allows us to avoid laying off artists between projects.

Further, the widespread distribution of our medallions markets our brand. When a job is too big for a local stained glass studio, they refer the customer to us. Also, other studios feel comfortable ordering custom and original art glass painting from Bovard Studio for religious and secular projects. Bovard Studio's custom medallions include 18 hand-painted and kiln-fired life of Christ and Old Testament scenes.

Collaboration creates progress much faster than individuals working by themselves. In the film industry, many work together to create the art of our times — movies. Google, Apple, and Microsoft bring brilliant people together to make revolutionary products. In the Renaissance, 10 to 15 artists surrounded famous artists to create the great masterpieces.

When I worked alongside artists in independent studios, we were locked in closets in our own world, each believing that we could be the next Picasso and that patrons would rush to our door. Things don't work that way.

At Bovard Studio, artists, glass painters, and designers collaborate on all projects. Talented artists work with other artists, each learning from the skills and creativity of the others. By working together on project after project, artistic talent flourishes. Finer work evolves than could have been created by individuals on their own. The synergistic output of our artists continues to inspire me.

At Bovard Studio, we have glimpsed the secret of the Renaissance.

Having restored stained glass from all different heritages, we can match the style and quality of any stained glass line.

For example, the windows of Louis Tiffany are up to seven layers of glass thick. Window on window on window on window creates the magic. During restoration, we have taken apart and rebuilt many Tiffany windows, learning the brush strokes, the techniques, and the art of the Tiffany craft.

Similarly, we learned the techniques of the great glass artists. This restoration experience provides the foundation for Bovard Studio to create new stained glass heritages for our clients' churches, courthouses, and libraries.

Marketing our custom stained glass services

When I began, I asked myself, *Who will be my stained glass window customers, and how can we reach them?* We couldn't survive as a local studio in our small regional area, so to stay in Fairfield, we had to become bigger. I identified churches, courthouses, and libraries as primary customers. I reasoned that pew salespersons sell pews to churches, benches to courthouses, and commercial seating to libraries.

I found a mailing list of about 600 reps who sold pews and chairs to my would-be customers. I did a direct mail campaign and followed up with phone calls. I signed six manufacturer's reps, several of whom still represent us 30 years later.

A manufacturer's rep works on straight commission and carries different non-competitive product lines. Currently, we have 14 of them across the country. That's how we built our client base. We also tried in-house salespeople, but lost money.

There are about 2,000 stained glass studios in the U.S. Most operate on a local level; only five or six of us compete nationally in the commercial public building sector. Our main competitor, the local studio, doesn't have to pay for transportation, food, or hotels. Local studios are well known in an area and usually have been around for generations.

It's challenging to win over a Catholic church to build their stained glass. Often, the church has used the same family for generations. Once we do get the work, our service and quality translate to lots of new business in the diocese.

We make stained glass windows the way it has been done for hundreds of years. Our products and restorations last a century without repair or maintenance. That means no repeat business unless that pastor gets transferred to a new church.

In the beginning, we exhibited at the Iowa State Fair, visited by close to a million people each year. The first year, the administrators gave us a tiny, out-of-the-way booth. The next year, they decided that our art was significant. For $600, they gave us a more central, 12- by 30-foot booth.

For 11 days, 12 hours each day, we couldn't leave our booth. It was exhausting. However, many people in Iowa came through, and we got a lot of Iowa projects. After four years, people knew about us, and exhibiting was such a grind that we stopped.

We've done many other trade shows over the years. Now we do the two that we know work — the small Catholic Facilities Managers Conference, where attendees represent hundreds of buildings in a diocese, and The American Institute of Architects national convention.

Rarely do we get into the residential market. It takes more effort to please a homeowner than it does a whole congregation. People are attached to their homes, which become part of their ego. That means if they're not happy with themselves, we aren't going to please them. Besides, home windows don't scale — we wouldn't travel across country to do one kitchen window.

I wanted to write about my experience starting Bovard Studio, the art of stained glass, including maintenance and restoration, and showcase the stained glass created by our studio. Authoring a book demonstrates status and expertise and a book can be an effective marketing tool.

I went to the largest publisher in our industry, selling him the book before writing it. (Anyone can write and self-publish a book, but then who will read it, and how will it get distributed?) For us, since a picture is worth a thousand words, we produced it in color. As part of my royalty, the publisher agreed to let me purchase as many copies as I wanted at cost for our promotional use.

The publisher successfully distributed the book — selling out the first edition and publishing an updated second edition. That distribution, coupled with using the book as a gift to prospective customers, helped grow the business.

Using challenges to advance our business

Either you overcome challenges or you don't exist. The greater the obstacle, the more creative the solution needs to be. We have turned the challenges of unreliable suppliers, hurricanes, earthquakes, and other unexpected events into opportunities that carried us through difficult times.

It would typically take six weeks to receive the new dyes required to bend our metal into ornate shapes for church window frames. If the dyes didn't work, we would have to wait another six weeks. My crew would sit on a job site with nothing to do for two or three days waiting for a New York supplier of frames and extrusions. Products would often arrive dented.

After a while, we started bringing these and other critical operations in-house, always improving the output. We created framing and glazing systems for different materials and built a frame shop, wood shop, and metal shop. We did our own tooling. We obtained a U.S. patent on 21 aspects of our framing and glazing systems for stained glass windows

Taking over from weak suppliers allowed us to become more self-sufficient and better able to serve our customers, delivering projects on time. By seeing supplier problems as opportunities, we created new aspects to our business that have sustained us during difficult times.

We recently completed a large church dome. We didn't realize when we bid that the dome had multiple radii within each of the panels. We did excellent work for them. They never knew what we had to overcome to restore this unique dome. And although we lost tens of thousands of dollars on the project, we learned something new; the experience adds to our knowledge base, which will prove helpful since we do many domes and skylights.

Stained glass is part of the architecture of a building, and our structural engineers play a critical role in the work. A stained glass window can last centuries. To do so, it must withstand wind load. That meant hurricanes brought us another opportunity.

Windows and doors are weak spots in a structure, and a dramatic pressure change from a hurricane can cause the roof to blow off. We developed a patented glazing storm window system to withstand winds of up to 150 miles per hour. Florida, the state with the strictest U.S. hurricane codes, approved it. To test our glazing and framing for hurricane-force projectile impact, the National Testing Laboratory shot two-by-four wood boards from an air cannon at our windows. The windows survived the shock.

We have developed a glass lamination product line that meets earthquake code in California. For example, we created and installed stained glass windows that met strict Los Angeles standards for the West Angeles Cathedral. The cathedral has a height of a 10-story building and a width of more than two football fields.

This largely African American church has 20,000 members, including Denzel Washington and Magic Johnson, co-chairmen of the building committee. It seats 5,000 people, has space for a 700-member choir, and fills to capacity for four services most Sundays. With all the new technology we had to develop, we broke even on the project. However, through it we got a lot of other business, including the Martin Luther King Memorial church in Selma, Alabama.

Visitors come from throughout the U.S. to see the West Angeles Cathedral and its stained glass.

Operations

Our customers finance our projects with down payments and stage payments. Even so, we sometimes need bank financing.

At the beginning, we asked Iowa State Bank, the only Fairfield bank in the 1980s that worked with meditator-based businesses, for a $5,000 credit line. The president, Terry Lowenberg, offered me 10. Now, 30 years later, we have a large credit line that gets us through the winter and slow times.

We received our first Small Business Administration (SBA) loan in 1990. With that type of loan, the local bank signs off taking 20% responsibility, the government 80%. We applied over the Christmas holiday.

The Cedar Rapids SBA loan officer was familiar with Bovard Studios. As a member of the architecturally famous Saint Paul's United Methodist Church designed by architect, Louis Sullivan, he saw me make a presentation. Subsequently, we got the contract and did good work. When the loan officer saw our application, he immediately OK'd it. Terry was astonished that the SBA approved our loan in three days.

Before doing a job, my production manager does the cost estimate. When we complete the job, I get a cost analysis of how it went compared to our estimate. With that feedback, we are always fine-tuning our estimation process.

We compute prices per linear foot on frames and venting. The complexity and quantity of glass gets factored into the stained glass square foot estimate. We take into account downtime because things don't always run smoothly. A broken truck can set back a project. Margin must be built in for the unexpected and for staff, accountants, pre-production work, management, and sales commissions. We add 40% to break even, and anything over becomes gross profit.

Every product is different. By being intimately involved in design, development, and manufacturing of the product, we know the business inside and out. Being there, running the numbers rather than guessing, having good accountants that give good feedback, and knowing the labor costs are essential.

Years ago, I contracted for custom bidding software. If I had known the cost and that it would take 10 years to build, I would never have done it. Even so, it's one of the best investments I've ever made.

Now, when I bid, we lay everything out by square footage, how many nails, how many screws. The software computes the cost of each element, and voilà, we create a bid. The software lets us bid a lot of jobs in a short amount of time.

As Art Director, I work with our team to come up with new products for our customer base. I often look over artists' shoulders suggesting this or that. Occasionally, as with the more contemporary West Angeles Cathedral, my design gets implemented.

I also do the critical job of recruiting and training the sales team. I keep reps motivated with meetings, calls, and direct contact in the field.

Our doors open at 6:00 AM and close at 6:00 PM. Employees name their hours, but must always show up at those hours, so we know when we can rely on them.

In the mid-1990s, I hired an employee who, as I found out later, had applied with the intent to unionize our small company. During the attempt, we were accused of 30 unfair labor violations, which was a delaying tactic since the union did not have the votes. I was expected to answer charges without being told specifics — I didn't know what I supposedly did to whom, when, or where. The union received only seven votes in the end, but the process cost me tens of thousands of dollars in legal fees plus a great deal of costly company time.

After that experience, I hired a Mexican engineer with an MBA and brought him to Iowa for three years as my production manager. Then, I set him up in a facility in Matamoras, Mexico, where a thousand stained glass workers built stained glass window inserts for large production door and window companies.

I pay double the local rate to hire and retain the best people. Counting transportation, the Mexican plant doesn't save money. Even so, the already trained and skilled available labor protects us from outside influences and the unforeseen. The plant also allows me to expand our production capability quickly for large and time-sensitive projects.

Slowing down

When I was younger, I was like the Energizer Bunny. It was go, go, go, 24/7, work, work, work. Eventually, I cut that in half.

A few years ago, I called myself semi-retired, and now I have a relaxed work schedule. I've replaced myself by training talented people in just about every aspect of the job.

Still, I don't know what I would do with myself if I left the business. I come to work every day at a more relaxed pace, enjoying life and finding time for golf and fishing.

WISDOM: Love what you do

PASSION FOR YOUR WORK IS NECESSARY FOR SUCCESS

Many people ask me how Bovard Studio became so successful. For a business to succeed longterm, you must have passion for it. I love my work and enjoy every bit of it.

I find creating jobs for artists and craftspeople most satisfying. Also, I love dealing with my customers, beautiful people with golden hearts, who endeavor to fulfill the spiritual aspirations of their community. It's an honor to be in this trade.

Few new businesses succeed, so pick something you love to do. That way, during the tough times, you'll see it through and be there long enough to have a chance to succeed. As long as you show up and put in a full day's work, you are still in business. The longer you do this, the greater your chance of success.

Most income generated by new businesses must be reinvested for growth and development. That means at first the company pays you little. Businesses have ups and downs, and those people who don't love what they do won't stick with it through the down times.

Maharishi once said, "See the job, do the job, and avoid the misery." I concur. Just do your duty, do what it takes, and do the right thing. Artists tend to think the world is here to serve them. We're here to serve the customer; they're not here to serve us. Do a good job. It's always rewarded one way or another.

If you are creative and flexible, understand the market, and are doing something you would do for free, you can make it.

Hire people smarter than you

A supportive family is also essential in any small business venture. Fortunately, my wife and I each grew up in a family of entrepreneurs. Well aware of the swings and cadence of small business, we witnessed first-hand its risks and rewards, its ups and downs, and the difficult times. We observed how perseverance turns failure into success.

My strengths lie in product design and development and in sales and marketing. My entrepreneurial father and uncles taught me to also know my limitations. I built the business by gradually replacing myself with people smarter and more skilled than I, recognizing others' talents, and putting aside my ego.

I hired exceptionally talented and gifted artists and designers who run circles around my artistic prowess.

I realized early on that I am not a good manager. When I ask someone to do something, I just think it is done and forget about it. That's not management.

I had started Bovard Studio to become an artist again. However, one of the most important realities an entrepreneur must face is their personal limitation. My experience as a child watching my father and uncles helped me to see the importance of this lesson early on. So, when the circumstance presented itself, I was mentally prepared to hire people who were more talented, with exceptional skills in areas I was lacking.

For example our business manager and Chief Financial Office (CFO) has a strong accounting, banking and small business background with more than 25 years of experience. He is one of the smartest businessmen I know. Our production director is a manufacturing engineer with a master's degree in business management with more than 30 years of work experience. He is also a gifted Apostolic Catholic priest and bishop. And we have several exceptionally talented and gifted artists and designers who run circles around my artistic limitations. Hiring these exceptionally talented people who love what they do and have important skills to contribute to Bovard Studios has proved the key to our growth.

Each of our staff has special gifts. As a bonus, they are fun to be around and love what they do.

Selling

If you know that you have a good product and are enthusiastic, selling comes naturally. You don't have to try. When you tell the truth and speak from the heart, people trust you. If you don't believe in the product, people can smell it a mile away.

You must have a thick skin because you will get a lot of rejection. You can't be desperate. You must be able to tell the prospect, "It's OK if you are not interested." No high-pressure stuff, especially if, like us, you're selling to a committee or government agency. My 10 years as a social worker in Pittsburgh served me well for sales. I enjoy meeting people and building the long-term relationships necessary for our business.

Politics and working with government

In 2003, I fired someone, and he started filing complaints about lead to Occupational Health and Safety (OSHA) and the Department of Natural Resources (DNR).

We always followed through with compliance, fixing things rather than paying fines. We invited the educational department of OSHA into our building in a voluntary compliance capacity. Unfortunately, when OSHA enforcement comes in, the work with the educational department is withdrawn and their educational staff must leave.

Our employees were cleaning our glass painting brushes in the sink, so there was a bit of lead going into our septic system. The Department of Natural Resources extrapolated that four pounds of lead a year was being placed into the environment. The DNR required us to tear up and replace the septic system, dump the contents in a toxic waste site, and stop cleaning our paint brushes in our sinks. We were happy to do this, as we had been unaware of the pollution we were causing. (Ironically, the 70 acres of land Bovard Studio sits on was prime, Iowa hunting land with more than four pounds of shot gun shell lead and bullets discharged each year.)

In my 10 years as a social worker, I learned how to work with the government. I wrote all the state legislators, the governor, our U.S. senators, our U.S. congressman, and George Bush, Sr. As a practical matter given the way politics works, in Bush's letter I put in a $500 campaign donation check.

Within a week, I had a call from the SBA in Cedar Rapids. I was the first one in Jefferson County to get a Ready Loan for $125,000 to take care of my obligations at 3% interest.

You've got to know how things work politically because the government has an enormous influence on our lives. You can get burned big time by the government. We use an excellent meditating tax attorney in Fairfield, Fred Schwartz, who knows how to work with the IRS.

It's also smart to be politically active. I've been a delegate at state-wide conventions. Those things help, and they're part of doing business.

Avoid lawyers like the plague

Any successful company will be copied. That's part of the risk. Several businesses have spun off from mine and are competitors. You can have non-disclosure and non-compete agreements, but they're not enforceable. I keep in mind that the copying of Picasso made his art more valuable and influential.

Courts waste time and money. We have never initially sued anyone but have been sued a half dozen times, mostly frivolously. I always entered a counter suit, which we won each time.

Avoid lawyers like the plague. I find that the only one who makes money in lawsuits are attorneys. Courts aren't predictable or necessarily just. For the time it takes, it's easier to earn the money than to sue somebody that owes you.

Success

For me, success is meeting payroll, and not worrying about it. It's also being able to buy anything from the grocery store or Walmart and not think about how much I spend.

Success for Bovard Studio has been creating a heritage for those around us. That heritage uplifts others, makes the world a more beautiful place, and reminds people of something more than stuff.

SPIRIT: Bridge Heaven and Earth

Excellence in any field, be it carpentry, software engineering, painting, photography, or rocket science, adds a spark of spirituality, connecting matter and spirit, and making life magical.

My art, my business, and my life share the common theme of bridging the terrestrial with the celestial. In my art, vibrations of consciousness surround human subjects.

My business creates and restores stained glass art, which uses light as a fundamental element. Stained glass protects those inside of buildings while uplifting spirits. In churches, stained glass art visually depicts stories of the celestial.

The Transcendental Meditation practice brings transcendental reality into daily life. The purpose of group practice of the TM technique is to bring Heaven on Earth.

Ron Bovard's twelve tweets

1. An entrepreneur must understand his limitations. He must hire smarter, more skilled, more talented people than himself and never let his ego get in the way.

2. Pick something you love and you will be able to work during tough times. If you don't make it, at least you did something you loved.

3. As long as you show up and put in a full day's work, you are in business. The longer you do this, the greater the chances of success.

4. I prefer to sell the product, sign a contract, and then produce it.

5. We estimate the job. To refine the estimating process, when the job finishes, we always compare estimates with the actual cost.

6. The initial income from a new business gets reinvested, leaving little compensation for all your entrepreneurial efforts. Loving what you do ·keeps you going.

7. A supportive family is essential for any small business venture.

8. Asking someone to do something, then thinking it is done and forgetting about it is not good management.

9. Do your duty, do what it takes, do the right thing. A good job is always rewarded.

10. If you know your product is good, and you are enthusiastic, selling comes naturally. When you tell the truth and speak from the heart, people trust you. If you don't believe in the product, people can smell it a mile away.

11. Failure is not a permanent state. Perseverance turns failure into success.

12. See what needs to be done and do it before the problem gets worse.

Ponder

1. Ron proved the possibility of making a business out of passion for art. What are your passions, and what possible businesses can you create from them?

2. Ron discusses the importance of a supportive family. How much support can you expect from your friends and loved ones as you experience the ups and downs of business?

3. Ron emphasizes the value of collaboration. Can you see anywhere in your business or elsewhere where results would be improved with collaboration instead of individual efforts?

4. Ron expressed strong feelings about outside influences such as the government, the court system, and unions. How able will you be to work with these large, sometimes unpredictable institutions?

Ron Bovard at project site of St. Mary of the Angel's Church in Chicago

Double door entrance opens to the West Angeles Cathedral steeple tower vestibule, allowing a view of stained glass panels that rise 108 feet overhead

Madonna

The Holy Spirit represented by a dove

Moses and the 10 Commandments

Handpainted ready-made medallions which are incorporated into stained glass windows. Used for glass-painting training at Bovard Studio

Bovard Studio replicated a favorite painting of Christ Knocking at the Door for the Berean Assembly of God Church, Des Moines, Iowa

Ganesha from the Vedas, destroyer of obstacles, representing knowledge, wisdom, education, and the fine arts, created for a Davenport, Iowa restaurant

Tiffany window restored and installed by Bovard Studio in St. Luke's United Methodist Church, Dubuque, Iowa

Jesus praying

Baby Jesus

Bard

Jim Davis
PHOTOS AT THE FINISH LINE

Jim Davis studied education at the University of Kansas and then taught high school. Later, to become an administrator, he returned to school to earn his master's degree. While completing his thesis he started his photography business. The entrepreneurial spirit took over, and he never went back to teaching.

I've known Jim as a friend, men's group colleague, fellow Chicagoan, and Cubs fan for 30 years. His photography is displayed in my office window. Jim combined his love for photography, entrepreneurial attitude, and special blend of humility, integrity, and niceness to create a company that makes people happy. Jim and his wife Diane are members of the Maharishi University of Management Board of Trustees.

JOURNEY: Chronicling personal triumph with pictures

SELLING ART FROM A YOUNG AGE

I grew up in the Chicago area in a family of teachers and farmers. We lived near a train station for downtown commuters where entrepreneurs peddled their wares. I started selling lemonade to passengers as they got off the train.

During the second day, I drew a picture and set it on the table. A passenger came by. He asked, "What's that?"

"The Mona Lisa."

"How much?"

"Twenty-five cents," which was like five dollars today. He reached into his pocket, and it wasn't for a nickel lemonade. Twenty-five cents bought him an original, one-of-a-kind, Jim Davis Mona Lisa.

Even back then, somehow, I knew I would sell art.

Every summer, a teacher and family friend would travel somewhere in the world with her camera. On her return, she would share her travel pictures with our family. She bought herself a new camera and gave me her old one for my 16th birthday.

Photography became a hobby. At the University of Kansas, I walked around campus with my camera to learn about the environment. Rather than study, I would photograph buildings and people, and became the local street photographer.

To make friends I joined a fraternity that resembled the movie *Animal House*. It had interesting characters who couldn't get in elsewhere. A frat brother had a business photographing parties on campus.

Three weeks into college, he pulled me aside. "Jim, what are you doing this weekend?"

I said, "The usual. A date, dinner, and a movie."

He said, "You haven't had a date yet. How would you like to go to a party, meet girls, take pictures, and get paid to do it?" I accepted. It was fun. I met people and got paid better than a Saturday night, pizza delivery-type job.

In college, I studied to be a high school teacher but dreamed of starting a business. My father counseled high school juniors about going to college or finding work. I told my dad about my dream of a career in photography. He said, "Jim, do it as a hobby. Photography is at the bottom of the list for making a living."

Taking pictures of graduates

After college, I became a teacher of the Transcendental Meditation technique, which I loved. To continue teaching, I needed part-time work. Besides my education as a high school teacher, I knew photography. So, I started my photography business to support teaching the TM program.

Saturday afternoons, I would have the sublime experience of initiating students into the simple, natural, effortless practice of the Transcendental Meditation technique. In the evenings, I would photograph some wild sorority parties.

One day, the lab I used to process party pictures sent me a promotional flier: "Make money photographing handshakes at graduations."

The program worked with a photographer taking pictures of grads as they received their diploma. Then the photographer would process passport-sized photos, paste them on promotional pieces, and mail the promotions to each home. Profitability depended on receiving enough orders of full-sized pictures to cover upfront costs.

At that time to get a photo, grads in gowns went to a photographer's professional studio. No commercial photographer took pictures of grads receiving their diploma, and none photographed on speculation.

In 1974, I started telling prospective schools that they had a choice. They could have parents pushing and shoving at the edge of the stage to take pictures, or they could tell disgruntled parents to stay in their seats with no pictures, or they could contract with us at no charge. We would conduct ourselves with the highest professional standards. Each family would receive a free picture of their loved one getting recognition on stage. We would even give a percentage of proceeds to the school scholarship fund.

The schools wanted to know my track record. The program had only been tested in Texas. Most of the Chicago schools told me, "When you get a list of local clients, come back, and we'll talk."

The first year I presented to 40 schools. Two said yes. I had enough parties, weddings, and other events to cover expenses through the first year.

The original promotional piece only taught how to sell the concept to schools. I called the lab, a small entrepreneurial business, and spoke to the CEO's wife. "I've got a graduation booked, but there are no instructions on how to photograph a graduation."

She said, "I respect you guys for sticking your necks out, given that so many things could go wrong."

Stunned, I replied, "Your husband never told me about things going wrong!"

She said, "Not much goes bad, but things do come up. I'll walk you through them." I took notes on her long list of unpleasant possibilities. After the conversation, I purchased liability insurance.

I reasoned, if the business worked in Texas, it would work in Chicago. The challenge was capitalization. The business required inventorying film and other supplies, processing each proof, and creating and mailing the promotional piece.

I didn't have the money. I turned to a friend, who backed me for a percentage of the profit. Gradually I built a business, figuring it out as I went along. My friend did quite well with his investment.

Only a percentage of people had to make the purchase. I would run into grads who would tell me, "I didn't order the larger photos, but we appreciated the little picture you sent." It's wonderful to have a career that makes everyone happy.

Marathons

I ran cross country in high school when no one cared about running as a sport. Later, while teaching the TM technique in the 1970s, I noticed an article about how people in the U.S. had begun running at major events. Then Japan, the rest of Asia, and Europe started having races.

I heard about an event in Cleveland with 15,000 runners and 100,000 spectators. It hit me: I could apply the same business model to marathon running that we used for graduations. I would photograph runners crossing the finish line, send them a passport-sized photo, and offer them larger pictures.

It turned out that graduates ordered more photos from their once-in-a-lifetime event than runners did. Even so, with 15,000 runners an event, we didn't need as high a percentage for profitability. Soon marathons became the second major part of the business.

At first, I hired other TM teachers to take photos. Eventually, we hired dedicated photographers, who now could make money doing what they loved. We did races in Boston, Chicago, Los Angeles, and New Orleans.

When I began the company, we would also photograph parties, dog shows, weddings, court cases, any event where people paid money for photos. It surprised me that weddings are not always happy occasions. Often photographers would find themselves in the middle of a family dispute.

In contrast, almost anyone who graduates or finishes a 26-mile race is joyful, excited, and appreciative. We soon focused only on graduations and marathons, happily giving up the other parts of the business.

Partnering

Four years in, the business was growing faster than I could handle. Part-time people worked in the office, but it wasn't enough.

John Narducci and I taught the TM technique together in a western suburb of Chicago. While teaching, John worked for me taking photos and doing behind-the-scenes office work. Always straight-forward, John told me, "You are great on the phone, but you are not good running the office. I'm really good at organization and hate sales. I'll run the office."

I agreed but would make suggestions. John would answer, "It's my office, and I'm running it. Just get on the phone."

This division of labor worked well. After a while, John said he wanted to be President. I yielded and became Senior Vice President. We started sharing the profit. Soon, John told me that for him to continue, he had to have a stake in the business.

While John was still working part-time, we photographed a race in New Orleans. A friend of mine, Brenda Franke, heard that TM teacher-photographers were coming down for a marathon. She figured it was me and met us at the train station.

Brenda and John hit it off. After the marathon, John told me, "I kind of like her. I'm going to spend a couple extra days. I'll catch a train later." Six months later, they were married in the MUM campus chapel in Fairfield.

In the meantime, John had become a partner. Brenda joined the team in marketing, mostly focusing on direct mail. Soon, Brenda told me, "I can contribute to the business, and I also want a stake."

Saying yes was a big deal. I would no longer be the majority owner. Even so, I figured it was worth it. It would be more lucrative to have a smaller stake in a bigger pie. Plus, I could focus on my strength in sales and going to events, and let Brenda and John take care of the rest of the business.

To maximize our marketing efforts, Brenda wanted to analyze the data we had been collecting.

All three of us knew Joe Mandarino. After finishing his Ph.D. and teaching a couple years in Kansas City, he became a professor at Maharishi University of Management. We called Joe to consult. He told us, "Guys, your data isn't good because your computer system is terrible. You have to get a computer system in place so I have good data to work with."

Joe became a partner. Our three-legged partnership became more stable with four legs. Joe was a brilliant mastermind. As we continued to grow, he spent years building and rebuilding systems to analyze the data.

Joe was unyielding about testing. John, Brenda, and I would come up with ideas that we knew would work. But, Joe would say, "We don't know what the customers will tell us." Joe would insist we roll it out with 50,000 people instead of 500,000. One year, if we had gone ahead with our original idea for everyone we would have doubled our profit. Another year, we were glad we didn't, because we lost 25 cents per person.

John and Brenda Narduci, Joe Mandarino, and I became the ownership and management team, each bringing a different set of skills. We also had "phantom" partners, key people underneath the actual partners. We formalized an agreement with them. They would receive revenue if we sold the company. This arrangement encouraged them to stay.

Growing the business

In 1982, we moved from Chicago to Fairfield. A five-hour drive, we loaded two U-Haul trucks from the Chicago office and dropped everything off in Fairfield. Within days, we were set up for business.

Competitors would approach us to buy their businesses. We started doing so and grew and grew. When we bought a business, John and Joe would integrate the two systems and refine our entire operation. Eventually, we had 75 employees in Fairfield, 15 elsewhere, and over 400 part-time photographers.

It took 20 years to get our first European account. We now have 40 such clients with three overseas managers plus, for a number of years, a partner in Japan.

During much of my 50 years in professional photography, film processing technology stayed the same. Then, almost overnight, email and digitalization changed everything.

At the very beginning of the innovation of digital technology, we still photographed with film and scanned to digital. We no longer had to pay for paper and passport-sized proofs. We could print the digitally created proofs directly to the ordering mailer. We saved the cost of labor to attach the proofs to the ordering form and the proofs were available to market in a shorter time.

As soon as the quality of images made with digital cameras was comparable with film, we purchased new digital cameras. The cost of film and processing was eliminated. Also, the images could be imported into the computer directly after the event, saving us the time to mail film to a lab for processing. We realized a saving in processing costs and were able to mail our solicitations more quickly. The speed of contact with the customers also improved sales.

Lastly, we were able to market more completely with a website, which also led to improved sales. In 1994, we set up our first website. It was basically just our order form that people could fill in with their order after they received our mail offer. With a completely digital workflow, we were able to transform our marketing and expand our product offering. To a significant degree, our profitability and ability to attract interest from equity investors was due to the transformation we made early on with digital technology.

Photographing the famous

Thanks to an official photographer press pass, I have taken many photographs of the powerful and famous. These opportunities include Presidents H.W. Bush, Clinton and Obama, Vice President Biden, Chancellor Helmut Kohl, Prime Minister Pierre Trudeau, and Mayors Daley and Bloomberg. Senator Edward Kennedy sent me a personal thank you note for sending him a particularly meaningful picture. I photographed Muhammad Ali many times, as well as numerous gold medal and world record holding athletes. I also took pictures of Cardinal Cody, various Bishops, Indian Saints, and lawyer Bobby Cochran of OJ Simpson fame.

One particular time, President Clinton was to be the commencement speaker at a university where we photographed the graduation. I mentioned to our contact that Clinton often liked to shake hands with the graduates, and I wanted to be prepared to photograph that event if it occurred. The contact's sources said that the president would not be shaking hands. Just in case, I left myself open that day.

The afternoon before the event, the school contact called me back saying that the President would be shaking hands after all and pleaded, hoping that we could send someone last minute. We already would be taking photos of the graduates with the university president. Now we would be taking photos of the graduates with the U.S. President. I gave him my social security number and in a couple of hours received another call saying I was cleared, since the Secret Service had previously vetted me. I needed to be at the security check in 12 hours (the event was a five-hour drive away). I arrived 5:45 AM.

The Secret Service was running late in setting up the metal detectors. The university invited me to come on in without inspection and set my equipment by the stage. I appreciated not having to stand outside in the rain, but I was concerned that I hadn't gone through proper security and my equipment case had not been cleared. About an hour later, I found a Secret Service person, introduced myself, mentioned I hadn't been inspected and thought he might want to bring a sniffing dog before someone became concerned about unapproved equipment by the stage. It took several inquiries and a long wait in a secure building before the White House staff person came and gave us "all access" credentials so we could take the graduation photos.

Not only was it fun to be only feet away from a President, sales more than doubled with everyone buying lots of photos. That event made a significant difference in our bottom line that year.

Another time, one of our longtime assistants said she couldn't help with a graduation because she was graduating herself. I told her she could still assist us and then jump in line at the end. She agreed. As we packed up our equipment to leave, she came over and thanked me for the wonderful opportunity. The actor, Danny Glover, had received an honorary degree. At the end of the recognition, he came to join the dean and greet the graduates. Since she was last in line, he spent five minutes chatting with her about what she had done and what she planned for the future. It was a graduation she would always remember.

Selling the business

To continue growing the business, we needed to buy larger competitors. That required cash and long-term commitments from our partners. Alternatively, we could sell the business. I wanted to keep going. Two of my partners were ready to move on with their lives. Despite their contribution, they did not share my passion for the business.

Market conditions were good, and the business large enough to afford a broker's commission. We found good representation. The partners and agent crafted a compelling story showing positive projections. The broker helped us to navigate the complexities of the sale and of the legal process.

We sold the business to an equity investing company. To grow the business, they merged it with a competitor and added capital.

After we had sold the business, I worked for the new owners as an ambassador, consulting with major clients and photographing events. I stayed because I enjoyed the work and they paid me well.

As a founder, I had done every job, spoken with everyone, and made sure that systems were working. After we sold the business, I was just another employee. I saw our owners make the same mistakes we had made years before. When there were problems, I shared my thoughts. Fortunately, my makeup lets me put my ego aside and allow others to call the shots, no matter how much I might disagree. After all, it was their money.

I am now retired. For fun and profit, I exhibit my photography and resell my prints. You can see several examples in the photos section or download at meditatinge.com/goodies the PDF containing the photos in color found in this book.

WISDOM: Do the right thing

DO WHAT YOU KNOW TO BE RIGHT

My grandmother had a farm in central Indiana. Like most farm people, she was goodhearted, conservative, and didn't mess around. Often after church on Sunday, we drove around the countryside to look at other farms. My father could tell right away whether a farm was doing well. To me, at nine years old, it all looked green and the same.

One day, I noticed small houses on a tomato farm. "Grandma, what's over there? That looks like a house."

She said "It is a house."

"You mean somebody lives there?"

She said, "Not someone, a family."

The shack was maybe 10 feet by 10 feet. "You mean like a mother, father, and one or two kids?"

She replied, "No, no, most have 8 or 10 kids."

I asked, "How can they even lie down?"

My grandmother said, "I don't know, but I grew tomatoes one year, hiring some of the migrant workers. When I saw how the people had to live, I decided never to do tomatoes again. It just isn't right."

She continued, "Other farmers say that the migrant workers expect to live like this. They move from south to north, following the harvest. If you don't use them, another farmer will, and he'll make the money from tomatoes, not you. I didn't care. No matter how much money I might make, it just wasn't right."

In business there were times I was tempted to make the money because everyone else was doing it, even though it felt wrong. Then I would remember my grandmother. Do unto others, karma, what goes around comes around — whatever you call it — do what's right. Try to minimize the bad and maximize the good. In my case, our business made people happy.

Yet, despite best intentions, our business wasn't totally positive. Before we digitalized, the chemicals used by outside firms to develop film had detrimental environmental effects.

On the good side, providing quality jobs with good people at a pleasant environment is extremely satisfying for an entrepreneur.

Money

Without a track record, banks won't loan you money. Banks are like pawn shops. You pledge the equity in your house or car and they give you money.

Self-finance as much as possible. Borrow from friends and relatives. Make good on whatever they give you.

Be as creative as you can. We showed our printer how our cash flow worked with payment history after we mailed out sample photos. With that information, we were able to negotiate a 60-day payback period.

Money is unrealized energy. If you try to hold on to it, it cramps up and doesn't benefit anyone. Keep the money flowing. That's what entrepreneurs do. As money comes in, let it flow to new business opportunities, and others will benefit.

Being successful isn't enough. Share your inspiration with others and share your money with good causes. Give money to the community that helped you be successful.

You can have a generous spirit and still be smart. Even with the best will, people remember conversations differently. Handshakes are nice, but in business, it is vital to create a clearly written agreement that both parties can refer to later.

Don't be married to ideas

As a child, I was first inspired to be an entrepreneur by the hula hoop. I thought that one good idea was all you needed. I soon learned that no one might buy your product even if it is brilliant. Don't be married to your ideas, be married to the market.

Don't take low sales personally. You may do everything possible, but the market just doesn't respond. Maybe you are ahead of the curve, and it will take years before people will want your product. Maybe your potential market is too small or too large. Stay alert. Sometimes it takes only a small shift to find the right segment.

Do the hard research. Ask if it is a good business model. Be careful sharing your ideas until ready. Others will tell you all the reasons why it's not going to work.

Be willing to cut your losses early. If the market says no, move on to the next idea. It's not like you're a bad person, they are just not buying now. Focus on what works. Something's going to click. Something's going to stick.

Sales

Sell benefits. Don't say that my product does this, this, and that and assume that people know the significance. The customer wants to know, "What does that feature do for ME?"

On the GradImages and MarathonFoto internet home pages, we don't discuss photo options, quality, or pricing. We sell the reason that the customer would want the photo. So our graduation messages include: "Remember your achievement — You worked hard for this moment. Don't let it fade away." And, "Proud grads. Proud Moms and Dads — No one is more proud of your achievement than Mom and Dad. Download and share your graduation day photos with them and other loved ones now." For marathons: "Remember your triumph — What lasts longer than a marathon? Great race memories."

When I started taking graduation photos, no one called me because nobody knew I existed. I knew that to move forward, I would have to make calls and knock on doors every day. If it went well, I hand-wrote a note. Now, I might send an email. People appreciate reading, "Thanks for your time. I enjoyed meeting with you. If we work together, I know you'll be pleased with the results." It shows you're serious about wanting their business.

As an entrepreneur, you must separate yourself from the competition. Find your strengths and make them your brand. Be true to yourself. Don't try to be something that you are not.

Say you write ads. Many people do that. What is your unique selling proposition? What distinguishes you? Maybe it is as simple as being on time and guaranteeing customer satisfaction. You'll figure it out.

There will be times when someone crosses you. You don't have to work with them but be gracious. Don't try to get even. You never know if you will have to work with them again. They will remember if you were ugly.

See the job, do the job

In the early days of the TM organization, Maharishi stayed as a guest in a home. The host saw Maharishi cleaning. She said, "You shouldn't be cleaning. That's my job. You are the teacher."

Maharishi replied, "The room needed cleaning, and I could do it. See the job, do the job, stay out of misery." That simple notion always stayed with me.

Through my young years, I worked as a janitor, scrubbed toilets, cleaned boilers, landscaped, made fast food, taught, and farmed. To earn the money to finish graduate school and become a teacher of TM, I worked as a stock picker in a giant Kmart warehouse. Train tracks led into the warehouse that housed the inventory for all the Kmart stores. We would traverse the aisles with a giant shopping cart, pick items that a store ordered, and load them on the train.

One weekend, we helped clean the warehouse. I worked with a manager whom I didn't know. The other workers left when they could. The job wasn't finished, so I stayed to help.

When we finished, he asked how far I was in school. I told him I was just finishing. He said, "Tell you what. If you're interested, come by my office. We can get you started in management at Kmart. I would love to have you on the team." I didn't want to work for a large corporation, so I didn't take him up on his offer, but this experience showed me that whether you own a business or work for someone else, be a partner. If something needs doing, don't try to get out of it. Just do the job and don't worry about it.

Partnerships

I eventually took on three full partners plus others with smaller ownership stakes.

People like my partners prefer working for themselves and tend to have strong personalities. They have ideas, vision, passion, and make things happen. Part of the entrepreneur's job is to work with a variety of egos both inside and outside the company.

We each had different strengths. As a team, all sorts of ideas flowed. With mutual respect, things worked. Group consciousness is much more effective than individual consciousness. Practicing the TM-Sidhi program strengthened our collective intuition and ability to work together.

When the chips were down, and business was tough, when things were not going right, we would differ. Yet, with compatibility and trust, we could move forward and make difficult decisions.

If you are not already part of a supportive team, I recommend forming or joining a mastermind group of successful people you trust. Use the group to share ideas. Allow the mastermind to hold you accountable for your commitments.

Lessons from Obama

In the summer of 2008, I had the opportunity to visit Barrack Obama's Chicago campaign headquarters. For a political organization, it was amazingly organized. There was no crazy energy. Stacks of paper were neat. People communicated easily.

The chief of staff spoke to the 60 of us taking the tour. "When we started the campaign, there were just a few of us. Obama pulled us aside. He told us to keep three things in mind:

1. Change begins from the bottom up, not from the top down.

2. It's not about winners and losers, placing blame, or feeling bad if something goes wrong. We work as a team, and we win together.

3. Have fun. If it isn't fun, it isn't worth doing."

These principles can be applied to any business.

Boston Marathon bombing

It's April 15, 2013. I am sitting on a small stool in front of the announcer stand at the Boston Marathon. There is an explosion. I feel the impact.

I think, *It doesn't sound good. People are probably hurt. It must be a gas line inside the building. I hope the people outside won't be hurt. Should I do anything? My job is to keep taking photos. I will let the emergency people take care of what they take care of.*

Twelve seconds later — it seems like two minutes — the second bomb goes off.

I think, *There may be more. This is not a good place to be. Should I try to help people?* I am positioned near many emergency responders. I don't want to be in the way. I think, *Take photos and when it's time, stop, and get out of here.* I find out later that others at more distant locations saved lives waiting for the emergency people to arrive.

I remember a friend living in San Francisco whose building caught fire. He escaped and then went back for his guitar. He never made it out. I think of my wife and daughter and decide not to take chances. With a camera around my neck, I leave the other cameras behind.

People are being carried on stretchers. I go to my colleague across the street who has been knocked over. We are both OK. "Should we take photos?" We took a few.

Then we both decide, "This isn't what we do. We don't take pictures of unfortunate situations. We take pictures of happy moments. Let the press photograph the tragedy. Let's make sure our crew is OK."

Now, the incident reminds me that I have no idea when I will be asked to leave this life. I take life more seriously and at the same time feel freer.

The future

Technology and circumstances continue to change. Even so, to a degree our service is locked in. For example, today everyone has a camera phone and people enjoy selfies. I have seen graduations where people use their smartphones to take selfies with the university president. After the 10th person, someone says, we can't have everybody doing this, or we'll be here all day.

We must just stay ahead. When visiting my daughter at the University of Iowa, I noticed an ad. Someone was offering to take photos for an organization's social media to help it recruit new members.

Fortunately, our core concept of finding events that people want to remember remains constant.

Final thoughts

You will work harder for yourself than for someone else. Put your heart into it and keep going. Even if the first business doesn't work, the second, third, or sixth business will.

Do the right thing, keep the energy flowing, and honor your spiritual path.

Being an entrepreneur is something you get a feeling for. I'm still getting the feeling for how to do it.

If you tell somebody that you will return the favor, return the favor.

You have control over your actions, not the fruits. Do your best, do right, let go, and let nature determine the fruit.

Why be an entrepreneur if you can't have fun doing it? If you don't have fun now, who knows when you will.

SPIRIT: Gain the support of nature

Maharishi speaks of the "support of nature." Others call it luck, grace, or good karma. Support of nature is something just dropping in your lap. It is avoiding misfortune as if by magic. Support of nature comes from regular TM meditation, past karma, and doing the right thing.

Having experienced support of nature, TM practioners have confidence that nature will continue to support them which makes it is easier to get to the next stage in business. People who meditate using the TM technique naturally develop a longer-term perspective which helps navigate the ups and downs of business.

In addition to regular TM practice, Maharishi has described other ways of increasing good fortune. Two of my partners got excited when they heard about creating a "Vastu" building. Maharishi advises that

Vastu architecture increases support of nature by applying fundamental ancient Vedic principles to the layout of the building. These include an east-facing entrance, special placement of rooms, room proportion, natural materials, slope and shape of the land, and best time to start building.

Each of the partners invested in a large log Vastu building for the good fortune of the business and its employees. After moving into this building, even non-meditating employees reported positive happenings that defied explanation.

I once heard a talk from a top business consultant from Japan. He said that while there is no guarantee that it will work, choose a partner with a history of success and good luck even if they seem not to be the best or most intelligent.

Business is about making right decisions. Effective decision making does not just come from analysis. It comes from the combination of mind, heart, and intuition. The TM-Sidhi program develops the heart and intuition. During the sidhis, the meditator goes deep within and becomes familiar with finer levels of feeling and intuition. That's not something you learn at Harvard or Stanford.

You might study a graph, and an idea comes. The hunch, initiated from analyzing the data, comes from intuition deep inside. Right intuition makes all the difference in business.

Trusting your heart and intuition brings wellbeing and success. Maybe you are not sure how to feed your family. Like my grandmother, you think you can grow tomatoes, but to do so, you need migrant workers to live in squalor in shacks. From deep within, your heart says no. Then you close your eyes, make your decision, and allow everything to fall into place.

Jim Davis' twelve tweets

1. Have as much fun as possible, share your passion, make people happy, do great work, and money will naturally flow.

2. No matter how much money is involved, do it only if you know in your heart that it is right.

3. Partner with those who have a history of good luck.

4. Don't be married to your ideas. If for some reason the market isn't buying, don't take it personally.

5. Show restraint in sharing ideas with others until you are really ready.

6. Show you care. Send a thank you note or email.

7. Sell benefits, not features. Don't assume the customer will figure out what the product will do for them.

8. Having confidence that you will receive the support of nature makes it is easier to get to the next stage of a business.

9. Whether you work for yourself or someone else, if something needs doing, just do it. Don't try to get out of it.

10. During the TM sidhis, the meditator goes deep within, becoming familiar with finer levels of feeling and intuition. You don't learn that at Harvard or Stanford.

11. Right intuition makes all the difference in business.

12. Keep money flowing or it cramps up and doesn't benefit anyone. Invest in new opportunities. Give money to the community that helped you be successful.

Ponder

1. Jim's father, who professionally counseled young people about occupational opportunity, discouraged Jim from a career in photography. How do you determine when to take the advice of someone more experienced and close to you?

2. Jim took on partners to expand his business, first giving up some

control and then the majority stake. Do you have the makeup to give up control and work with strong-minded partners?

3. How do you relate to Jim saying, "Whether you work for yourself or someone else, be a partner. If something needs doing, don't try to get out of it. Just do it."?

4. Jim talks a lot about support of nature. He even says, "Partner with those who have a history of good luck." What is your experience?

5. When Jim sold the business, he came back and worked as an employee. What do you think about his choice? Could you do that?

Jim at the Brandenburg Gate in Berlin, 2011

Above left: Young Jim Davis taking photos

Above right: Jim at Los Angeles wheelchair competition

Left: Paul, David Lynch, Ringo, and Betty Lavette at a David Lynch Foundation event

Sir Richard Branson at The Virgin Money London Marathon

Chicago Marathon

Clouds

Vista

Mystical Purple hills rocks

Mystical Purple road

Left: Maharishi greeting in Fairfield, fall 1975

Below: Maharishi speaks in Fairfield, December 1979

Right: Maharishi at Taste
of Utopia Celebration
in Fairfield, January 12,
1984

Below: Maharishi
inaugurates the
Maharish University of
Management meditating
dome during construction
in January, 1980

PART FOUR
Making Business Work

Steve Winn
Monica Hadley
Peter Huggins

Steven Winn
SERIAL ENTREPRENEUR

Steven Winn has worked as an accountant, info-mercial pioneer, no-money-down real estate expert, home-based business seller, pizza restaurateur, and seminar organizer. In the process he made, lost, and made again, millions of dollars. As half-owner and operations director for Seminar Crowds (seminar-crowds.com), he now works on average less than an hour a day.

Steven and I are longtime friends. As I explain in the chapter about my own journey, Steven played a key role in helping me to let go and sell my company.

JOURNEY: Making and losing millions

THE BECKLEY GROUP

In the early 1980s, my friend, Ed Beckley, had written a book and was starting a company in Fairfield that gave seminars about how to buy real estate with no money down. Ed had learned the financing techniques of large contractors and big developers: when the big players build a huge hotel, they use other people's money, not their own. Ed taught individuals to do the same for starter homes and for creating real estate portfolios. In the 80s, real estate values kept increasing and many craved this kind of knowledge.

At the time, I was working as a CPA for one of the major "big eight" accounting firms in San Francisco. But the work wasn't a good fit, and I didn't enjoy it. On top of that, I couldn't afford San Francisco rent, so I lived across the bay in Oakland and commuted. After several years, I had had enough.

Ed offered me a 20% stake in the company and asked me to run it. A former high school teacher, Ed had made a fortune in real estate and seemed to know what he was doing. I liked him and said yes, and my wife and I moved to Fairfield.

At first, Ed traveled around the country and gave free workshops that he advertised in local newspapers. Then, at the workshops, he sold his weekend no-money-down seminars. In 1983, President Ronald Reagan deregulated the TV airways, putting The Beckley Group in the right place at the right time. We could now use half-hour TV commercials to promote our seminar sales presentations, so Ed began using info-mercials to draw people to the free talks.

Ed went to Denver in October to do a weekend seminar. The course materials and for-sale audiotapes got lost on the flight. Ed waited and waited and waited at the airport. Finally, the materials arrived, but the guy at the counter, said, "Sorry we're closed now, come back Monday."

Ed was panicking. When I joined Ed, things seemed to be going well, but I soon discovered Ed was financially overextended. His real estate holdings looked great on paper, but he was cash poor. This huge business event could make or break the company, and some bureaucrat was saying, he wouldn't open up. Ed followed him to his car.

The guy kept saying, "No, no, no," and got into his car.

Ed jumped on the windshield and said, "I'm not leaving until you get me my books." Dumbfounded, the man got them.

We did OK in October, but November and December were disasters. We were out of money, and creditors were demanding payment. We had no idea what to do. It made no sense, but we temporarily closed the business to attend the December 1983 Taste of Utopia course in Fairfield. The conference was led by Maharishi and attended by 7,000 practitioners of the TM and TM-Sidhi programs from around the world. During the course, we enjoyed extended group meditation practice and lectures from Maharishi.

Come January, we still couldn't pay our creditors. The prudent thing would have been to quit and declare bankruptcy. Instead, we scraped together enough for one more seminar, and we killed it.

New to the industry, we hadn't known that the seminar business typically dies in November and December and roars back in January. The same infomercials that barely drew a response in November brought massive crowds to our January seminars. At the beginning of the year, everyone resolves to change their lives, and we provided a vehicle to do that. From then on, we just kept rolling.

Infomercials bring big success

In 1984, Harvard grad and TV director Tim Hawthorne found he had few opportunities in Fairfield to make money, so he applied to be a speaker at our seminars. Tim had created several successful vignettes for *That's Incredible*, a 1980s prime-time TV show.

We hired Tim to produce our next generation of infomercials. We taught Tim the infomercial business — how to buy TV time, how to track results, and so forth. Tim was fantastic, producing fabulous infomercials for us.

By this time we were selling books and cassettes directly from info-mercials rather than doing seminars. This was a much better business model, and our business soared. The Beckley Group was one of two companies that made infomercials big in the U.S. In the 80s, half of the infomercial talent in the country came from Fairfield.

When our business eventually crashed in 1986, Tim started Haw-thorne Direct, which as of 2018 is still going strong. Tim was a re-markable businessman and became a principal architect of the modern infomercial and direct-response industry.

Thanks to the successful infomercials, at our zenith, The Beckley Group had nine Fairfield locations and employed 600 people in a town of 10,000. In our first full year, we had $1 million in sales. We did $4 million the second year. Then, $16 million. In 1985, we sold $41 million in product.

I made sure all the details of the business were properly handled with a lot of long-distance organizing. No minor task before the internet, I managed four teams doing seminars in four different cities each week.

Business success can bring great emotional satisfaction. My mother had been unhappy that I quit the accounting job; she had no clue about the business. On her first visit to Fairfield, I took her to one location and announced to the team, "This is my mother." They all clapped and cheered.

My mother asked, "Who are all these people?"

"My employees, Mom."

I repeated the exercise nine times.

Failure

In 1986, because of bad decisions and the end of the no-money-down real estate fad, The Beckley Group collapsed.

We had been the town heroes, having brought many people to Fairfield from the east and west coasts. There were now 1,700 in the meditation domes each day. (Maharishi had predicted that if 1,600 people, 1% of the square root of the U.S. population, practiced the advanced TM-Sidhi program in the domes each day, there would be a significant influence of peace in the United States. The Soviet Union collapsed during that time.)

Then we shut down the business and laid everyone off and became the town goats.

We hated laying off our employees. They were not only good employees but friends and good people. But, we had no choice. If we kept them on, we wouldn't have been able to pay salaries.

Becoming the town goats was not as traumatic for me as it was for my business partner. Ed's name was on the business. He had people hounding and harassing him, knocking on his door late at night, broke, and blaming him.

Even for startups that don't shut down, at times harsh decisions must be made. In the world of entrepreneurship, the owners may have to choose between laying people off and closing the business. If the business closes, everyone loses their jobs and creditors don't get paid.

From 1986 to 1994, I semi-retired. Having made a bunch of money at The Beckley Group, I thought money-making was easy. I invested time and money marketing a beautiful futon bed with a Japanese shoji screen that was featured on several magazine covers. It didn't sell. I also started a mail order business for union members to buy union goods. Unfortunately, members found price more important than union loyalty.

Déjà vu — Home Business Technologies

Ed Beckley and I teamed up again in 1994 to form Home Business Technologies, where we taught people how to start a business from their home. Without renting an office and with minimal inventory, our clients could start their home-based businesses with little capital. We encouraged clients to keep their jobs until their businesses were successful. Instead, we asked them to make a different kind of sacrifice — to give up TV, stop wasting time, and spend 10 to 15 hours a week on their part-time business. Because of ingrained habits, making optimal use of time is hard for most people. Further, every business requires some kind of selling, and most people resist selling. Our course helped people learn to carve out time and feel more comfortable selling.

Our program was straightforward. Even so, most people in home-based business opportunities, such as Amway, don't make money. Because of the many scammers, the government closely regulates the home-based business industry.

We promoted the course through infomercials and direct mail. Ed and I share a similar philosophy — identify a fad, grab it, enjoy high profit margins, and exit. We know that eventually someone comes along and does the hard, detailed work with a reasonable margin to maintain a long-term business. That just isn't who we are.

Ed and I repeated our adventures of the 80s. The first year, we did $3 million in sales. In the second year, we did $51 in sales million and employed 125. We grew so fast that we couldn't keep up and made mistakes.

Then, in 1996, we had a run-in with the government, and the business crashed. Ed called Iowa Attorney General, Tom Miller, a liar in the Des Moines Register for going back on a promise that he had made to Ed. After the Register article appeared, the FBI raided us looking for fraud. They couldn't find fraud, because there wasn't any. But when the government takes action, they can't back down, or they look stupid.

The FBI and IRS agents were investigating every detail of my financial life looking for some tax fraud so they could force me to testify against Ed Beckley. I have always been straightforward on my taxes and financial dealings, so there was nothing for them to find.

It's common in hypergrowth companies to have things fall between the cracks. The Feds saw over 200 customer complaints, which represented a small percentage of our over 200,000 customers. They charged us with conspiracy to commit fraud. We had done nothing illegal or fraudulent, but the government has more power than any individual. Within 30 days, the government took down Home Business Technologies. Our employees lost their jobs and promised bonuses, and many customers didn't get their refunds.

After they shut us down, we were town goats again — and I learned that fighting the government is foolish.

The experience shocked me. I saw us as running a straightforward business with a strong desire to help our clients become financially secure.

In 1992, I had become a part-time minister of the local Unity Church. There, we teach a lot about forgiveness. I began practicing what I had been preaching. I would spend three or four hours a day praying that I could forgive the FBI and IRS agents, the judge who made some marginal rulings, and the Iowa Attorney General who instigated the shutdown.

It took months for me to forgive and make peace with all the prosecutors. Once I did, my life started to fall into place. Still, I judged that the State and the Feds made a mistake and shouldn't have done this to us. I didn't resolve it completely until 2014 when, during a meditation, the investigation, the agents, judge, and attorney general appeared. They merged into me, and all of my judgments dissolved into the oneness of my Being.

Pizza born from bankruptcy

After losing a lawsuit with the IRS for half a million dollars, I declared personal bankruptcy. Even in bankruptcy, the IRS has three years to collect after the final assessment. If I started anything new and became successful, they would take it to pay off my debt. I collected unemployment insurance and sold off everything of value from past entrepreneurial adventures. Broke, I had no clue what to do next.

I am fortunate to have a committed wife who stuck with me through the fat and lean years, during high profile success and the embarrassment of my name splashed in the headlines. It seems like it was my effort that brought us business success. Yet, I often think it was Geri's deep presence that made everything happen. The world only seems to operate through cause and effect at the surface of life.

Support from the universe is not about trying to make something happen; it's about receptivity and openness to what comes. Together, we decided to try a grand experiment: we would put our trust in the universe, and we would do the complete advanced TM program every day.

Don Schmidt, a friend who lived five doors down, would often ask me to walk with him. A longtime meditating entrepreneur and founder of Angel Graphics, Don sold prints and posters to retailers and the craft industry. He had figured out how to get printers to use extra ink so posters looked brilliant even with inexpensive paper.

During these walks, Don would ask my opinions about various business challenges. Finally, he said, "Why don't you just work for me?"

There had been no trying on my part. My intention was only to be of service.

We all have different strategies for running a business. Don's strategy was to cut costs everywhere, all the time. If he thought employees were wasting paper clips, he would refuse to buy new paper clips and have them reuse them. This approach worked for Don. He was successful for decades.

My strategy was to focus on sales and to stop having meetings about cutting costs. When Don would leave, the sales staff had more time to sell, and sales skyrocketed.

After working for Don for a while, I told him that for what he was paying me he could hire four secretaries and get a whole lot more done. Don refused. He wanted to take three months a year off, and I was the only one he trusted to run the business. After about six months, I showed him better solutions, and we had a friendly parting.

I listened to my intuition and left without a backup plan. The grand experiment was teaching me to trust the universe to take care of me. And that's what happened.

Mark Delott, my future Seminar Crowds business partner, approached me with a creative scheme to create a pizza business franchise. He would provide the finances and strategy, and I would manage the day-to-day business. We planned to take the franchise public and do it inexpensively by taking advantage of certain loopholes. The first store would be in Fairfield.

I didn't have anything else going on, so I tossed pizza.

I put my heart into it, made terrific pizza, created strong marketing, and did everything else that needed doing. I made two grand a month with all the pizza I could eat. Then, the loophole disappeared. My partner Mark Delott said there wasn't enough money in the pizzeria and I should keep any profit.

Very kind of you, Mark.

Seminar Crowds — Knowing my value

Mark started looking around for something else to do. His cousin was promoting seminars to senior citizens taught by financial planners. Mark's cousin bought mailing lists, designed, printed and mailed promotional postcards, and handled the reservations for the financial planners. The planners would then do the seminars and offer their services. Mark and I saw the opportunity. We thought these seminars would become popular, and jumping in at the start of a fad is my entrepreneurial strategy.

Mark is right-brained, very creative, and not someone to run operations. Mark said, "I'm going to start the business. Come work for me and run it."

I responded, "Mark, I'll help you create a system to get you started, but that's it."

After a few weeks, I told Mark, "Here is what to do. Now hire someone to do it."

Mark replied, "I want you."

"I'm not for hire."

Even though he would double what I made tossing pizza, I was clear: I was going to be an equal partner in my next business. I didn't want to work for anyone or be a minority partner with little say. That clarity let me say no. Nature can only support you if you know what you want.

Whatever work you do, do it impeccably, and offers will come. Having seen how I threw myself into the pizzeria, Mark said, "All right, I'll give you half the business." We each put up $100 and became 50-50 partners.

Both Mark and I had been beaten up in business. We both had massive successes and failures. We thought if we could make $40,000 a year without working hard that would be fine. We agreed that Mark would do the marketing, and I the operations. We had a contest to see who worked the least.

I worked directly with the financial planners. Powerful people, they could stand in front of 40 or 50 people and convince 80% of them to make an appointment about investing. Our financial planner clients continually pushed me around, and I hated it. We had closed the pizzeria because this looked more promising, but I was unhappy.

I said to Mark, "I'm not coming into work until I have transformed my emotions into love for all our clients. OK?"

Mark, God bless him, looked at me like I was crazy. He said, "You do what you gotta do."

For two weeks, I stayed home and dealt with my thoughts of being bullied and disliking our clients. I kept doing internal emotional work until I got to a place where I loved these people. I would even have been willing to recommend another mailing house if I thought it would be better for them.

Upon returning, I had the most fun in my life with these same financial planners. They started appreciating me and business just skyrocketed. In the first four years, we made a profit of $3 million.

Most marketing companies in our industry mailed out brilliant, full-color, fancy, expensive pieces. These pieces promoted the financial planner and his seminar. Instead of a brochure, we mailed a four-by-six, black ink on yellow stock postcard. The card, like the brochure, advertised a free meal and fabulous information from the planner about the financial future.

With the postcards, we offered a free lunch at Denny's. Nobody showed up. Then we tried Olive Garden. Good response. Then we tried Ruth's Chris, a big fancy steakhouse. A crowd came. The quality of the restaurant, not how the invitation looked, made the offer compelling.

We optimized the system. Rather than sending one-dollar brochures, we mailed customized 29-cent postcards. We designed the piece, found leads, and organized the reservations. The client just showed up and gave the seminar. We later expanded to include lawyers and chiropractors — professionals conducting seminars to sell high-end products.

People aren't stupid. They understand they are being provided lunch for an hour of their time. A fancy brochure can trigger the thought, *Somebody's* making a lot of money. Instead, with a postcard they think, *That's a nice restaurant. I'll listen to the guy. The topic sounds interesting.*

As with the infomercials in the 1980s, we were in the right place at the right time. This time, it was the technical revolution of digital printing. We could now create customized print mail pieces quickly and inexpensively.

Today, with so many new technologies, it's even easier to strike gold. I recommend that entrepreneurs find a unique application of an emerging technology and be the first to apply it to a marketplace need.

As of 2018, Seminar Crowds continues to pull in millions of dollars in yearly sales.

WISDOM: Complement your strengths

DO YOU OWN A JOB OR A BUSINESS?

As an entrepreneur, you either own a business or you own a job. If your business requires always being there, that's a job.

Most entrepreneurs start a company and work 60 to 80 hours a week, doing the various tasks of their business. They do them because they're better and faster than anybody they can hire, and there's not enough time to train others. When they do finally hire, often these hard-driving, frazzled entrepreneurs can't keep people. The dream turns into a nightmare.

A variant of that experience showed up for me with the two hyper-growth multi-million-dollar businesses in the 80s and 90s. I directed operations, making all the decisions so that everything would get done. I thought quickly, knew answers, and would say, "Do this, do that." Employees normally followed through. I had five chairs outside my door, and people would sit in line waiting to ask me questions.

Did I feel important? Yes. Was it emotionally satisfying? Yes. Was it a smart way to run a business? No. I was micro-managing everything.

In my current business, I got smarter. The first year, I immersed myself, working many 14- to 16-hour days. After all, I reasoned, as the digital printing revolution evolved, how could I train someone when I didn't know the answers myself?

In the second year, as with the other businesses, I realized that I was still micro-managing. However, this time, I didn't want the glory. I didn't need to feel I was the most important person in the business, and I stopped believing that only I could make things run properly.

We hired good people. One day I told them, I'm not coming into the office in the mornings anymore. They panicked. They were used to asking me what to do, and I'd tell them. If it didn't go right, I assumed responsibility.

I told them, "You are smart. You know the business as well as I do. You are going to do this. If you have questions, give me a call." They called me a lot the first week, called some the second week, and then they stopped calling. Suddenly, I had a life. My employees ended up doing a better job and putting in better systems than I could have done by micro-managing. Now the business pretty much runs itself. I have the freedom to travel and study. Recently, I received a master's degree in Vedic Science from Maharishi University of Management. I would go to school and at three o'clock head over to the business for an hour to check on things and answer questions.

Some entrepreneurs may desire stability, self-expression, or being a difference-maker in the world. Each case requires a different strategy. Knowing why you are in business brings clarity to decision-making.

What are your strengths? What kind of business do you want to have? What are you willing to do?

Personally, I want to earn plenty of money, so I have the time to meditate, take care of my family, and engage in other spiritual pursuits.

I understand the idea of *following your passion* for a business. What if your passion is about spiritual growth and taking care of your family? Does that mean you can't start a business? I don't think so. For me, business is not about money, but about freedom, spiritual growth, and personal integration. I've seen many people following their passion, creating businesses, but not creating freedom. The business owns them. A business must be properly structured, so it allows you to use your time how you wish.

Some may ask, can you make money from a fad and still be spiritual? Of course. Businesses only succeed by providing a service. Do you have to be poor or passionate about your business to be spiritual? Maharishi taught that spirituality is not about poverty or giving things up. Rather spirituality is about the expansion of consciousness and happiness, creating a full heart as it expands into Unity Consciousness.

Complement your strengths

Understand your strengths and your weaknesses. If you don't have a necessary talent, partner with or hire someone who does. I can work with all sorts of personalities, which allows me to find wildly talented partners. These partners balance out my shortcomings and weaknesses.

Salespeople usually don't make good managers, and they don't like following rules. Not surprisingly, they are often looking for work. About 20% of the population are natural salespeople. I know how to work with them. As an entrepreneur, good salespeople have made me a lot of money. A good salesperson doesn't have to be the classic extroverted glad-handing guy. Effective salespeople are clear about who they are inside and know how to tell their story to the right people.

Ed Beckley, my partner for the two fast-growth companies, was a phenomenal marketer and salesman. He was aggressive and pushed things to the limit. My current Seminar Crowds partner, Mark Delott, is a terrific marketer with crazy right-brain ideas. He is not strong in operations and knows it. Operations is my core strength.

Many people have great business ideas, but nothing happens because there is no execution. Once you have a reputation for executing and doing things well, people bring you great ideas because they don't want to do it themselves. I held out for 50% of the business with Mark because I understood my worth.

Honesty is one of the real success forces in life. I always tell the truth. If I make a mistake, I don't try to hide it, and I'm always honest with Mark.

I do B+ / A- marketing. Mark does A+ stuff. 90% of his ideas are outlandish, crazy, unworkable. The remaining 10% are fantastic, and we have made a fortune on his outside-the-box gems. I give Mark the freedom to play around and brainstorm and am honest when it's not a good idea. He's happy to receive the feedback because he knows himself.

As a result, in addition to being business partners we have become close friends, always watching out for the other.

Hiring and firing

I hire people based on my sense of their emotional "tone." I know that if I feel a certain way, so do others. I look for presence and poise and reject negativity and cynicism. I assess if they will be blown sideways when things go wrong.

Because of the process of going within, meditators often exude a unique passion, conviction, and softness that others don't have. Their tone opens doors, but they still must be able to follow through. Skills are transferable and trainable, but I can't teach tone. Assuming new employees have the necessary required skills, I can train them on business tasks and watch them blossom.

I assume resumes are 90% hype. Best case, resumes are specific about accomplishments: "In this position, I accomplished this, this, and this." If the resume shows a great fit, but the interviewee doesn't have the right emotional tone, I don't hire them.

Yes, I have hired the wrong people; I've made some real whoppers. What did I do to correct the situation? I let them go.

Also, I tend to hire people in their 20s. They do not have preconceived notions about what's possible or how to do things. Their enthusiasm, vision, and out-of-the-box thinking are priceless. And my experience helps them avoid mistakes that they would otherwise make.

At the Beckley companies and now at Seminar Crowds, we encourage people to follow their dreams and do what fulfills them even if it means leaving us. This perspective pays off — we attract good people. At work, we give people incentives and a lot of freedom to fulfill their quotas. They love the flexible time and opportunity to earn money on their terms.

Firing people is always an emotional thing. Everybody's afraid of change. Yet, I've noticed that fired employees usually find more suitable positions.

If people aren't performing, they aren't happy. One thing to remember: it's business, not personal. The people who work for me are my friends, and I care a lot about them. Yet, I separate business and friendship. I respect the fundamental law of business — make money or fail.

If we get to the point that my partner and I have to invest money to pay people, we will close the business. That's why we're careful every step of the way, watching sales and being ruthless about cutting expenses, even if it means letting people go.

Contracts

I only do business with people I like and trust. If I don't trust someone, I can't expect a contract to control their behavior. In today's world, enforcement costs much more than the value of the deal. That said, the advantage of a contract is that both parties are clear about what they are agreeing to, and most people honor what they put in writing.

Often, something isn't addressed in the contract. I would never expect contracts to force people to do what's not in their long-term interest. When issues come up, the parties need to discuss and change the agreement or go their separate ways. If I create a contract that's not good for the other party, it won't work for long.

We always honor our side of a contract, renegotiating if necessary. People sense our trustworthiness and continue doing business with us.

Once, one of our competitors expressed interest in buying us. It turned out they were trying to learn about our business. After that experience, if a competitor expresses interest in our business, I request reciprocal information from them. If they want our sales figures, we want theirs; if they are snooping, we find out quickly.

Raising money

One way to begin a business is to raise lots of investment money, and then raise more. It took FedEx five years before they hit a critical mass to become profitable.

I don't recommend raising money from investors when starting your first small business. Instead, plan on making money right away. It may sound impossible, but find a way to do it. Focus on what you can sell, and sell the heck out of it. Sell it and sell it and sell it until you can expand your line. Then expand, expand, and expand from a position of strength, always paying your bills.

If you do decide to raise money, you must understand the psychology of it. When you chase something, your emotions and ego are in charge. Instead of chasing it, decide to have it.

There are two kinds of wanting. "I want a glass of water" and "I want to raise a million dollars by the end of the week." In the U.S., anybody can get a glass of water in a few minutes. With a million dollars, fear and resistance come up. We think, *How can that happen? It's impossible.*

Wanting water is a decision: I want it, and I know I will have it. Wanting a million dollars for most of us is a desire based on the stressful feeling of needing it. I once spoke to a successful bond trader. For him, raising a million dollars was emotionally similar me to wanting a glass of water.

If you want the million dollars, you can decide: "I will raise a million dollars by the end of the week." When you are clear and certain, it's as if it were done. Nature responds to all-in decisions. You take the necessary action and allow it to come, and, as if by magic, channels open up.

If you are desperate, the sharks gather. Your posture should never be, "Please, oh please, help me, I hope this is going to work." Were you ever in high school, anxious for a date? Did you get the date? Instead, if you were cool and didn't care, schoolmates could relax and respond to your attractiveness.

By deciding, you are no longer chasing the million dollars. Instead, you are drawing investment to you, attracting money, investors, partners, and clients. "I've got this phenomenal thing here, and a few people are going to make a lot of money. I want to know if you're interested or not."

The second habit in Stephen Covey's, *Seven Habits of Highly Successful People* is "Begin with the end in mind." From the depths of a quiet mind, picture the result with the same certainty that you would have if you wanted a glass of water. Let go, and allow the universe to support you.

SPIRIT: Stamp your intentions on the infinite

MASTER YOUR FEELINGS

Much of business is about mastering feelings. Warren Buffett once said, "My biggest secret to making money was learning to manage my emotions." Emotions are not trustworthy or reliable friends; that quiet voice within is. If we make decisions based on our feelings (ego, stress, karma), our internalized programs dictate the results.

Most of us act based on how our families and society programmed us. If we had terrible grades, came from a poor family, or experienced early trauma, then we don't believe it possible to make a fortune in business. We believe we don't know how, don't have the ability, and don't deserve it. If we only refer to our programming, our fate is all but determined.

Once we start making decisions from the Self within, freedom increases, and karma's impact is limited. If we refer to that unbounded quiet spot inside us, we take control of our lives.

In the 1980s, I made a fortune that in today's dollars would be $5 million. I was 33 years old and just couldn't keep it. I bought good stuff, traveled, donated, paid taxes, put money in commodities, and invested in startups. I went through the money in five years. If I had dwelt on losing so much money, I would have repeated my failures. Continually referring to the loss would have colored and controlled my life. Instead, I looked at the loss, transcended it, and released the picture of it.

Then, I focused on the experience of making millions. I internalized it and believed it would happen again. What we put our attention on grows.

Many things in business make us feel uncomfortable and scared. Maybe it's failing; perhaps it's firing someone; maybe it's asking a for past-due payment. Thinking about success can also bring fear. The thought of making $1 million by the end of the year might bring up anxiety. The fear comes from our conditioning rather than from our true Self. If we are afraid of having money, we are telling the universe we don't want it, we don't deserve it, and we can't handle it right now. If we let negative feelings run our career, we're referring back to our emotions and stress. When fear captures us, we base our decisions on negativity.

I learned to make decisions from calm rather than from fear. I would get quiet and ask myself, "What's the next step?" Maharishi speaks of Self-referral. He says to meditate and return to the unbounded, infinite, unlimited Self. From the silent place within, we can think and act and effortlessly gain the support of nature.

Like fear, greed limits us. If we let greed instead of our vision motivate us, we never get enough. If we are functioning from greed, greedy people join us. Greedy people take advantage of us and don't stay. If we catch ourselves being fearful or greedy, we don't need to fight the fear or greed. Instead, we can go to a quiet place within and release the emotions. If we keep going back to quiet, the world is ours.

Giving freely from a pure heart is an antidote to fear and greed. I've always donated a lot. By donating, we're telling the universe that we have plenty of money. "Give, and it will come back to you," is a principle found in every major religion.

If we think small, we are letting fear govern. Instead, think big. All things are possible when we engage in Self-referral and tap into the unbounded awareness within.

Business is phenomenal for personal development

Business riches come and go. What's important is who we become. Ask yourself, "How would having a business help me become the person I want to be?"

A friend told me that the three major personal growth initiations in life are learning the TM technique (experiencing Transcendental Reality), getting married, and having a child. I would add a remarkably transformative fourth area — starting a business. Business is phenomenal for personal evolution and for developing the Self-referral process. In business, we learn to focus and go deep within to make decisions. In the quiet, we ask and get results. Daily practice of the TM technique cultures that quiet.

Business appears to take place during day-to-day operations. But business actually happens in the quiet moments when we stamp our intentions on the infinite. When we go within, our infinite potentiality shows up again and again.

Maharishi taught that the first sense of creation takes place in the silence of Pure Consciousness, when "existence becomes conscious, then intelligence becomes intelligent." Those words affected me profoundly.

I look at business as a way to cultivate the divine qualities of infinite intelligence becoming intelligent. Success in business requires the development of the qualities of truthfulness, strength, creativity, kindness, compassion, courageousness, flexibility, stability, and intuition. I have applied the divine qualities developed in business to my relationships, raising children, and making a difference in the world — all places I have experienced darkness.

Business can get dark, dismal, and hopeless. The entrepreneur thinks, "I'm never going to make it through." Then comes intuition and trust — faith. It's a subtle impulse that says, "I should go this way," even though the facts may not support it.

The ability to fulfill our desires depends on how well we establish the habit of referring back to the Self. We can create again and again from unbounded awareness, the field of all possibilities. Once we master this Self-referral process, the world is ours.

Steven Winn's twelve tweets

Listen to the quiet voice within

1. Emotions are not trustworthy or reliable friends. The quiet voice within is. If we make decisions based on emotions (ego, stress, karma), internalized programs determine the results. Instead, we decide by going deep within, getting clear on the goal, and asking for the next step.

2. Decide what you want and know it's done. Nature responds to all-in decisions. If we are sure we will get it, channels open up, and we can simply allow it to happen.

3. Business appears to take place during day-to-day operations. But business actually happens in the quiet moments when we stamp our intentions on the infinite.

4. Riches from business come and go. What's important is what we become.

5. If we use greed instead of vision as our motivator, we never get enough. If we function from greed, greedy people join us. Greedy people will take advantage of us and then leave.

Execute

6. Whatever you do, do it impeccably, and offers will come.

7. Many people have great business ideas, but nothing happens. With a reputation for executing and doing things well, people bring you great ideas because they don't want to do it or can't do it themselves.

8. As an entrepreneur, you either own a business, or you own a job. If your business requires you always to be there, that's a job.

9. What kind of business do you want? What are you willing to do? Do you desire stability, self-expression, being a difference-maker, or making a lot of money? Knowing why you are in business guides daily decision making.

10. The fundamental law of business must be respected: make money or go out of business. The people who work for me are my friends, and I care a lot. Yet, I separate business and friendship. It's not personal; it's business.

11. Do business with people you like and trust. If you don't trust a person, you can't expect a contract to control their behavior. Enforcement costs much more than the value of the deal.

12. Always tell the truth. If you make a mistake, don't try to hide it. Honesty is one of the real success forces in life.

Ponder

1. Steven's story had a lot to do with his relationship with success and failure. How do you deal with success and failure? What can you learn from Steven's up and down journey?

2. Steven states that his goal in business is to make money so that he can spend time pursuing his interests. His main strategy is to look for "fads" and make money quickly and easily. Do you have a judgment about that approach?

3. In addition to making money to have free time, Steven gave other reasons to go into business — stability, self-expression, and making a difference in the world. Why are you in business? What business decisions do you and will you make because of that?

4. Steven has a simple, direct approach to both hiring and firing. He hires on the basis of "emotional tone" and fires with the mindset: it's business, not personal and it's probably best for everyone. Do you agree with his thinking? How do you approach hiring and firing?

5. According to Steven, developing Self-referral is key to business success. Developing Self-referral means going within for answers. Can you relate? Can you think of examples of Self-referral in your life?

Steven Winn uses own marketing piece to promote Seminar Crowds post cards for financial planners

Steven Winn's Seminar Crowds mails postcards inviting folks for a complimentary gourmet dinner hosted by a financial planner

Steven Winn partner Ed Beckley and his no-money-down real estate system

Monica Hadley
TRANSFORMING IDEAS INTO BUSINESSES

Monica Hadley became an accidental entrepreneur at the age of 22, when her father's death thrust her into the role of running Sunsprout Systems, a supplier for sprout farmers.

Since then, she has launched and run businesses in a variety of industries. Her current portfolio includes Aeron Lifestyle Technology, which designs and manufactures consumer products; SEO Design Solutions, which offers a Wordpress framework; and Fairfield Accounting Services.

In her spare time, Monica and her mother have a weekly radio show, Writer's Voices with Monica and Caroline. She also founded a non-profit organization, The Iowa Justice Project.

JOURNEY: Adding structure to a half-dozen business and non-profit partnerships

FROM YOUNG MOTHER AND COLLEGE DROPOUT TO ACCIDENTAL ENTREPRENEUR

I didn't set out to be an entrepreneur. In fact, I began my adult life as an 18-year-old mother and college dropout. My goals were to make a decent living and to make a difference in the world. Entrepreneurship provided both.

At 22, I had just moved to a new town with my husband, four-year-old son, and infant daughter. My husband worked 12 hours a day. We didn't have much money and lived in a basement apartment beneath our landlords.

One day, after visiting my grandmother, I returned to discover that my landlady had left a nasty note in my apartment. I was angry and upset. She had invaded my privacy and criticized my housekeeping. I called home and told my father what happened.

He said, "Why let this woman upset you? You did nothing wrong. You're giving her power over you. Forget about it."

A few weeks later, my dad died while hiking in the Grand Canyon. That last conversation with my father remains with me. I am the one responsible for my happiness, and I have complete control over my attitude.

When my father died, I became an accidental entrepreneur. He left his business, Sunsprout Systems, to my younger brother Bryan. Sunsprout manufactured and supplied equipment, seed, and packaging for independent alfalfa and bean sprout growers. Previously, I had been doing the accounting for the company and my brother had grown sprouts. Together we took over operations and got a sink-or-swim education in every aspect of business from sourcing to sales.

Sunsprouts was the beginning of my business career. Since then I have founded or been involved in building five successful businesses and two nonprofit programs.

Fairfield Accounting

I have a real affinity for math thanks to a rich childhood exposure to numbers. I took a bookkeeping class in high school and Intro to Accounting as a college correspondence course. At 18, I trained with H&R Block to prepare people's taxes. At the same time, my father's bookkeeper taught me the real-world basics of accounting, which really helped when I took over Dad's business.

In the early 1980s, I bought one of the first personal computers, the Osborne. QuickBooks didn't exist, and accounting software cost thousands of dollars, so I taught myself to program and wrote general ledger and payroll programs.

I met a woman with a bookkeeping service in Des Moines. She wanted a partner in Fairfield. Soon after we set up shop, she left the state and I took over. In 1983, I ran my small accounting business in a basement. I needed help but had a hard time attracting anyone.

A competitor, Nick Wolfe, convinced me to merge with his firm. That way we could better serve Fairfield's emerging entrepreneurial community. When Nick left Fairfield in 1984, I formed Fairfield Accounting with Nick's original partner, Margie Wood.

I was still running Sunsprout with my brother when I started Fairfield Accounting.

Many new businesses have no accounting system. Without numbers, you don't know where you stand, what the real costs are. It is tough to make good decisions. Still, people say they'd rather go to the dentist than to their accountant. It's understandable. Accountants know the intimate details about a client's money situation. Money affects a client's status and personal and business survival.

It takes a certain kind of personality to work with accounting clients. Women make up most of Fairfield Accounting, and women tend to be more nurturing. Several of us do most of the hand-holding. Our clients may get a tax notice and freak out. Often the problem is insignificant and we spend time telling clients not to worry.

Tax problems we can solve; there's not much we can do about

financial problems.

Over 30 years in business, Fairfield Accounting has consistently employed between 10 and 15 people.

Country Fresh

In 1987, Bryan came to live in Iowa for a year to take over Sunsprout, which he then moved to Houston. Bryan morphed Sunsprout into Country Fresh as he expanded to specialty imported produce, then to organic produce, and finally to cut fruit. He was so successful with those products and Country Fresh that he eventually discontinued Sunsprout.

I was involved with Country Fresh from the beginning until retiring in 2017, mostly serving as the Chief Financial Officer (CFO). Today, Country Fresh promotes healthy snacking by making it easier for people to consume fruits and vegetables. The company cuts up fruits and vegetables, packages, promotes, and distributes them nationwide. They have multiple facilities, hundreds of employees, and distribution to some of the largest and best retailers in the country.

After serving as Chief Financial Officer (CFO) for most of the company's life, I recently retired from that position.

Aeron Lifestyle Technology

By 1996, I was newly single with two children. I owned Fairfield Accounting with Margie, had no debt, and needed a better car.

My close friend, Jeffrey Smith, was passionate about an idea — an aromatherapy diffuser that plugged into the car cigarette lighter. He had been trying to get his invention to market for two years. He had no money and a lot of debt, but he wouldn't give up.

Instead of buying a car, I decided to invest in his idea — even though manufacturing a new category of consumer product is the most difficult type of business to start. When we started Aeron, "fragrance diffuser" wasn't even a term in business lexicon.

We quickly learned that my $15,000 investment was not nearly enough to design, tool and produce the product. From my experience at Fairfield Accounting, I knew how to persevere to be successful. With that confidence, I cashed in my Certificates of Deposit and borrowed money from my brother. Still short, I funded Aeron on my credit card — something I would never advise anyone to do.

Over the next three years, the company refined the product's design, created the tooling, and manufactured it. The DriveTime™ diffuser looked and worked great.

I had over six figures invested.

We made only modest sales in the U.S., UK, Australia, Japan, and Thailand. Our big break came when I went on the Home Shopping Network. Shortly after the successful show, the buyer got fired, and the replacement never returned our calls.

We found a distributor in Thailand who promised to do great business in Asia. Then the Thai currency collapsed, and the distributor disappeared.

We raised another $60,000 to produce a TV infomercial. Selling aromas in a television commercial totally flopped.

We didn't give up. Until you quit, you haven't failed. I borrowed more money from my mother, got more credit cards, and worked harder at Fairfield Accounting. We ended up moving our manufacturing to China to lower costs. I dug into my Fairfield Accounting retirement account to pay for that.

With a lower price, we landed a spot with Best Buy as it tested selling automotive products. Our DriveTime diffuser sold well. Then Best Buy canceled the test.

It seemed like every time we turned a corner, things fell apart. We kept going. As the year 2000 approached, it was getting iffy.

Then, finally, the tide turned. In January 2000, we found a new partner, Patrick Kosar, who was then a Vice President at Books Are Fun. Sharing our vision, Patrick invested in Aeron in exchange for the majority of the equity. In 2002, he became Aeron's CEO. Our sales topped four million dollars, almost 10 times as much as the first five years put together. In 2016, sales were $30 million and we are still growing.

In the early 2000s, we stopped trying to build our own brand of consumer products. Instead, we became a company that designed custom products for large retailers. Aeron is now an industry leader in developing home, auto, and travel fragrance programs for major retail chains worldwide. For our retail clients, we conceptualize, design, prototype, perform market analysis, test, set up a global supply chain, provide tech services, and assist with compliance.

Pivoting from building our own brand to designing products for others wasn't an easy decision, but it brought us success for years.

We bought an equipped factory in Mason City, Iowa, three and one-half hours north of Fairfield. Price-wise, we purchased it at the right time, and were able to get financing late in 2008, during the big credit freeze.

We invested millions of dollars into the Mason City factory. Shortly after opening, a fellow came up to me and said, "Thank you for giving me a job." Another employee, I was later told, had been coming to work and living under a bridge before he could change his situation.

Now, between our Fairfield design headquarters and the factory, we offer services from concept to prototype to full production runs in the USA. In Fairfield, we use a 3D printer to build a prototype, or in some cases a pilot mold. We send the mold to our factory and within days create samples from the actual resins to use in production.

Before 3D printing, we spent thousands of dollars to cut the mold in China and then had to wait four weeks for samples. If a product requires significant manual labor, we still have it molded and manufactured in China. If we need a labor-intensive product quickly, we also work with Mexican suppliers, a truck drive from Iowa. We manufacture the final product in our Iowa plant and include a "Made in USA" logo.

It took 15 years, but now we're back to our roots developing our own branded products. In 2015 we launched a product line under the brand, Scentual Living, and in 2017 we re-launched DriveTime. We sell long-lasting home fragrances and home and car diffusers directly on Amazon and to wholesale accounts.

SEO Design Solutions

From the start at Aeron, Jeffrey Smith did the web work, making sure that we ranked high on the early search engines.

Though he remained on the board, in 2006 Jeffrey left Aeron and started a Search Engine Optimization (SEO) company. Knowing Jeff's dogged persistence, I partnered with him. I backed the company and helped with the infrastructure.

The company consults and sells a WordPress framework with SEO built-in, as well as one of the most popular SEO plug-ins for WordPress sites, SEO Ultimate. Brands such as Michaels, Comodo, American Express, and *Food and Wine Magazine* have hired SEO Design Solutions for consulting and SEO services.

Writers' Voices

In 2006, meditating entrepreneur James Moore started Fairfield's KRUU-LP 100.1 FM, a "solar-powered, open source, independent, non-commercial, listener-supported, grassroots community, low-power radio station, broadcasting 24 hours a day and seven days a week." A hundred volunteers hosted and produced 70 KRUU shows a week.

In the beginning, James asked me to do a talk show. "Anything you want."

I wanted to do something with my 82-year-old mother, Caroline Kilbourn, who had a long career on radio. At first I thought we would do a call-in advice show about business, but because my mother and I are both avid readers and sometime-writers, we started a show where we interview writers from all over the world. Afterward, we post it as a podcast. Early in the life of Writers' Voices I hoped to expand the brand by creating a social network for writers, but I didn't have the time to devote to it so had to shelve that idea.

KRUU closed down in 2018, and we've moved the show to the Maharishi University of Management station, KHOE. We also broadcast on Iowa City's community radio station, KICI -LP 105.3 and post our podcasts on writersvoices.com, our YouTube channel, and on Apple iTunes.

Iowa Justice Project

In 1984 in the U.S., 34,000 people were serving life sentences without the possibility of parole. In 2016, that number quadrupled to over 140,000 out of 2.3 *million* U.S. incarcerations. Latinos and blacks made up two-thirds of the people serving life sentences.

Some in Iowa were serving life sentences because of its felony murder rule. The rule has been ruled unconstitutional by the Iowa Supreme Court, but the courts have thus far refused to apply that principle retroactively.

A member of the Iowa State Penitentiary chapter of Toastmasters International inspired me to found the non-profit, Iowa Justice Project. This inmate, a man of color, is serving life without parole for a crime committed when he was 19. His white co-defendant, the guiltier of the two, received a much shorter sentence and served only a few years. Due to the felony murder rule, if my friend were being sentenced today, he would receive a shorter sentence than the time he has already served.

The Iowa Justice Project applies legal support services and promotes efforts to ensure that the courts treat people the same for the same criminal act.

My three types of business partnerships

Each day I am involved with one or more of my businesses and non-profits. These businesses fall into three broad categories, each more challenging than the previous.

1. Filling a Market Need

In this type of business, the entrepreneur sees a need and fills it. Fairfield Accounting came about because many Fairfield small businesses needed basic accounting. My two non-profits, the Iowa Justice Project and Writers' Voices, also fill an existing need.

With each of these, already having the skills, I just started doing the work.

2. Improving on an existing idea

Cutting up fruits and vegetables is not a unique thing. Country Fresh just does it better. They developed new and more efficient equipment, sanitation processes, quality control, and packaging to extend shelf life. Also, by tighter control of purchasing and faster turnover of raw product inventory, a fresher product is available to consumers.

SEO Design Solutions improves on SEO by building it into the framework of websites. As opposed to doing SEO as an afterthought, the framework allows the webmaster to optimize the most important aspects of the site and information architecture as part of the construction process.

3. Creating a new product

Starting a business based on a new idea is the hardest way to go. Such a business requires building a product from scratch and then educating the public to create a market for it. Aeron Lifestyle Technology and its brands, DriveTime and Scentual Living by Design, fall into this category.

Aeron is the most successful of my businesses. If I had known the effort and struggle involved, I'm not sure I would do it over again. It's like having a baby. Over time, you forget how hard it was. In the end, it turned out well for me, my partners, and the people working for Aeron.

WISDOM: Show the Universe You Mean Business

INVEST IN YOURSELF AND YOU CAN'T LOSE

George Bernard Shaw said, "Life isn't about finding yourself. Life is about creating yourself." Whether you win or lose today, the skills you develop, the experience you gain, and the friends you make form the basis for future success.

Investing in yourself means getting in the arena and taking action so you can learn. My brother started over three times before he created the mega-success of Country Fresh. Knowing that you gain from every failure helps you get through the hard times.

For a Transcendental Meditator, consistently practicing the TM technique is another way to invest in oneself. By experiencing the universal silence within, a meditator gains the support of nature. Of course, if you want nature's support, you must also give nature something with which to work — you must take action.

If you can show the universe that you mean business, and nothing can stop you, the universe will take note. Winston Churchill said, "Success requires going from one seeming failure to another without loss of enthusiasm." Jeffrey Smith and I never gave up on Aeron.

Ideas are easy, execution is hard

Sometimes people jealously guard their ideas, which I think is foolish. Ideas come easily, and similar ideas tend to surface at the same time. I have come up with what I thought a brilliant idea, only to read about it the next week. Turning ideas into successful businesses is the hard part.

If it were simple and anyone could do it, no one would need you or your business. If it were easy to keep up with the changing tax code, then our clients wouldn't need Fairfield Accounting.

Thomas Edison said, "Genius is 1% inspiration and 99% perspiration." With perseverance, anyone can succeed. Give everything you have, no matter how challenging, no matter how tedious, no matter how long it takes, even if you have to change directions.

When you understand what it takes to persevere, problems become opportunities. You know that if you have a problem, other people have the problem — and if you can solve it, you'll get more business.

A complaint is another chance to turn a problem into an opportunity. Customers aren't always right, but we can make them feel right. Most people are invested in being right and can't admit to a mistake. We take responsibility for everything in our businesses, even for things not our fault. Blame doesn't solve problems. For example, when a Fairfield

Accounting client calls up angry, we accept responsibility, are as kind as possible, and do whatever we can to fix the problem. As a result, we gain the client for life.

When Aeron employees make a mistake that affects a customer, we approach the customer with a conciliatory attitude. That gets us much further than being defensive or offensive. If an employee messes up, it's really our fault. Either, we chose the wrong person for that job, didn't give proper training and support, or didn't manage properly.

We realize that each mistake allows us to refine systems and win over customers and employees.

To successfully execute a business, it is important to be aware of the 80/20 Pareto principle law of the vital few. It tells us that

- 80% of profit comes from 20% of customers;

- 80% of problems come from 20% of customers;

- 80% of sales come from 20% of products.

At Fairfield Accounting we applied this principle. The top 20% of our customers were business clients and the most problematic 20% were individual clients. After our analysis, we cut almost 80% of our client base — our individual clients — so we could focus on our business clients.

We became more profitable with less stress.

The structure and flow of business

I think of business as structure (operations) and flow (fairy dust.) Operations and accounting make up structure, and sales and marketing are flow.

Having a structure in place means you can walk away from the business, and the business continues. Flow is vision. It's the element you can't define. The business tends to be more dependent on individuals providing flow.

Success usually comes from a pairing a visionary sales-type person and a strong financial person. The two aspects are hard to find in one person. Successful partnerships include mutual respect for the other's strengths, trust, and compatibility.

My strength has always been with structure. In my businesses, I work in finance, production, property, legal, IT, and HR — the structural elements. I like to work in partnerships because most people are not good with structure. I've been fortunate that my visionary, sales-oriented partners respected the importance of structure.

At Aeron, we started out based on flow. Jeffrey made things work; when things went wrong, he fixed them. That got us only so far and made us dependent on him. I started focusing on process and procedure.

Fairfield Accounting is a little different since, by definition, it is a structural service. Still, there is a flow component. My partner, Margie, does a great job keeping our clients and employees happy. Part of my work on the structure side is to add systems.

Systems can be as simple as written checklists, which we have in all my companies. With checklists, nothing gets forgotten. At Aeron and Country Fresh my accounting staff uses a detailed monthly accounting checklist. At Fairfield Accounting, we have all kinds of checklists: lists for new clients, lists for reviewing returns, lists for financial statements.

That said, it is easy for systems to fall by the wayside. Recently at Aeron, I sent out three reminders to use systems. People started using them again because their boss reminded them. Eventually, they will forget and will need to be reminded again.

I have people that are better than I am in implementing systems. My son does an excellent job making step-by-step rules that anyone can follow. At Aeron, I have an employee that records all meetings that discuss process.

Also at Aeron, I recently created a system that allows me to order the proper tooling. Someone starts by entering the tooling authorization into our company database. The authorization gets passed along to the engineers and others involved. With each step, the system generates an email to alert the next person. When the work is ready for me, I have the necessary information to decide on the tool size and place the order.

Without structure and systems you end up solving the same problems over and over again.

Structure and flow are both critical to success in business. Although I am analytical (structure), a lot of my success comes from intuition (flow). As important as analysis is, you have to listen to your gut deep inside. Just be sure it's not your emotions talking.

I can view a general ledger at Fairfield Accounting for a few minutes and things other staff missed just pop out. At Aeron, I seem to know the right people to hire and the right choices to make.

Knowing what to do requires pulling together everything you know and going inside for the answer. I give my Transcendental Meditation program a lot of credit for inner clarity.

In the past few years, with support from Margie, my brother at Country Fresh, and my partners at Aeron, I have fewer day-to-day operational functions. I now have a more strategic role, which is a lot of fun for me. After being an accountant these many years, I enjoy my involvement in product design, website creation, and other creative flow activities.

When to pivot

Part of the flow of business success comes from knowing whether and when to pivot.

Entrepreneurs sometimes get stuck on their plan. They don't want change because they are in love with their ideas. Listen to the marketplace. If you're running into something where there's no progress, then you probably need to change direction.

For example, after years at Aeron of trying to launch a product line, we had the opportunity to redesign and manufacture an existing product for a retailer. We saw that we could leverage that experience with other retailers, and we pivoted to great success.

Incremental progress eventually builds to success. Look for hints of progress before making the change. It's a delicate balance to keep focused and not get distracted by the next great opportunity. Stick with something long enough to see if it works.

At Fairfield Accounting, we also pivoted. I examined revenue charts, hours worked, and profit from that work, and then assigned a numerical value to stress level. From that analysis, we dropped our individual tax clients to work only with business clients, which frees us to take more year-round business.

Being a woman

You don't need to deny your femininity to be successful in business. I do think women tend to be better at the essential business skills of collaboration and cooperation. Women are also competitive, but for me, the collaborative side works well with all my partnerships.

The most important thing is to believe in yourself, to have confidence. Then it is easy to ignore whatever anyone says or does. I try to follow Eleanor Roosevelt's advice: "No one can make you feel inferior without your consent."

When I was younger and less confident and running my dad's business, some guy on the phone called me "honey." It infuriated me. I got hives and turned red. I wanted to phone him and tell him off. Now, it doesn't bother me. I just take it in stride.

Shortly after moving into the Mason City Aeron factory, we developed equipment to build a particular product. It did not work, creating a million dollars of bad product. We lost money for a couple of years and it seemed like we might not succeed. We had been profitable and had an excellent relationship with the banks. One of our lenders came from out of town. In a room filled with male bankers and colleagues, the banker focused on me: "Do you know what you are doing?"

I didn't cause the loss, I was reporting it. My colleagues later agreed that he focused on me with condescension because I was a woman.

In 2011, my brother at Country Fresh sold a minority interest to a private group on Wall Street. I was the Chief Financial Officer but got questions like, "How would you know?"

At times it was hard, but I stayed true to myself. I never confronted them, but continued to give my input — even when they ignored me.

Over time, my persistence and confidence paid off.

In 2015, the Country Fresh managing partner told me that they were always looking for people that could add immediate value. He said, "I could drop you into any of our companies, and you'd add value overnight."

I have hired men who have a problem working for a woman. I can usually tell in the interview, but occasionally someone slips through. While working in my brother's company, I shipped one such man down to Texas.

In the future, I would like to mentor younger female entrepreneurs. There are many powerful women CEOs and high-level executives working in Fairfield businesses and nonprofits. Most didn't start the businesses, but they have a lot of business skills.

SPIRIT: Be happy whatever you do

The lesson my father taught me about being responsible for my happiness has governed choices made in my business life.

People mistake achieving goals for happiness. You must ask yourself, what is success? What are you going for? Is it income level or status or happiness? To me, happiness is success and success is happiness. Yet, success is not the key to happiness. Happiness is the key to success.

If you enjoy what you're doing, you'll be successful. Some people think that means they must find the thing they love to do. I say, you just have to enjoy whatever you're doing.

You're not always going to love what you do or have fun. Creative people may not want to get stuck in the details, but the details are important. If you can find a way to enjoy the details, you'll have a better shot at success.

I like all my work, but I enjoy most making a difference in people's lives. Giving employees great opportunities and contributing to my partners' success has brought me the most fulfillment in my business life.

Monica Hadley's twelve tweets

1. With perseverance, anyone can succeed. Give everything you have, no matter how challenging, no matter how tedious, no matter how long it takes. Until you quit, you haven't failed.

2. Many new businesses have no accounting system. Without numbers, they don't know where they stand, and it is difficult to make good decisions.

3. Take responsibility for everything in your business, even things not your fault. If an employee messes up, take responsibility. You either chose the wrong person, didn't give proper training, or didn't manage properly.

4. Trust, compatibility, mutual respect, and complementary skills are what makes partnerships work. Success usually comes from pairing a visionary sales-type person and a strong financial person.

5. Meditation helps, but if you want nature's support, you must give nature something to work with. Show the universe that you mean business, that nothing can stop you. The universe will take note.

6. Investing in yourself means getting in the arena, taking action so you can learn. Win or lose, the skills you develop, the experience you gain, and the friends you make form the basis for future success.

7. The problem is thinking you have a problem. Problems are opportunities. If you have a problem, other people have the problem. If you solve it, you have more business.

8. Knowing what to do requires pulling together everything you know and then going inside for the answer. Just be sure it's not your emotions talking.

9. As a woman, you don't need to deny your femininity to be successful in business. The most important thing is to believe in yourself, to have confidence.

10. Customers aren't always right, but you can make them feel right.

11. Some people think that they must find the thing they love to do. Instead, you need to enjoy whatever you do. Love what you're doing, and you'll be successful.

12. Business success comes from knowing when and whether to pivot. Stick with something long enough to see if it works. Look for hints of progress before making a change. It can be challenging to stay focused and not get distracted by the next great opportunity.

Ponder

1. Are you a structure or flow person or both? What does that mean for your business?

2. In creating your business, would you prefer to partner or do it yourself? What are the pros and cons?

3. Monica never gave up at Aeron. Persistence is the one quality that all entrepreneurs have. Is that a quality you have or are willing to develop?

4. Can you be happy whatever you do?

5. Monica says that dealing with sexism is one situation where her father's final words of advice are very useful. No matter how condescending or paternalistic a man may be, rather than get upset or lose confidence, she continues to provide her expertise and input, without backing down — whether or not they ignore her. What do you think of this strategy?

Aeron team with Monica Hadley, front center

Car aromatherapy
diffusers sold by
a Monica Hadley
company

Monica Hadley with registered trademark certificates from the U.S.
Patent and Tradwemark Office

Peter Huggins
PUTTING PEOPLE FIRST

I met Peter as his T.A. instructor in 1974 at Maharishi International University in Fairfield. Ten years later, Rita and I briefly lived in a small guest house in the back of Peter's Palo Alto home. Rita helped Peter's wife, Susan, with their newborn. Upon arriving in Fairfield, Peter, a mutual friend Jonas Magram, and I started a men's support team.

Peter had worked with Jonas in the oil and gas industry in California and Iowa. Later, Peter took a position with close friend Earl Kaplan at Books Are Fun. Seven years later, Reader's Digest bought Books Are Fun for $380 million dollars.

Several years after that, Peter began offering oil and gas limited partnerships to friends and family. I don't know anything about oil and gas, but I know Peter, so I invested.

Peter has a simple business success sauce — people come first.

JOURNEY: From a $380 million sale to oil and gas partnerships

FIRST MIU GRADUATING CLASS

I gave up my surfboard and hang glider in 1974. Maharishi International University (MIU) had just moved from Santa Barbara, California to Fairfield, Iowa. My girlfriend, Susan, and I drove cross country to our new Midwest abode.

In 1977, Susan and I graduated in a ceremony that awarded the first MIU bachelor's degrees. The day after graduation, we married. Forty years and four kids later, we are still going strong.

I left MIU with a degree in Interdisciplinary Studies, which prepared me for nothing and everything.

Racquetball club manager

I moved back to San Francisco and took a job managing a racquetball club. Like bowling in the 1950s, racquetball was the hot new thing in exercise. Venture capital firms built racquetball clubs and hired MBAs to run the business.

The club I managed had 12 courts and was open from 6:00 AM to 10:00 PM. Like hotel rooms and airplane seats, profitability depended on the racquetball courts being occupied. It was easy to rent courts to business people before and after work. However, from 9:00 to 5:00, the courts remained empty, so the economics didn't work. I solved the problem, which set in motion my business career. Like most things, the solution was simple and based on common sense.

The previous manager was intense and a great racquetball player. He related well to the guys at night. However, he did not connect with women customers.

I started by hiring two amazing childcare providers. I considered them key to the business and treated them like goddesses. Moms would bring their kids and play racquetball knowing that their children were well cared for. And the business grew. It turns out that I had discovered the key to making racquetball clubs profitable — fill the daytime courts with happy moms. The happy moms told all of their friends, and soon the club was busy all day.

The MBAs in charge named me Manager of the Year. I had understood that it wasn't the sport that made the business successful — that would take care of itself. It was the human part that required sensitivity and awareness.

Getting my MBA

From my time at the club, I learned that I was good at working with and managing people. I also learned to appreciate the business acumen of the high-powered MBAs in charge.

I decided to get an MBA and learn the language of business. The University of California, Berkeley, Hass Graduate School of Business, a top MBA program, accepted me. I enjoyed the program. It gave me familiarity with the terminology and stature. Even so, I saw the MBA as just another tool in my bag. I knew my success would come from who I was as a human being and how I connected with people.

The fixer for an oil and gas partnership

In 1983, after receiving my MBA, a team of three Bay Area TM teachers hired me to manage oil and gas industry limited partnerships. I oversaw the details of the drilling operations. This was on-the-job training, but I loved the challenge of learning a new industry. I found that my ability to connect with a drilling hand or the local geologist allowed me to learn the oil and gas industry very quickly.

My friends selected me because I was flexible and good with people. I could pick up new information quickly, process it, and make conclusions.

I spent several years traveling throughout the U.S. Then, the company got into a major conflict. One of the chief operators committed fraud, and their business went bankrupt. We had raised around 15 million dollars. Our investor partners were furious. The three guys I worked for didn't want to deal with difficult clients or the aggressive lawyers. They told me, "Fix this, and we'll give you half the company."

It took three years of dealing with people, their differences, their stress, and their confrontations. I would sit in groups of three or four people who wanted to kill each other. I walked them through the situation, got to the other side, helped resolve their conflicts, and brought agreement. I credit MIU and the Transcendental Meditation program for much of my success.

The week of the final settlement, we had several successful Texas oil wells come online. Along with 50% of the company, I received a big check.

I took the risk, dealt with the stress, and came out on top. I was successful because I could connect with all the people involved. Putting relationships ahead of numbers has paid off big-time throughout my career.

The move to Fairfield

When I graduated from Berkeley, Hewlett Packard offered me a position. I had to decide between the corporate route and working for inexperienced meditating friends. I chose my friends. Because of that decision, in 1984 Susan, our baby son Evan, and I moved to Fairfield. There, I continued working for my friends in the oil industry.

Using profits from the sale of my Palo Alto home, I purchased land in the Fairfield countryside and built a home on it. Our kids grew up on 20 acres, something that couldn't have happened in California.

Humanizing Books Are Fun

I started working for Books Are Fun in 1993, when it had 20 employees and four million dollars in annual sales.

The founder and CEO, Earl Kaplan, was the best man at my wedding at MIU. Earl had been bugging me to work for him for some time, but I never believed his company was for real.

In the early 1990s, before Walmart and Amazon, Earl started Books

Are Fun by purchasing books at 70% off retail. How did Earl get 70% off? Bookstores receive books on consignment and pay publishers only when the books sell. The publisher absorbs all printing expenses without guarantee that anyone will buy. Earl proposed to book publishers that they sell us books at 70% off. We would pay cash in advance and promise no returns. All the publishers had to do was print the books and receive a guaranteed profit.

We told publishers it wouldn't affect their Barnes & Noble or Borders sales because we sold books in teachers' lounges. For a week, we would display 20 to 25 best sellers, cookbooks, and fancy coffee table photo books in the teachers' lounges for 50% off retail. A teacher would like a book, fill out an order form, and receive it in five days.

The first couple of publishing companies were hard to convince. That changed as soon as Earl demonstrated that the model worked.

Eventually, we developed our own products, mostly gift items. We would discover something cool, and get it manufactured in China at little cost.

We began selling our products in corporations, where we would set up a book fair of several hundred titles for two or three days. Employees would come and buy books and gifts during their break.

Earl, a master strategist and negotiator, wasn't particularly good at managing people directly, so he hired me as VP to manage his sales team.

Earl developed a system for testing books to determine the ones that would sell. We'd buy a couple hundred copies of a book, and the sales reps would put them out at schools. Depending on how well a book sold, we might buy 100,000 copies for the next school year.

We created systems so we could grow quickly. We had systems to train sales reps, to assign routes, to ship books to reps, to process sales, to create reports, to FedEx sales commission checks, and so on.

We bought books five to six months in advance. If we didn't sell them, we were stuck. With little margin for error, too much excess product would kill the business. It took great courage to move forward at our aggressive pace.

Earl's twin brother, David, and their father provided seed capital.

Earl didn't know anything about business operations or accounting but was smart enough to know what he didn't know. He hired Ted McLaughlin, a CPA, as the CFO. Ted spoke the lingo. As the company doubled and tripled in size, Ted would show Chicago bankers our testing, analysis, inventory projections, salaries, overhead, and unexpected expenses estimate. He convinced the bankers to keep loaning us money.

Information flow was critical. We had as many as 500 reps around the country. Every Friday night, each rep would call headquarters and give their sales manager the results over the phone. It was like a rah-rah party as the numbers came in. We witnessed how the whole thing grew from week to week.

Saturday morning all the managers would meet with Earl. Together, we reviewed an Excel spreadsheet with the consolidated weekly results, seeing how well our tester books performed. Before the internet and E-Commerce took off, it was the right business model at the right time.

The company was good at driving sales and making decisions by the numbers. We understood the profit needed to grow the business.

However, as mentioned before, Earl wasn't great with people and hated having to fire anybody. When I arrived, they didn't have a Human Resources (HR) person, and no one had much concern for the wellbeing of the employees. There was a need for someone to see the business in terms of people not just numbers. In any business, human connection, the "heart value," is critical. HR problems ended up in my office.

Earl did have a deep understanding for how self-motivated people work best. Many managers micromanage. They look over your shoulder and expect you to do things a certain way. They almost want to do the job for you. Earl knew that people work much better if you leave them alone, so he created a structure of independent sales representatives. That approach allowed the company to grow to $240 million dollars in revenue in seven years.

Anyone could become a rep and independent contractor for Books Are Fun without business experience. We looked for people with the desire to run their own business and found a strong base in Fairfield.

Earl wanted the reps to be excited and see the business as their own.

He gave them a good product but didn't make them buy books or sign a contract. He told them, "It's your business. You can earn as much as you want. You spend only for driving around. We ship the books to you and pay you a 22% commission. You will receive your commission check within five days after you make the sale."

Earl understood that paying the reps right away motivated them to make more sales the next week. As a group, Earl treated them generously, with respect, and as the most important part of the business.

The reps worked hard and made $70,000-$100,000 during a nine-month school year.

With three to four hundred employees, we sometimes had to fire people. Earl hated doing it, so he would ask me to let them go. For dark humor, the sales assistants tacked a noose to my door. They told people going into my office, "You're done if he closes the door."

We could easily identify poor performing salespeople and other problem employees by their mistakes. I would help an employee see that they were not well-suited for their position. Together we discussed what else they might do inside or outside the organization. If we didn't have an internal solution, I had to let them go. It could be emotional, but I tried to do it in a heartfelt way. People appreciated that I cared.

My job was to empower the staff, educating team leaders in sales data and logistics. We gave leaders authority and responsibility for their team. If someone didn't get along, the leader would try to find another position where the person could be happy and successful.

Connecting with people cultures respect. People caring about people in an organization creates a fluid energy, and that helps generate business.

Closely aligned with his CFO, Earl focused on the numbers. From the start, Earl planned to sell the business and took the risks necessary for steep growth.

In August 1999, Reader's Digest bought Books Are Fun for $380 million dollars.

Reader's Digest was big in the publishing industry, much bigger than we were. They put accountants in charge (something I would never recommend). The accountants wanted to manage everything to the penny.

Reader's Digest completely missed that we were a people business based on relationships with reps and publishers. Management never showed the reps much respect and quickly lost their support. They tried forcing the reps to buy books and sign a contract. Reader's Digest never understood that what made the business work was creating entrepreneurs who grew their own businesses.

Within five years, Books Are Fun was bankrupt.

Earl Kaplan bought back the company that he had sold at $380 million for $17 million, mostly for the inventory.

Genetic ID

When Books Are Fun sold, I made money from the stock. Like many others, I left the company a few months after the sale. Earl said that when I left, Books Are Fun lost its heart.

In April 2000, Genetic ID offered me the Chief Operating Officer (COO) position. Genetic ID, founded by John Fagan, a MUM professor, pioneered testing foods for genetically modified organisms (GMOs). Genetic ID helped create the first non-GMO certification program.

I liked the idea of working for a company that would make a difference in the world by helping safeguard the food supply. My focus was to build Genetic ID's infrastructure, support the company's global expansion, streamline operations, and expand the laboratory's capacity. This blueprint helped lead to Genetic ID's subsequent success.

I worked at Genetic ID for about a year and a half. At the time, with its lab on the MUM campus, Genetic ID was more of a cause than a business.

With four kids to put through college, I still needed to make money and wanted to start my own company. I asked myself, "What do I like? What am I good at?" The oil and gas business had treated me well. Once you drill a well and it produces, cash flows in whether you work, sleep, or are on vacation. That's a nice way to live.

In 2001, using the proceeds from Books Are Fun, I started oil and gas drilling partnerships.

My oil and gas business

Finding investors is about sharing your vision and finding people who relate to it. My plan was to raise money from Fairfield friends and family. Friends naturally wanted to know the risk, the upside, and the downside. The first investor is always the hardest. After that, other people join. I raised $600,000 in my first deal but went on to raise over $12 million dollars over the next 12 years.

For my first deal, I met with geologists in Texas and found a low-risk drilling prospect. To demonstrate my confidence and commitment to the process, I put up over 40% of the money.

My first investor, Ken Sewall, had been a professor at MIU and had a Ph.D. in economics. He ran the numbers and thought the deal made sense. Four other guys joined because they believed in Ken. Since that time, I've created over 20 different partnerships with a 150 investors.

I asked myself, "What's my purpose for creating the business?" Of course, I wanted to make money.

Going deeper, I realized that I was in business to serve my friends and family, who became my partners. Like Books Are Fun, I knew my business would grow if the partners were happy, felt well-treated, and made money. At some level, my potential partners realized my concern for their welfare, and that allowed me to raise money.

I studied other oil and gas promoters. The industry has a shady reputation. There are many Wall Street types selling oil and gas deals in large multi-million dollar packets. The salespeople take as much as 30% upfront for putting the deal together. They don't invest any of their own money, so they don't care if the deal works. I did not want to follow that model.

My partners have standing. I educate them about the risks and rewards, and I always have skin in the game with 10% of the investment. If I do well, my partners do well, and they want to invest again.

Relationships are key, both for finding investors and discovering good drilling prospects.

Oil and gas is a risky business. To minimize the risk, rather than putting the partners' money in one well, I diversify and find 10 wells. Only a few wells must come through for success.

I started by flying down to Texas and meeting with operators who had identified land that was prospective for oil and gas. Over time, I came to care for these operators as people.

When I began in 2001, low oil and gas prices made for a somewhat dormant industry. It was a good time to meet with the people selling prospects.

The oil and gas business became more popular. Over time, it would have become harder for a small operator like myself to find good oil and gas prospects to drill. Operators don't make good opportunities public. They sell them through their personal network.

I was a good partner. In the same way that we quickly paid sales commissions at Books Are Fun, I paid my bills immediately. When an operator asked me for something, I always cooperated right away. My geologist supplied valuable information for each project. I regularly met with my geologist and operators in rural Texas, which they appreciated since I came from Iowa. They liked me.

I connected with the operators even though we may have voted and worshiped differently. Like local Iowans, rural Texans are really good people. My work and life are more fulfilling because of my day-to-day interactions with them. As these relationships developed, operators would call me with good deals they could have sold to someone else.

It's a simple business. A consultant in Texas does my geology. I employ two accountants in Fairfield. We have 150 investment partners and a bunch of people I work with in Texas.

The hardest part is finding good oil and gas prospects to drill. Once successful, a well can produce income for 15 to 20 years without much work from our side.

The oil business is cyclical. As of 2018, prices have been depressed for several years. Everyone focuses on today's price, but I plan for the long-term. As oil prices slumped, I structured my business to minimize expenses. We have wells that could produce but don't because of prices. Having oil and gas in the ground is money in the bank. It's there and has value, but we can't withdraw it now.

I keep in communication with my operators and investors. With the operators, we adjust and cut maintenance costs. Eventually, there will be a good return. I tell my partners that oil and gas have gone through many up and down cycles. Prices will rebound.

WISDOM: Discover what you do well

BENEFITS OF THE *TM* PRACTICE AND MIU

Before MIU, I bounced around, attending three different colleges with no idea what to do with my life. That changed at MIU. I practiced the TM technique twice a day, took classes based on MIU's holistic approach to education, and lived in an environment of meditators. At MIU, I gained self-confidence and learned how to treat people.

A few years later, Berkeley accepted me into their MBA program even though MIU wasn't yet accredited. My Stanford and Harvard MBA racquetball club bosses recommended me, referencing my maturity, common sense, leadership, and ability to work with others. I developed those fundamental but hard-to-teach traits at MIU, which educates the whole person. At MIU, I came to know myself from the study and direct experience of pure consciousness. That inner knowingness proved a big advantage in the competitive workforce.

Find your place in the world

I enjoy my work life in the oil and gas industry so much that it doesn't feel like work. I like the people and the excitement of drilling a well.

Life becomes so much easier if you find a vocation that suits you. Know your uniqueness; know what you are made of. Find what's fulfilling, what's natural, what's soothing. Discover what you do well and makes you happy. Honor that discovery, and life will work out.

Find a career that allows you to give the most of who you are. That giving will be the most fulfilling part of your life. Don't let worldly aspirations push you into objectifying others or dishonoring your values. Come from your strength and volition.

Always treat people as you would like to be treated.

Hire people smarter than you

I hire people smarter than I am. Rather than being threatened by smart people, I know that smart people make me look good.

As at Books Are Fun, I don't micromanage. I make sure my accountants understand the job and then I get out of their way.

Make money by leveraging time

As an employee, you only get paid when you work. Even if you charge $250 an hour as a consultant, time limits your ability to make money. As an entrepreneur, you can make money each time a product or service is sold, whether or not you are working.

However, being an entrepreneur isn't easy. You must be patient and thick-skinned to survive the uncertainty, volatility, and cyclical nature of the marketplace. If that is not in your makeup, then you should work for a corporation where someone gives you a paycheck.

Win-win

Some say to be successful, you must be super aggressive and always negotiate the best possible deal. You can't be soft.

I think that's short-sighted. Yes, you want a good deal, but it is more personally fulfilling to treat others well and make sure they also get a good deal. A reputation for creating win-win transactions keeps the door open in the future, and that makes for a business that lasts.

Effective selling

Your mindset determines your effectiveness at selling products and finding investors. Just wanting the prospect's money doesn't work.

Rather, you must want to give your customer something of great value.

I always try to put my financial and drilling partners' needs ahead of mine. Then, no matter what happens, I've served them. This approach is more fulfilling and leads to success.

Managing money

Understand how your money comes in and goes out. Whether the money you manage is yours, your business's, or other people's, know the basics of accounting, budgeting, and working with Excel spreadsheets.

To function in France, you must speak French. Business school taught me the language of business. To raise money, you must understand cash flows, finance principles, and financial and tax accounting. Even if you hire financial experts, you need a basic understanding. You must be able to manage them and understand their limitations.

Entrepreneurs can pick up a lot of financial knowledge on their own from books and online courses.

The Environment

We need oil and gas to power the modern world. Without oil and gas, much of the world would starve. Natural gas is a clean fuel, much better than coal. Yet, natural gas still comes out of the ground and destroys the environment.

When I started in 2001, I attended a three-day wind conference in Washington DC. I soon realized that as a small entrepreneur I wouldn't be able to raise the 100 million dollars necessary to do a wind project.

I don't frack because of its destructive environmental effect. I work with operators who are very conscious about the effect their drilling has on the environment.

It will be some time before we are able to replace conventional fuels. Until that time, there is a trade-off, and I will continue to drill for oil and natural gas.

SPIRIT: Lead from the heart

The wellbeing of employees is critical to the success of any business. Yet, businesses, particularly small ones, view the Human Resources position as an unnecessary expense that doesn't generate sales. Wherever I worked, I tried to help people. I would become the HR department even though no one knew it.

Earl didn't care much about that human element at Books Are Fun, but I did. I didn't get a lot of recognition, wasn't the highest paid or most respected. Yet, I was one of the happiest people there, because everyone loved me and I cared about them.

Many people with MBAs are great at driving business but could not care less about people. For them, people are just a means to an end. But I value my personal and business relationships more than my accomplishments and financial success. I believe that business is about taking care of people. Success comes from how well you treat and serve the needs of your secretary, your accountant, your boss, your customer, your supplier, your partner. A caring attitude brings happiness and success in any field you choose.

Books Are Fun was successful and made a lot of money. Reader's Digest took over with everything in place for ongoing profitability. Yet, how did Reader's Digest drive the $380 million business into the ground in four years? They stopped nurturing its people, the most basic component of the business. I've seen that same mistake repeatedly in my career. The human factor gets lost in operations, accounting, finance, and marketing.

Few people listen. Many times a sales assistant would come to my office crying because something happened. I sat and listened. That's all that was needed.

Sitting and listening without judgment can go a long way to resolving conflict and personal problems. Give someone space to unburden their heart. You can reflect back what they say. You can share a perspective or experience, but mostly just listen, even if it pushes your buttons.

Listening allows the person to open up. Being a vehicle for them to let go of their stress can make a huge difference.

We live in a cocoon in Fairfield where people smile and care about one another. Such a friendly and compassionate environment is rare. Like in a warm bath, we forget we're in this cocoon. Every time I travel, I notice that people don't smile. It's a whole different world.

When traveling, I try to connect with people — the car rental employee, the in-transit passenger, the food vendor. It doesn't take real energy. It doesn't take extra time. A small kindness may bring a little bliss to someone's tedious and stressful day.

Touch people's lives. The rest of business is a game to play.

Peter Huggin's twelve tweets

1. As a student at Maharishi International University, I developed hard-to-teach traits of maturity, common sense, leadership, and teamwork.

2. Life becomes so much easier in a vocation that suits you. Ask yourself, "What do I like? What am I good at?" You can't fake it. Discover what you do well and makes you happy, and life will work out.

3. Being an entrepreneur isn't easy. You must be patient and thick-skinned to survive the ups and downs. If you can't stand the uncertainty, then work for a paycheck.

4. Understand in detail how the money in your business comes in and goes out. Even if you hire financial experts, you need a basic understanding of finances to manage them.

5. Don't let worldly aspirations push you into objectifying others or dishonoring your values.

6. Being able to communicate is more important than anything you learn at business school. Success comes from who you are and how you connect with others.

7. You want a good deal, but it is more fulfilling to treat others well and see that they also get a good deal.

8. Effective selling is not about wanting your prospect's money. It is wanting your prospect to have something of value.

9. The most underrated thing in business is personal relationships. Success comes from how well you serve the needs of your assistant, accountant, boss, customer, supplier, and partner. A caring attitude brings happiness and success in any field you choose.

10. When traveling, it doesn't take much extra time or energy to connect with people and bring a little happiness.

11. People work much better if you make clear the task and leave them alone.

12. Passive income means cash flows in whether you work, sleep, or are on vacation. That's a nice way to live. Employees and contractors get paid only when working. Even at $250 an hour, time limits earning potential.

Ponder

1. The main theme of Peter's story is the importance of human connection in business. Is relating with people one of your core strengths? If so, how will that show up in your business? If not, what will you do about it?

2. Obtaining appealing products at a 70% discount for resale was the basis of success for Books Are Fun. In the digital age, after initial costs, it is common to create and sell products with an even higher margin. Are there other lessons from Books Are Fun that could be applied to selling digital products?

3. What abilities do you need to develop and what skills do you need to master to be able to raise money for your venture?

4. Do you agree with Peter that the Human Resources (HR) function is critical to business success?

PART FIVE
Selling Knowledge

Eva Norlyck Smith
Hal Goldstein

Eva Norlyk Smith
YOGA UNIVERSITY ONLINE

I first met Eva in 2008 when she interviewed me as part of her Maharishi University of Management (MUM) Psychology Ph.D. dissertation. An early inspiration for this book, she interviewed Fairfield meditating entrepreneurs for her paper on inner development and entrepreneurship.

Eva taught the TM technique in the early 1980s. Later, she helped launch a TM-based business college in Kenya. Soon after, on the MUM campus, Eva co-managed a $1.5 building project of two four-plexes.

Prior to her Ph.D., at MUM Eva studied professional writing and then blogged for the Huffington Post and other websites.

Eva became a Yoga instructor in 2006 and soon after helped create a DVD course, "Healthy Back, Healthy Body."

In 2007 to market the DVD, she started a website with resources about therapeutic yoga. In 2010, the website became YogaUOnline, an online business that offers continuing education to yoga teachers.

JOURNEY: Applying lifelong learning to creating a successful online business
TM TEACHING PREPARED ME FOR ENTREPRENEURSHIP

In the 1970s, most TM teachers were recent college grads. Those of us who became teachers were often asked to accomplish tasks that seemed daunting because of our youth and inexperience. At 25, I organized courses in a new city and coordinated a talk from a famous psychologist — finding a hall, negotiating the fee, generating publicity, and handling all the follow-up. 200 people showed up.

In 1991, my first husband, a professor at MUM, and I were sent to Kenya to start a MUM sister school. We had no campus, no students, no money, and knew no one. We had one contact, an Indian businessman who had run a private primary school.

Somehow within a year, we created a residential school for children on a beautiful campus. Through bootstrapping, we continued to expand the school, ending up with a hundred students when we left two years later.

Later, a MUM trustee and I initiated a 1.6 million dollar construction of two fourplexes on campus. I became the project manager during construction.

These projects helped give me the experience and confidence to launch and run my own business venture.

Starting YogaUOnline

I didn't set out to start a business.

In 2005, my second husband Terry and I, both body workers, attended a 200-hour yoga teacher training. Soon after, we created a program called "Healthy Back, Healthy Body" and taught the program in Fairfield.

One of our students, meditating entrepreneur Tim Hawthorne, had founded Hawthorne Communications, a direct marketing and video production company. Tim and his wife were going to New Zealand.

They asked if we would video the class so they could review it while they were away.

It ended up being a rather involved DVD production with voiceover, music, and five different takes. We wanted to sell the course but didn't want to be one of a thousand mostly unsuccessful people selling yoga DVDs. So, I decided to create a website that would be a resource for the therapeutic benefits of yoga. We would highlight various yoga teachers' work and sell our DVD via the website.

Serendipitously, I ran into a MUM student who had been working on a similar idea and had created webinar teleclasses with well-known yoga teachers. She had gone bankrupt and wanted to save some of the original elements of her website.

I bought the webinars from her and put them up online on what eventually would become YogaUonline.

What we do

YogaUOnline offers continuing education classes for yoga teachers.

Hundreds of studies extol the benefits of yoga, and doctors refer patients to yoga classes with ailments ranging from emotional stress to back pain. But most yoga teacher training does not cater to the needs of those referrals. For example, 40-year-old Americans are likely to have tight hamstrings and other limitations with bio-mechanical consequences. Yet, half of all yoga poses risk hurting the lower back of someone with tight hamstrings.

I recognized the need to educate yoga teachers with a focus on the limitations of the American body.

We began by offering online quality instructional videos taught by well-known and well-regarded yoga instructors and other health professionals. At the time, nothing of quality existed online, but soon we had many copycats, as the main yoga marketplace players began offering online yoga courses as well.

Fortunately, we have a different business model than most of our competitors, focusing on training yoga teachers with emphasis on therapeutic yoga. By staying true to our core audience, we increased our base of instructors and customers.

To educate yoga teachers, we don't just teach yoga postures. We offer basic courses in anatomy, body functions, body mechanics, and teaching methodology. For example, Judith Hanson Lasater, Ph.D., P.T., and author of eight books, trains yoga teachers in kinesiology and yoga therapeutics. Dr. Loren Fishman, a famous back-pain specialist and diagnostician — a physiatrist — deals with the biomechanics of the body. He has written a number of books including *Yoga for Osteoporosis*.

We have two different live webinars each month. Each course normally features two live webinars with slides and lectures, as well as accompanying yoga videos illustrating the topic.

At YogaUOnline.com, people register for the courses, which they have permanent access to in their dashboard on the website.

In 2013, we started selling monthly subscriptions. Subscribers can access all new content. Despite a small number of initial subscribers, persistence paid off. The stable monthly income from subscriptions has become our bread and butter, allowing us to hire permanent staff instead of just using contractors.

When we launched YogaUOnline in 2010, my partner had a database of 5,000 email subscribers. By 2013, we had 12,000 email subscribers and $250,000 in sales. As of 2018, we have 70,000 email subscribers and over $1,000,000 in sales.

Getting a business education from online marketing gurus

If you just put something up on a website, nothing happens. In 2010, we uploaded my partner's webinar recordings and emailed everyone on her list, inviting people to visit the website.

We had one sale in a month.

I soon learned about online courses that teach internet marketing. A core concept with most such courses is to "move the free line." Unless you're selling toilet paper or another must-have consumable item, don't expect people to just come to your website and buy from you. You have to establish a relationship with them first.

On the internet, since you never meet people in person, the best way to do that is to give something away for free. Then give something else for free and then something else. By delivering real value to people, you establish credibility. That establishes a basis of trust that makes people pay attention when you then later send them an offer.

I took the "30-day Challenge" for free with Australian, Ed Dale, who taught me how to research keywords for Search Engine Optimization (SEO). Our "Healthy Back, Healthy Body" course emphasizes posture. My research revealed many people searched for "posture support," and few websites wrote about it.

We posted articles on a new website that we built around the "posture support" keyword phrase. We put the keyword in the article's website address, title, first paragraph, and throughout the piece. We got several other websites to link to each article. Within a week of launch, we were number 11 on Google for the "posture support" search.

With his free course, Ed offered value and developed trust. He was a perfect example of what it means to move the free line and the kind of relationship you can build with people by giving something of real value without asking anything in return.

Ed started sending me offers about his courses and on behalf of his many friends. Clicking the offer's link meant free reports and videos and learning about the great things the online marketing system would do for me. Then, boom. If I joined in the next two days, I would get $7,000 worth of product for only $2,000.

I never spent so much money with anyone as I did with Ed and his affiliate friends. I was happy with the results; it turned into a good business education. But you really have to have the time to follow up if you enroll in a course like that or it's not money well spent.

I benefited the most from Jeff Walker's Product Launch Formula. Jeff continues to be one of the leading pioneers in the field of internet marketing. He posits that having the greatest offer in the world isn't enough. You must give people a reason to take action. Otherwise, folks are on to the next website, having forgotten about your great offer.

We use his Product Launch Formula to sell our webinars. We engage our prospects by giving useful information for free — an exclusive teacher interview, relevant articles, and whatever we come up with to establish the conversation and familiarize the customer with the teacher. The more expensive the product, the more time we spend.

Only towards the end of a marketing sequence do we send people an actual offer—but we generally don't keep the doors open that long, again, to force people to make a decision so they don't just forget about it and move on to something else.

Mailing list and SEO

We continue to grow and build our mailing list since an email address can have a limited lifespan. We regularly partner with non-profit Yoga Alliance and also advertise on Facebook. Depending on the quality of the lead, we can afford to pay up to two dollars for a qualified lead. One new customer who purchases our courses can pay for an entire promotion.

We also use our website and SEO to get new customers. For example, a New York Times article made exaggerated claims and stirred up controversy about yoga injuries. In response, we promoted a free online tele-summit: "Yoga Injuries — Fact or Fiction." From that event, we added 2,000 people to our email list.

We continue to add new articles and videos to our website, which helps SEO and engagement. We also repurpose that content for our email newsletters. Our newsletters provide yoga knowledge and inspiration plus information about upcoming courses. We send emails twice a week since twice a week tests best for course enrollment.

We survey our list to get a sense of where people want to go, what they enjoy, what courses they want to see. And we regularly check our list's open rate to monitor engagement.

Consumer videos

We also offer videos of traditional yoga practices taught by our yoga instructors. Consumers can log into the Practice Channel and watch anything with an $18-a-month subscription.

Many other websites offer similar content for consumers. Consequently, our consumer sales are modest, averaging 250 subscribers a month. Still, the Practice Channel adds to our credibility and increases the amount of searchable content. We include the $18 channel in the $50-a-month yoga teacher subscription, increasing its value.

Seeing the opportunities

Only masters from India taught yoga in the U.S 30 to 40 years ago. Now, mainly Americans teach yoga. People from all over the world come to the U.S. to take the latest courses. Yet, there's no authority and no leadership in yoga teacher training.

Becoming a massage therapist requires certification, which means you pass certain tests. The closest thing in yoga is a registry run by Yoga Alliance, which verifies that you took a 200-hour yoga teacher training course. There's no consensus about what you should know to teach yoga and no testing. It's a crisis in the yoga world.

A *Yoga Journal* survey showed that 36 million people practiced yoga in 2017, up from 20 million in 2012. Looking deeper, 30 million say they haven't practiced yoga in the past six months. I believe the quality of yoga instruction has much to do with the drop-off.

But it has created a great need for quality yoga teacher education, which is one of the gaps we fill. We see a great opportunity for expanding yoga teacher education, but that is a larger, long-term project.

WISDOM: Be a pro

FIND YOUR PLACE IN THE WORLD

Some people find out early what they should be doing with their life. For others, it's a constant exploration, and they may never completely find out.

It took me a long time, and I had to trust the process. I would find something I was passionate about, do it for a while, and then move on to something else. There were many forks in my path. Even after I finally decided to get a degree and become a writer, there were choices. Should I write scripts, novels, non-fiction, advertising copy, blog posts, technical manuals?

To choose, I asked myself, "Do I enjoy this? Am I attracted to it? Does it bring me happiness? Is this something I would do, even if I weren't paid?"

"Follow your bliss" may be a tired cliché but also a profound truth. You can trust your bliss. Stay in tune with it, and eventually you will gain the support and guidance to make your best possible contribution.

Running a business is the most challenging and fulfilling thing I've done. Looking back now, it seems like all the experiences I gained along the way were steps that gave me the skillset to make it possible.

Learn a Skill in Depth

An entrepreneur who gives her or his all attracts others who give their all. Giving everything you've got as an entrepreneur or employee translates into success in life.

Becoming a professional takes time, hard work, practice, and in-depth learning. Pros learn to do things to perfection, keeping the big picture in mind while focusing on the details.

I earned a master's degree in Professional Writing at MUM and then wrote professionally. As a student, we wrote and rewrote articles 10 to 12 times. It seemed a terrible waste of time, but it structured a skill level that has been useful in every single project I've done.

At the school in Kenya, I wrote the marketing materials and structured the lectures. When I was project manager for the construction of two fourplexes, I created a 150-page specifications manual that brought the cost down from $150 to $85 per square foot. To solicit bids to program YogaUOnline, I wrote a specifications document which kept the cost down.

Writing well is a huge boon for the entrepreneur. It provides a systematic way to structure thoughts and communicate with other people.

I have a friend, not much of a writer, who excels at spreadsheet modeling. He raises money for solar energy plants in Chile by creating sophisticated and detailed spreadsheets.

Once you master a skill, you know what professional-grade work looks like. You can recognize mastery in others, and business success depends on attracting other pros.

Grow the business organically

It's easy to get ahead of yourself, trying to develop a sophisticated website. We've been lucky that we've been able to take baby steps and let YogaUOnline grow organically, expanding the site with income from the business.

Organic growth lets me evolve the business based on market response and on my current skill level. There's an infinite amount of work that could be done at any one time. A large part of managing growth is managing your own energy, because it's easy to get burned out. By growing organically, you're not beholden to investors and specific financial goals, which gives you a whole other level of freedom.

It takes four legs and eight arms

Running a small business is a work in progress. You're never done. The marketplace changes; the customer base turns over; competitors come in; disruptive technology emerges.

That's just half of it. If you're successful, you must grow four legs and eight arms. There are so many things to be done, you cannot possibly do all of them. Further, many entrepreneurs get to the point where they don't have the skillset to do what needs to be done. Taking the business to the next level often requires different skills and a stronger team.

I interviewed meditating entrepreneur, Fred Gratzon, for my Ph.D. dissertation about Telegroup, his company that eventually went public. From the start, he knew that it would be big and that he couldn't do it himself.

Fred said, "I had the fire, and I looked for the guy with the firewood."

He found Cliff Reese. For years, they built a successful company. Then the marketplace changed, and they came up against their own limitations.

Entrepreneurs must know when they can deal with things themselves and when they have to find "the guy with the firewood." Finding partners has been a dream of mine.

In the past, I worked with someone who seemed perfect. The more I got involved, the more I realized we had different styles. I have learned that when hiring or partnering with people, it's a good idea to do a couple of projects together to see if the partnership is a good fit.

Entrepreneurs tend to be mavericks — self-starters and self-motivators. They like working for themselves and may not do well in a team context. Yet, growing a business requires maintainers and team builders.

Learn to Delegate

As we grow, I learn more about managing and delegation.

Early on in 2012, a friend in Philadelphia took on many production and customer service details for the business. She's independent, well-organized, and takes care of daily operations so I don't have to think about it.

I try to eliminate busywork and tasks that others can do. I chop activities into small pieces and use a Google spreadsheet to track assignments. A content editor and several freelance writers take responsibility for creating articles. We have several marketing coordinators and assistants handling various tasks.

Overall, I've found, it's better to fit the job to the person than the person to the job. Each person has unique skillsets and propensities; if you use those, rather than trying to fit them into a specific bucket, everyone ends up happier. We can do that, since we're still a startup business with greater flexibility of how things get done.

Certain tasks can be delegated only with skill and care. For example, creating a website is complicated and has been a constant learning process. You can't just hire a developer and walk away.

We've been through three iterations of YogaUOnline.com. I would give the programmer instructions, and he would hear something different. To not waste time and money, I learned to go slowly and catch problems right away.

Recently, I found a translator, a programmer who understands me and can communicate with the contracted programmer. Once the translator knows my wishes, I leave it in his hands.

Handling stress

I love what I do and can see working on YogaUOnline for the rest of my life. At the same time, I recognize my physical limitations. I can work up to 40 hours a week as long as I don't work at night. I must take time to have fun, or I get fried to a crisp.

Entrepreneurs learn the hard way the importance of stress management. I've been on adrenal burnout enough times to know that I don't win by overworking and must take time to recover.

TM keeps me sane. I couldn't do YogaUOnline without my daily practice.

SPIRIT: Focus, transcend, and you can do anything

Business is about addressing a constant continuum of problems, big and small.

The number one thing I learned from meditating and working for the TM organization is that anything is possible. Any problem can be solved.

Problems are not solved at the level of the problem. I go deep in meditation and tune into where the solution resides. Then, at work, I put all my attention on the challenge, allowing the pieces of the solution to come together.

My motto seems to be "Fools rush in where angels fear to tread." I consistently put myself in situations where afterward, I wonder, *What was I thinking? What was I thinking to take on a million-dollar construc-*

tion project at MUM without any building experience?

I have structured within myself a can-do attitude. I know if I sit down and focus, a solution will emerge. By moving ahead, things work out. Once I commit, it is as if my guardian angels hold their hands over me.

Eva Norlyk Smith's twelve tweets

1. An entrepreneur who gives her all attracts others who give their all. Master something, and you will be able to recognize mastery in others.

2. Becoming a pro takes time, hard work, practice, and in-depth learning. A professional sees the big picture while impeccably attending to the details.

3. Writing well, to systematically structure thoughts and communicate them to others, is a boon for the entrepreneur.

4. Do you enjoy it? Are you attracted to it? Does it bring you happiness? Would you do it even if you weren't paid? Trust your bliss. Stay in tune with it and gain the guidance needed to make your best possible contribution.

5. You don't win by working on overdrive. With adrenalin burnout, you will need time to recover. The TM practice helps keep you sane and able to do your work.

6. Organic growth lets you evolve the business based on market feedback and the development of your skills.

7. Business is a work in progress, a continuous solving of small and large problems. The marketplace changes; the customer base turns over; competitors come in; disruptive technology emerges.

8. If you're successful, you will need to grow four legs and eight arms to do the many things you need to be doing. Many entrepreneurs get to the point where they don't have the skill-set to take the company to the next level.

9. Anything is possible. Any problem can be solved but not at the level of the problem. If I sit down and focus, I know the answer will emerge. I put my attention on the challenge, tune into the solution in meditation, and allow the pieces to come together.

10. If you just put up something on a website, nothing happens. The greatest offer in the world isn't enough. You must give a prospect a reason to take action.

11. Create a free product line. Give away useful stuff. Once you establish credibility, you can charge for advanced services. The more expensive the product, the more time must be spent at the beginning building trust.

12. Creating a website is complicated and is a constant learning process. You can't just hire a developer. In order not to waste time and money with web development, go slowly and catch problems right away.

Ponder

1. Have you purchased online classes? If so, have they been worthwhile? If not, why not?

2. Eva says pros give their all and do their work to perfection. Is this too high a standard? Do you have a field in which you are a pro?

3. Have you followed your bliss or taken a more conventional path? Does following your bliss make practical sense?

4. Do you think there is a solution to every problem?

Eva Norlyk Smith uses Instagram infographic to promote YogaUonline

YogaUonline Marketing Skills course

Hal Goldstein
MAGAZINES ABOUT LAPTOPS, PALMTOPS AND THE IPHONE

In 1970, after graduating from the University of Wisconsin, Hal hitchhiked through Europe and North Africa for almost a year. He spent the next 14 years earning three master's degrees and applying them as a social worker, a teacher of the Transcendental Meditation technique, and a Hewlett-Packard software engineer.

Hal married Rita Schwall in 1984, and they honeymooned by driving from Palo Alto, California to Fairfield, Iowa to participate in Maharishi Mahesh Yogi's World Peace Project. The following year, Rita and Hal founded Thaddeus Computing, publisher of magazines about mobile computers and reseller of used mobile equipment.

In 2011, Hal semi-retired. He remains a minority partner after selling *iPhone Life* magazine to former employees. He continues to consult and write for the magazine, as well as run a part-time business that resells legacy mobile equipment.

Hal's latest venture is this book and website, which are based on a class on entrepreneurship he teaches at Maharishi University of Management. In class, Fairfield entrepreneurs speak to students about what they learned on their journey.

JOURNEY: Dancing with Hewlett Packard, Microsoft, and Apple

THE FIRST 37 YEARS

I grew up in a comfortable, supportive middle-class family that valued education. Two recurring childhood thoughts set the direction of my life. First, I believed that I was incomplete inside, and that growing up meant I would learn to be whole. Second, in the 1950s we were taught to hate and fear Russians and communism. I reasoned that if I had grown up in Russia, I would have hated and feared America and capitalism. I never understood why no one discussed this obvious paradox.

Those thoughts formed the basis of a lifelong quest for inner and outer peace that opened me up to meditation and moving to Fairfield.

In the late 60s at the University of Wisconsin, Madison, I loved the Beatles and Dylan, experimented with drugs, and non-violently protested the Vietnam war. Upon graduating — confused, disillusioned, and trying to find my way — I hitchhiked for nine months through Europe and North Africa, hearing about the Transcendental Meditation program in my travels. My adventure ended when my father died and I returned home.

A few months later, I learned the TM technique and decided to move forward with my life.

In the 70s, I received master's degrees in mind, heart, and spirit — Computer Science and Social Work at the Universities of Illinois and Wisconsin, and Interdisciplinary Studies at Maharishi International University.

Subsequently, I counseled, taught TM, and programmed computers.

In 1975, in Columbus, Ohio, I instructed over 200 people in Maharishi's Transcendental Meditation program. Teaching the TM program was sublime and rewarding. In the process, I became comfortable speaking in public and running the *TM* Center as a business.

Two years later, having just come off the advanced TM-Sidhi six-month course in Switzerland, I stayed at my mother's house near Chicago. Broke, I looked for work.

I applied to be the Assistant Professor of Social Work at New Mexico State University, Las Cruces. The position, funded by a last-minute grant, involved teaching and work-study supervision. In August, the Social Work department flew me down for an interview, which went well.

During the interview, I hit it off with the two faculty with whom I would be working. Two weeks later, I called one of my new friends. She told me that the university search committee liked me but probably wouldn't offer me the job. I was under-qualified, having only one year of social work counseling experience.

My cousin happened to be driving to college in Arizona. I asked her to drop me off at the university in Las Cruces where I had interviewed. I walked into the hiring professor's office. He was taken aback. "There must be some misunderstanding. I didn't offer you the job."

I replied, "If you hire me, I'll do a great job for you. School starts in a week, and I know you don't have anyone. I'll be at the nearby motel if you decide to call."

The next day, I got the job.

That experience taught me that with a clear intention and unshakable commitment I could manifest what I set my mind on.

I returned to school in 1981 and graduated from the University of Illinois in Computer Science. I interviewed with many companies, including Hewlett Packard (HP), the premier Silicon Valley tech company.

For three years I worked as an HP software engineer. The challenging but invaluable experience confirmed again that I could do what I set my mind to.

Maharishi continued to ask practitioners of the advanced TM-Sidhi technique to move to Fairfield and meditate together and create an influence of peace in the world. My fellow engineers thought I was nuts when they heard about my intention to leave prestigious HP for a meditation project in the middle of nowhere.

During my HP tenure, I had started dating my future wife, Rita

Schwall, who had an excellent position in health care. In Autumn 1984, we married and quit our secure jobs. We honeymooned with a leisurely drive from Palo Alto, California to Fairfield, Iowa.

There, Rita and I bought a small two-bedroom home for about 20% of what we would have paid in California. It turned out, funnily enough, that Fairfield property owners rejoiced as the crazy "Ru's" (short for "gurus") swooped in from the two coasts to pay inflated property prices.

Setting up shop

Before leaving HP I bought, at heavily discounted employee prices, the first LaserJet printer (70 pounds) and the first PC-compatible laptop, The HP110 Portable (9 pounds). Few individuals had such computing power. With the LaserJet I could create professional looking documents without an outside service. With the laptop I could write, create spreadsheets, and play games anywhere. At the airport, years before ubiquitous mobile computing, other passengers would stare when I pulled out my laptop.

To my surprise, from The Portable I could not print bold, change fonts, or produce graphics on the LaserJet. I reasoned that maybe I could earn income by writing software that allowed the laptop to take full advantage of the LaserJet. Unfortunately, few people owned such an odd combination of equipment which together retailed for $7,000 in 1985 dollars. I had no way to reach potential customers. Even so, I programmed "PrinterTalk" for my own use.

I had been in Fairfield six months, writing PrinterTalk and selling personal computers for ComputerLand of neighboring Ottumwa, which I didn't enjoy. Rita spent a lot of quiet time visualizing a solution.

One day, I burst out of my office. Excitedly I told Rita that I would create a newsletter for HP laptop owners who didn't have the time to figure out The Portable's many possible uses.

I knew nothing about running a business or publishing. I just felt strongly that ardent HP customers would appreciate a newsletter. From the newsletter, I could sell PrinterTalk. Just as I followed my intuition and moved to Fairfield when it did not make sense, I went forward with the project. Still thinking of myself as a programmer rather than a publisher, I named the company "Personalized Software."

HP understood the value of a newsletter devoted to their laptop. With a tradition of supporting former employees in startup ventures, a tradition that helped build Silicon Valley, HP agreed to send me addresses of the 2,000 HP Portable warranty registrants.

In the mid-1980s, mail order solicitations filled mailboxes of typical middle-class families. I studied every piece I could get my hands on, noticing what made me want to buy things. As an enthusiastic, professional, geeky HP Portable owner, I fit the demographic and psychographic of my audience. Effective wording that moved me would probably work on my potential customer.

With my laptop, LaserJet, PrinterTalk, and some editing help, I created a mailer. In it I asked people to subscribe to a not-yet-existent newsletter about their HP Portable. I included a two-sided page jammed with tips and tricks.

Without knowing anything about writing, designing, printing, or mailing a newsletter, I decided that we would be able to produce six issues a year. My intuitive wife, Rita, suggested a $55 subscription price. That number seemed as good as any. These avid HP fans spent over $4,000 on the HP laptop and necessary accessories. I reasoned that many would be willing to subscribe for $55 to learn how to use their equipment more effectively.

In the summer of 1985, Rita and I sent out the mailing and left for a TM course in Washington, DC. We came back and found a post office box full of checks for $55.

We hadn't realized that a 1% response would have been good and a 2% percent response tremendous. In two mailings, 20% of the HP laptop registrants sent $55 to an unknown company in rural Iowa for a newsletter that existed only in my head.

With the money, we had enough to start the company, so we cashed the checks.

After sending the initial mailing, I received four dense pages of HP Portable tips and tricks from Ed Keefe of Ankeny, Iowa. Ed wrote that it pleased him that a fellow Iowan was creating such a publication, but he didn't think he needed to subscribe.

I immediately called Ed, a computer science instructor at a community college. I said, "How would you like to share your knowledge with others by writing for our magazine? Oh, and I can't pay you."

Ed said, "Sure."

I now had another writer.

At the same time, I had been talking on the phone with other knowledgeable enthusiasts who were calling to subscribe. The light bulb went off. My customers would be my editorial staff.

Doctors, engineers, lawyers, managers, teachers, and CEOs called and told me how they used their HP Portable professionally and personally. During the call, I asked if they would write up their findings for other users, and I started using their editorials in issue one.

Working with a volunteer staff had its downsides. We did a lot of editing. Also, we had to cajole writers to meet deadlines. Despite the drawbacks, their contributions expanded the breadth and depth of our magazine at minimal expense.

The Portable Paper, 1985-1990

We cashed the first subscription checks in July 1985. By October, customers were calling, asking when they would receive their newsletter. I had lined up a local printer and written most of the articles but still had a lot to do before publication.

One foggy Fairfield morning, a small truck plowed into the driver's side of our car as Rita and I crossed an intersection. Rita sustained broken ribs and collar bone. Knocked unconscious, I escaped with a headache.

Besides maintaining the house, Rita also helped me with the business. Attending to Rita as she recovered from the accident and producing our first issue would have been impossible, so my mother flew in to take care of Rita and the house. She also helped in the office.

In late October, I asked my artist friend, George Foster, if he could lay out our newsletter. George said yes, although I found out later he had never done anything like it before. I gave George a printout with the articles. A decade before reliable desktop publishing, George specified the fonts, spacing, and graphic placement for a fellow meditating entrepreneur, Ron Flora. Ron retyped the text into his gigantic typesetting machines.

Together, George, Ron, and I edited, produced, cut out, pasted, and re-edited "type" on glossy white boards that we would give to the printer. The three of us produced the first 28-page issue by staying up three days and nights, sleeping only during TM time in the meditation dome. Without the heroic efforts of George, Ron, and Ron's wife, Susan, I would not have had a business. We mailed our first issue right after Thanksgiving, 1985.

I had chosen a creme colored paper to help create a warm connection with the reader. In that first issue, I promised that together, in the pages of the newsletter, the reader and I would embark on an exciting, pioneering technological adventure.

As it turned out, PrinterTalk could take the files from The Portable's limited built-in word processor and make use of the font and graphic capabilities of the new portable HP ThinkJet. I advertised PrinterTalk and a maze-type game, TigerFox, written by one of the engineer architects of the HP110 Portable. I worked out an arrangement where we published TigerFox and paid him a royalty.

Our customers and Hewlett-Packard liked the first issue a lot. However, even given our incredible 20% direct mail response, not enough new owners sent in warranty cards for our business to be sustainable. Somehow, in the pre-internet, pre-social media 1980s, we had to reach more HP Portable users.

Before leaving HP, I had worked with the customer support team. I thought, *Why not offer a free issue to the many HP Portable users who call HP for help?*

The General Manager of the support division loved the magazine, liked me, and understood the benefit of the newsletter to callers. However, because of strict company policy he was unable to provide me with customers' contact information. I mentioned the dilemma to a former colleague who worked on the phone in HP support. A week later, a large unmarked envelope arrived containing a printout of names and addresses of over 9,000 HP Portable users.

We were buzzed! Not only would we benefit, but HP and HP customers would be better off with a wide distribution of *The Portable Paper*. Sending the mailing would mean prosperity for the business and the ability to support ourselves and others in Fairfield.

Yet, Rita and I hesitated.

We were reminded of Maharishi's advice: "Always do what you know to be right." We wanted to feel good about the company we had just begun. We didn't want the business to be founded on a lack of integrity. My friend at HP had gone against company policy to help us.

After considerable soul-searching, we devised a ceremony. We built a small fire in a burn barrel in the backyard of our modest two-bedroom home. Then, page by page, taking turns, Rita and I threw the 9,000 names in the fire.

In my 27 years running the company, "the burning" was the most important thing we did. Ignoring common sense, Rita and I felt that destroying those ill-gotten leads was the right thing to do. That integrity served as the foundation for our business, still successful nearly 35 years later.

After the burning, we felt both relief and concern. Had our idealism taken the business from us? How would we survive with well under 1,000 subscribers?

Using the newsletter to sell products

When Portable users called our office to subscribe, they would tell me about the non-HP apps and accessories that they made work with their HP laptop. In the newsletter, we would review those products and publish how-to instructions.

Installing those apps and accessories often required patience and technical knowledge. Many readers didn't want to spend the time to figure all that out. These readers trusted us and were not particularly price sensitive. With the success of PrinterTalk and TigerFox, we began selling software and accessories at premium prices. We included simple instructions and often supplemental software.

Within a year, we were making more income from selling products than from newsletter subscriptions. In a few years, we were publishing separate catalogs to supplement the dense price list included in each issue of *The Portable Paper*.

Shortly before publishing our first issue, HP replaced The HP110 Portable with the superior HP Portable Plus. It came with a larger screen, more expansion options, and greater compatibility with the IBM PC standard.

That meant that our readers, visionaries who just spent $3,000 on their Portable, would have to pay another $3,500 to $4,000 for the new HP Portable Plus. These people, more than anyone, understood the advantages of the new Portable Plus. Yet, how could they justify the price, and what would they do with their $3,000 HP110?

The thought came: *Buy the HP110 from our readers for $1,000.* Then we could sell it to our readers' colleagues, friends, and family for $2,000, bundling a subscription and other extras from our product line.

Before eBay and Amazon, we became the HP Portable Equipment Exchange. We advertised the Exchange to our core newsletter audience. Soon, we were staffing a second business that bought, tested, refurbished, sold, and supported used HP Portables. There were times in the coming years that the profits from this auxiliary used device business kept our magazine afloat.

One of my strengths is persistence, refusing to accept "no."

We wanted HP to include our free issue offer in the HP Portable Plus packaging. Unfortunately, HP had a policy of keeping extraneous material to a minimum in the packaging of its products. I sent *The Portable Paper* subscriptions to engineers, marketers, and managers in the HP Portable Plus division. I followed up weekly, reminding HP that knowledgeable and enthusiastic customers translate into more sales.

After about a year, I finally got a "yes."

Starting in 1986, when someone opened the packaging of their newly purchased HP Portable, HP Palmtop, HP Handheld, or HP Pocket PC, they found an invitation to receive a free issue of our publication. Having no other cost-effective way to reach our targeted audience, that free issue brochure sustained the magazine business until 2002.

Since 2002, with no brochure, we have had the ongoing challenge of depending on the internet and newsstand sales for new customer acquisition.

Rita saves the business and our marriage

Starting a business is all-consuming. Like caring for a helpless, totally dependent infant, it requires love, nurturing, and patience at all hours.

In the first year of the business, I worked non-stop writing the news-letter, marketing it, making sure it got to customers, creating Portable products, managing the fast-growing Portable Equipment Exchange, training new employees, and tracking the money. Rita helped during emergencies.

After that intense year, Rita and I made two decisions that saved both the business and our marriage. First, we realized that both of us liked to be in charge; neither liked being subservient. We agreed that Rita would take care of the house and the rental properties, and I would run the business. Second, after watching me work from early morning to night seven days a week for about a year, Rita stood firm. Unless I took one full day a week completely off and away from the business, she would leave me. Ceding to her demand was the smartest thing I did for the business, my sanity, and our marriage.

We relaunch the business with a new vision

Off the record, in 1989 several contacts at HP warned me that HP was going to stop building The Portable Plus. Instead, the same HP Corvallis, Oregon division that invented the calculator and The Portable Plus would begin manufacturing a handheld-sized, fully-functional, MS-DOS computer with lots of great software built-in.

Instead of being devastated, since our business completely depended on The HP Portable, I saw opportunity. Instead of selling the $3,500 Portable Plus, HP would be marketing pocketable devices for $700. By leveraging our relationship with HP, we could start a new publication and end up with far more customers.

HP agreed to offer a free issue of our as yet non-existent HP Palmtop newsletter in the HP Palmtop packaging. Their only request was that we include "HP" in the title and add a tag line. The publication became *The HP Palmtop Paper — An Independent Publication for Users of HP Palmtop Computers.*

On April 29, 1991, at 1:30 PM, we relaunched the company with a new HP Palmtop focus. We changed our company name from the PrinterTalk-inspired "Personalized Software" to "Thaddeus Computing" to honor my wife's devotion to St. Jude Thaddeus (the saint of impossible cases and St. Jude hospitals).

Inspired from deep within, I unveiled the Thaddeus Computing vision:

"Curving back on ourselves again and again, together we create a model Fairfield Heaven-on-Earth business.

Bliss (Enjoy)

Knowledge (Learn)

Right Action (Do Right)"

I posted signs of the Thaddeus Computing vision in my office and our meeting area.

"Curving back on ourselves again and again, together we create a model Fairfield, Heaven-on-Earth business" refers to a passage from the Bhagavad Gita. Our success would come from the team repeatedly going within through regular TM practice and then together building a great company that other businesses would emulate.

I used "Bliss (Enjoy)," "Knowledge (Learn)," and "Right Action (Do Right)" as the daily standard for us to assess how well the company was doing.

- Enjoy: Is Thaddeus Computing a fun place to work? Do customers like dealing with us?

- Learn: Are employees continually upgrading their knowledge and skills? Are customers more adept at using their mobile devices?

- Do Right: Does our behavior reflect the highest standards as we interact with each other, our customers, and our suppliers?

In the midst of daily business challenges, the Thaddeus Computing vision reminded me of the decision to move to Fairfield for peace on the inside and the outside, and that I wanted to create a special place to work. I used the statement as a standard, a practical guide for making difficult business decisions and for hiring like-minded people. At the same time, the displayed sign could embarrass me when I perceived the business or myself falling short of the vision's ideals.

The vision kept me on course during our many business highs and lows. Turning my business over to employees in 2011, I am most proud that these values continue to be part of the company DNA.

The HP Palmtop Paper, 1991-1999 (the golden years)

I consider the 1990s and *The HP Palmtop Paper* our company's golden years. It was a time of profitability, prestige, and product innovation. We were close to our customers and close to HP. We applied what we learned in the 1980s with 2,000 HP Portable customers to 20,000 HP Palmtop customers, and we continued using the contributions of our readers for editorial. Throughout my years publishing, non-paid guest professionals wrote most of the content for our magazines and website.

The HP Palmtop Paper became more like a magazine. We used glossy cover stock, printed in two colors, hired ad salespeople, lowered subscriptions to $35, and increased the page count. We expected a good response with the free issue card inside HP palmtop packaging but were soon overwhelmed with up to 1,000 phone and mail sub-scriptions a week.

We weren't prepared for fast growth. We didn't have the expertise, the procedures, the software, the training, or the personnel to process orders and fulfill them promptly. Piles of orders would appear in the baskets of our growing number of data entry employees. A call from an unhappy subscriber wondering about an order could grind the entire operation to a halt. At one point, we were over a month behind processing new orders.

Fast growth was a blessing but caused an incredible amount of stress. The "Bliss" from our vision statement was not experienced by our staff or our customers. It took almost two years to get a robust system in place to process orders, send free sample issues, and mail proper subscription and renewal sequences.

In February 1993, we received a pleasant surprise, a letter from Richard Hackborn, Executive VP and Board Member, Hewlett Packard:

> "The HP Palmtop Paper is one of the very best written
> and organized user publications that I have ever seen in
> my 25 years in the computer business. Every issue is full
> of useful articles, and even the advertising is interesting.
> Each time I receive a new issue, I am compelled to read
> it from cover to cover within a few days."

We used the letter for years on all our subscription advertising. After the letter, any resistance by HP personnel to working with our small company faded.

With the 1993 introduction of the HP200LX Palmtop PC, we received another surprise. *The HP Palmtop Paper* name and our phone number were built into the HP200LX contacts app, a number that still works 25 years later!

History repeated itself. Shortly after its introduction, HP replaced the initial HP95LX Palmtop with the more powerful, larger-screened, PC-compatible HP100LX, which soon became the HP200LX. We began buying, refurbishing, repairing, and selling used palmtops.

In 1993, I gave several employees The Portable Plus-based Portable Equipment Exchange business in exchange for royalty payments so I could focus exclusively on the HP Palmtop market.

A reader and engineer from Alabama, Mack Baggette, developed the hardware, software, and procedure to upgrade the speed and the internal storage of the HP200LX. He trained our staff to do the 20-minute upgrade and sold us parts and software. Soon, we began advertising Palmtop upgrades in the magazine.

Also, once again, our readers informed us about commercial and privately developed software that worked well on the HP Palmtop. It did not take us long to produce catalogs chock full of used Palmtop options, apps, accessories, and upgrades. With the birth of the World Wide Web, we created www.palmtoppaper.com — still operational today — with a shopping cart.

To help expand our audience, my first contributor and longtime columnist Ed Keefe agreed to edit a book, *PC in your Pocket — Best of The HP Palmtop Paper.* We self-published the book before self-publishing was popular.

Then, in 1993, a big change came. The HP division responsible for the famed HP Calculator, Portable Plus, and Palmtop moved from Corvallis, Oregon to Singapore, near its Malaysian manufacturing operation. The move meant establishing a new set of relationships with HP Singapore employees. Rita's and my regular journeys to Corvallis became treks to the other side of the world.

Despite the Palmtop's popularity among a core audience, HP continued to be disappointed with overall HP Palmtop sales. In 1997, HP Singapore announced that they would join forces with Microsoft. HP and other major manufacturers would produce handheld devices running a new, Microsoft Windows-like mobile operating system, a formula that had been incredibly successful with desktop Windows. HP reasoned that, given its two decades of experience with Palmtops and calculators, it would become a dominant player in a huge new market.

Microsoft and *Pocket PC* magazine, 1998-2008

I became friendly with the HP Singapore division manager, Khaw

Keng Joo. He encouraged me to start a generic magazine about handheld devices. He promised to include our free issue offer in the new HP handheld packaging, even though the magazine would cover all the Microsoft-based handhelds from different manufacturers, and he introduced me to key Microsoft management.

In 1997, HP announced its HP 300 Handheld PC using Microsoft Windows CE. Except for the introductions, we didn't know anyone at Microsoft and had little understanding of its culture. After 14 years, it would prove difficult to wean ourselves from HP.

We reasoned that our premium pricing newsletter model would no longer work. Since handhelds were becoming mainstream, the publication also had to be mainstream. That meant becoming a full-color, glossy paper, ad-based magazine with broad newsstand distribution, reduced subscription pricing, and a professional website.

Surprisingly, after the 1997 Handheld PC introduction, Microsoft wouldn't talk to us. They ignored my many, many attempts to establish contact and create a relationship. We were producing an expensive, glossy publication supporting the mobile Windows platform, a platform that had been panned by the press and was not selling well. From Microsoft, we wanted content to share with our common customers, help with circulation, and a financial partnership for co-marketing projects.

Early in 1999, out of total frustration and uninvited, I flew to Redmond, calling, emailing, and faxing Microsoft contacts of my arrival. Showing up had worked to get the teaching position in Las Cruces. Maybe it would work again. But, Microsoft refused to see me. If it weren't for our strong Palmtop aftermarket business, we wouldn't have survived.

In Spring of 2000, out of the blue I got a phone call from Microsoft. Would I like to meet with their team to discuss their plans for a new class of devices to run on their mobile operating system?

I flew to Redmond and signed a non-disclosure agreement. This time, a gracious product manager took me through Microsoft's Pocket PC specification and strategy. The Pocket PC looked like the popular, keyboardless Palm but had extra features and expandability.

The manager wondered if I had an interest in changing the name of our magazine from *Handheld PC* Magazine to *Pocket PC*. Microsoft was not going to trademark "Pocket PC." They wanted "Pocket PC" to replace "Palm" in the popular lexicon to generically refer to handheld devices. Our magazine would be part of their strategy. Microsoft wanted to see wide distribution of our magazine, especially in places like airports and trade shows where industry leaders traveled.

From 2000 until 2006, Microsoft proved an excellent partner. They helped us with end-user stories and bought thousands of issues for industry trade show giveaways. Microsoft contributed a significant portion of the $200,000 that airport newsstands require before they will place a new magazine on their shelves. A magazine normally remains on airport newsstands without additional fees as long as it sells. Until recently, *iPhone Life*, the current incarnation of our publication, had a strong airport presence.

Our tradition of using volunteers continued both in print and online. We had around 20 regular magazine contributors and bloggers plus guest articles from Microsoft, webmasters, software developers, and accessory manufacturers.

During rapid technological change and Microsoft's ongoing repositioning, we kept changing our name. In 1997, we launched *Handheld PC Magazine* about devices using the Windows CE mobile operating system. In 2000, we were Windows Powered *Pocket PC* magazine. By 2005, we became Windows Mobile *Smartphone & Pocket PC* magazine. Our website followed by switching domain names from HPCmag.com to PocketPCmag.com, and then to Smartphonemag.com.

We applied *The HP Palmtop Paper* philosophy to become a hub for all things Pocket PC. As the hub, we saw growing the Pocket PC platform as our mission. We did so by supporting its various stakeholders including end-users, Microsoft, hardware manufacturers, app developers, gear manufacturers, websites, and even magazine competitors.

This strategy allowed potential internet rivals to view us as friendly. We had web pages devoted to the best Pocket PC websites and invited webmasters to promote their site by submitting articles to *Pocket PC* magazine.

We opened our website for developers to describe their Pocket PC software and gear, whether or not the vendor advertised.

Consequently, PocketPCmag.com received many links back. We often bested Microsoft's PocketPC.com as number one on a Google "pocket pc" search. I even made friends with the publishers of our closest rivals, *Handheld Computing* and *Pen Magazine*. The communication helped us avoid our ad sales staffs trashing each other, and when their magazines folded, allowed us to acquire their mailing lists.

As the Pocket PC platform became popular, apps appeared, which at that time sold for between $20 and $70. With review sites and centralized app stores in their infancy, consumers had no good way to evaluate these expensive purchases.

We already had the PocketPCmag.com Encyclopedia of Software and Accessories database. The natural next step was an evaluation system.

In 2001, I came up with a plan for the "Best Software Awards," in which much of the Pocket PC ecosystem participated. A *Pocket PC* magazine editor and I nominated products from our online database. We used its groupings to create voting categories. Then I reached out to Pocket PC webmasters and other experts to vote for best mapping software, best chess games, best calculators — 48 categories in all.

The awards soon took on a life of their own with plenty of headaches for us. Vendors would lobby us and then complain if they didn't do well. Judges would tell us the many things we did wrong. Customers who didn't like the winning product would grumble. As we added more products, the process became more complicated. Each year, I would vow not to do it again, By the eighth year, out of a database of over 4,000 products, we had 83 experts judging 936 apps in 194 Pocket PC, Smartphone, and Developer categories. We programmed a web interface for the team of volunteer, impartial, expert judges to communicate and vote.

The awards process demonstrated the power of collaboration on the internet with so many volunteering their time. It also solidified our role as a hub for all things Pocket PC.

After several years of doing our Pocket PC software awards, we created a $300 app package that contained virtually all of the over several hundred finalists and winners, at a time when mobile apps cost between $20 and $70. We obtained copies of the top software by trading a year's worth of advertising for the app unlock codes. Both the developer and our company benefited by exchanging software and ad space that cost neither of us anything to deliver.

After the initial setup costs of CDs and a web interface for customers, the revenue from the package was almost pure profit. Each year we offered a new package which attracted repeat customers.

In 2008, we got double-whammied. First, the economy tanked. Second, despite the HP and Microsoft headstart of two decades, Apple's iPhone quickly dominated the smartphone market.

Within a period of four months, cash flow from *Smartphone & Pocket PC* subscriptions, advertisements, and newsstand sales all but stopped. Our UsedHandhelds business did well but was not strong enough to keep us going.

After over 20 years of being responsible for employee payroll and customer product, I was exhausted and wanted out. But I don't like losing. From a team of 15, I paired down to a staff of five, and we were still in trouble. Only a stroke of good fortune kept us solvent.

Back in 2001, our UsedHandhelds buyer and I had gambled and made an expensive purchase of HP Handheld computers when we couldn't keep up with demand. As soon as they were delivered, the market became flooded with the devices. Over 1,000 handhelds languished in our basement.

In 2008, at a time when we were most desperate, we received a call from a broker. It seemed a client needed a chip found only in the handhelds in our basement. The customer, who had unsuccessfully tried to have the chip manufactured, was willing to pay us $70 each. We only had to take the device apart and ship the motherboard.

With that $70,000, I could have shut down the business, paid my print bill, and not owed anyone anything. But I wasn't yet ready to let go.

iPhone Life, 2008

Richard Hall, my *Smartphone & Pocket PC* editor, had been with me for 20 years starting with *The Portable Paper*. Marge Enright, customer service rep, had been with me for 13 years. She was so warm and engaging, customers used to call customer service just to talk.

I told both Marge and Rich that there was no cash coming in from *Smartphone & Pocket PC*, and I was ready to shut down. I did have an idea, but it would mean they would have to go on unemployment insurance and work for free. If things by chance worked out, there would be a bonus.

Starting in 2007, we put an iPhone on the *Smartphone & Pocket PC* magazine cover every couple of issues. Each time, newsstand sales jumped.

In July 2008, we sent the final issue of *Smartphone & Pocket PC* to the printer. To keep the business going, we planned to produce another issue but make it exclusively about the iPhone. We already had a subscription base and wide newsstand distribution. We would keep the same bar codes, and it would become *Smartphone Magazine's iPhone Life*. We wouldn't miss a beat except that it would be published quarterly instead of bi-monthly. *Smartphone & Pocket PC* subscribers could request a refund.

Richard agreed to start working on the issue, even though none of us knew anything about the iPhone. Marge, who had never sold anything, agreed to be our ad sales rep. Both worked as volunteers, trusting I would make it right if we were successful.

Once again, with Apple we hooked our wagon to a huge, daunting, successful company about which we knew little. As with Microsoft, I tried making contact with Apple and was ignored.

We soon learned that Apple prides itself in self-sufficiency and does not partner with other companies unless absolutely necessary. We reached out to websites supporting Apple products. Most companies in the Apple ecosystem modeled Apple. They valued their independence and did not want to partner. I no longer had the internal drive to make the effort, week after week, month after month to penetrate Apple and its ecosystem as I had done with HP and Microsoft.

We were selling about 20% of the copies of *Smartphone & Pocket PC* magazine that we sent to the newsstands. We sold 42% of the first newsstand issue of *iPhone Life*.

Only 15% of our subscribers requested refunds, and we had a normal renewal rate. In 2009 and 2010, with a small staff publishing just four issues per year, we were quite profitable. With few employees, no iPhone products to sell, and no Pocket PC Awards, my workload relaxed.

Given the fast pace of iPhone adoption, I decided to go all in. I wanted to sell the business and have a substantial retirement income.

Deciding to go back to a six-issue-per-year schedule, we hired more editorial, marketing, and ad sales people, some quite experienced and expensive. Based on potential, I also hired several exceptionally talented, recent graduates of Maharishi University of Management.

Then, in early 2011, we had unexpected competition on the newsstand from oversized overseas publications, slower than expected advertiser adoption to six issues a year, and delays in newsstand payment. Our income could not keep up with our higher payroll, the print bill, and new marketing projects.

I knew I could weather the storm but was out of energy. I didn't want to lay people off, restructure, and start over again. Besides, I didn't like the isolation and lack of communication among those in the Apple iPhone ecosystem. I no longer enjoyed my work.

Rita and I had accumulated enough savings to live comfortably. Yet, my identity was tied to the business. I wanted to finish on top.

I turned to friend and serial entrepreneur, Steven Winn, also featured in this book, for some coaching. When I was willing to completely let the business go, an incredible transformation took place.

Retirement: 20-Somethings take over

In spring 2011, I was prepared to shut the business down even though it had assets of value. I brought in David Averbach, Raphael Burnes, and Alex Cequea, my three talented, 20-something employees.

I shocked them with plans to close the business, asking if they could do something with the website. Given Raph's web expertise, they said, "sure." Then, we started looking at the money we were getting from digital subscriptions. I said, "With Alex as the editor and without the expense of print, maybe you can make it work."

David, a business major, loved spreadsheets and started playing with the numbers. He eventually looked at printing costs. With reduced staff and David, Raph, and Alex initially working for little, they could soon make the business profitable again.

We decided to move ahead. The three of them took over with David as the CEO. We planned to divide ownership and income into fourths. I would have no day-to-day responsibilities but be available for advice. I would loan the company the money necessary to operate until it could stand on its own.

The four of us spent several days discussing the terms of the agreement; it was the most remarkable negotiation in which I have participated. We all genuinely wanted the arrangement to work for each of us. Each side made concessions without prompting from the other.

I knew a top meditating lawyer in town, an expert in mergers and acquisitions, who was a friend of David's family. The four of us, clear about the agreement, decided to use this one attorney. The lawyer wanted none of it. He felt we should have separate representation. We finally prevailed, and he did his best to represent each of our interests.

I credit an innate goodness in each of us, and lack of fear or greed, for allowing us to form the agreement so easily. Our mutual trust, appreciation, and respect have only deepened through the years, even through challenging times.

I soon realized that my retirement was a much bigger deal for me than for anyone else. The world didn't stop. My partners had their hands full. A few readers of my farewell column sent kind notes. Even my biggest fans got over it quickly and moved on.

Within a short time, the business was profitable, and in 18 months my partners paid their loan back.

While I didn't initially receive money from the sale of the business, I received a legacy, something of great personal meaning. Jobs stayed in Fairfield for the next generation. The way my partners run the company perpetuates the Thaddeus Computing mission of creating a model business characterized by bliss, knowledge, and right action. As an equity partner, a financial windfall remains possible.

David and Raph, along with Noah Siemsen and Donna Cleveland, who together replaced Alex, have done an extraordinary job assembling a dedicated, talented, harmonious team. They run a tighter, more disciplined, and better-managed business than I did. They have moved the company forward in the declining magazine industry which has experienced a double-digit decrease in newsstand sales each year since 2008. While continuing to publish the print magazine, my partners transformed the business. The website, online subscriptions, and ad sales form the new digital-based profit-center for the business. iPhone-Life.com has over three million unique visitors each month.

Today, I still own the UsedHandhelds portion of the business which operates with a part-time staff and little input from me. Given exponential advances in technology, it is remarkable that as of 2019, we still have a profitable business supporting HP Palmtop users. We also sell Pocket PCs and other older devices on eBay, Amazon, and UsedHandhelds.com.

David Seagull, who worked for me on three different occasions, had another idea to leverage the reputation and expertise of Thaddeus Computing. David identified a customer, a consortium of small Verizon stores, for a digital magazine about Android phones. The plan was for the stores to give the magazine to their smartphone customers. David and I were 50-50 partners, although David did most of the work. We had one very profitable year before the client backed off.

In 2011, the Fairfield Entrepreneur's Association named me Entrepreneur of the Year, mostly for modeling a business transition that kept jobs in Fairfield.

In Spring 2012, I began teaching "The Successful Entrepreneur" to Maharishi University of Management undergrads, in which I invite local Fairfield entrepreneurs to tell their stories. This book and future volumes are based on the transcripts from their talks.

WISDOM: Keep your word

INTEGRITY MAKES BUSINESS WORK

Integrity — always putting core values first — makes business effective, meaningful, and life-supporting. From integrity comes trust, the glue of business. Trust allows for the frictionless flow of business activity. Without trust, a business falls apart.

In my case, our employees were confident they would be compensated. Our customers believed they would receive a useful magazine every two months. Our printer knew we would pay for 120,000 copies. Our banker had confidence that we would pay off building mortgages and our short-term loans.

I always wanted my customer, employee, lender, partner, or supplier to get more out of a transaction than I. If I screwed up, I'd admit my mistake and make good.

Keeping one's word builds trust. I practiced making only those promises that I knew I would fulfill. Building my keeping-my-word muscle increased my self-confidence, power, and trustworthiness. After a while, I knew that anything I committed to would come to be.

I evaluated my employees on how well they kept their promises. Those employees who followed through or warned me of delays 100% of the time were godsends. If employees kept commitments only 70% or even 95% of the time, I worried and had to track their promises.

Running a business means making decisions all day long. In the heat of daily business activity it is easy to cut corners to save time or money. Yet, I found that sooner or later there were consequences for ignoring my inner compass. As Maharishi once said, "The laws of nature cannot be deceived." We made right action a company standard, and I told our staff to tell me if they saw me doing something they didn't think was right.

I practiced following my inner conscience with customers, employees, partners, lenders, and suppliers. Not only did that translate to better sleep, I believe an air of integrity surrounded our business. In over 30 years, we have never been involved in a lawsuit. Honesty and a generous spirit have served our business well.

Create a wow product. Know the customer. Connect the two.

When someone asks my advice about their business idea, I question them about the product, the customer, and the link between the two.

First, is the product or service a "Wow?" Will people buy it rather than spend their money elsewhere? In the case of the *The Portable Paper*, each page communicated the knowledge and enthusiasm of HP Portable users worldwide.

Second, who are the customers, and why do they buy? Our HP Portable user customers were educated, geeky, ahead-of-the-curve professionals with a thirst for knowledge about their laptop.

Third, can customers be reached in a cost-effective way? The connection between product and customer is the magic, the spark that makes a business work. We used HP registration cards, in-box free issue offers and, later, the internet and newsstands to reach our potential magazine customers. Then we used our magazine to sell apps, gear, and used devices.

A business has a life of its own

A business reflects the collective consciousness of its owners, employees, customers, investors, suppliers, and community. Often, I would walk into our office, witness its vibrancy, and be in awe. Even though I created and nurtured the business in its infancy, it expressed its own character, survival mechanism, and penchant to find purpose.

To understand the culture, strengths, and weaknesses of an entrepreneurial business, look to the values and personality of its founder and CEO. Our business culture mirrored my personal qualities, which included tolerance, loyalty, inclusiveness, focus, calculated risk-taking, looking for the next new thing, messiness, and a desire to please. I was (and am) a learner, teacher, creator, under-valuer of details, generous, idealistic, practical, and bottom-line oriented.

I was happiest brainstorming a new initiative with our team and then working on the project. Yet, as CEO, much of my time was taken up with problems. Problems inevitably involved cash, people, or rapid growth.

It was difficult to maintain equilibrium when we were short on cash. Fear and concern for survival would take over, even if I could see that the cash flow issue was temporary. Truly lean times meant worrying about salaries, cutbacks, and layoffs.

In over 27 years, I employed several hundred people and faced many challenges. A difficult personnel situation could distract me for months. Employees had problems with their health, their family, their finances. Sometimes they weren't suited for or committed to their job. Others were chronically late or sick or had difficult personalities that affected the team. I did my best to balance business wellbeing with kindness and loyalty.

When the business grew too fast, we had unhappy customers, disgruntled employees, and headaches. I would have to balance battling the chaos of the day with building systems for growth.

Business is something I did to survive, prosper, and find meaning. When I tied my happiness to its ups and downs, I lost my center and suffered. I was most effective when I viewed business as a game. Deep down, thanks to the TM technique, I was an observer. I knew I was playing grown up Monopoly. I had only to give my best and stay true to my values, enjoy the process, and not over-identify with the results.

Managing employees

The business succeeded thanks to the contributions of our employees and contractors, although sometimes in the midst of day-to-day challenges, I would forget. At one point, we had 21 full-time people working for us along with a half dozen part-time contractors.

The print shop for The HP *Palmtop Paper* resided across the alleyway. The owners and I would commiserate about our employees' lack of common sense, poor time-management skills, and laziness.

Meanwhile, our employees discussed their crazy, demanding, disorganized bosses.

The printers and I often didn't recognize that most people prefer to work their eight hours and then enjoy home life. Our employees agreed to give us 40 hours a week in exchange for a salary. Rather than doing a better job inspiring and training our employees, we somehow expected that they would think about the business with the same obsession we did. If they thought like we did, with the same commitment, why work for us?

Smart businesses hire carefully and fire quickly. I often did the opposite. In our growth periods, when desperate, I hired quickly, which could be a big mistake. In a small company's family-like atmosphere, success comes from its people liking each other, doing jobs effectively, and representing the company well.

I found the best question for checking references is, "Would you hire them again?" Any hesitation is a red flag requiring elaboration.

When hiring, I would often "fall in love" with the interviewee, especially when I saw an inner spark coupled with an enthusiasm for my business philosophy. Rather than focus on resume qualifications, I looked for potential and had a soft spot for undervalued misfits.

As a result, I got some extraordinary people who did great things for the company. I also got some management headaches. What I would view as tolerance and understanding for talented individuals, other employees saw as unfairness.

Our policy of promoting from within flowed from my hiring on potential and creating a learning environment. Motivation, raw talent, and company familiarity compensated for a lack of skill and experience in the new position.

In my business, Brian Teitzman ran The Portable Equipment Exchange and moved to selling ads for *The HP Palmtop Paper*. Accountant Wayne Kneeskern complained about typos in the magazine and became the company proofreader while also running UsedHandhelds. Colleen Rodibaugh started in data entry and ended up managing circulation operations and working as my assistant. David Seagull, who worked for Brian in the 1980s, returned to become my marketing manager. David Brooks in I.T. joined farmer and Wayne son-in-law, Jamie Snyder, to repair palmtops. Biba Dangol started in shipping and receiving and became my UsedHandhelds buyer and comptroller.

I was too slow to fire, always hoping that things would work out. With the peace that followed a firing, I would realize that I should have let the person go six months before.

The whole company met two to three times a week for department updates, learning sessions, and birthday celebrations. The meetings built trust and coherence among the team and made for a more enjoyable environment.

Operations and marketing

Most people seem to have either a marketing or an operations mindset. A business needs both. My marketing, entrepreneurial, let's-just-do-it way of thinking moved the business forward. Yet, it needed balance from a practical, hands-on, what-systems-do-we-need-to-create mentality.

Without marketing, there would be nothing for operations to do. Without operations, the business would not keep its promises to customers. Marketers often want to bypass the rules and trivialize practical concerns. Operations people don't like change, special cases, or complex sales offers.

The operations and marketing departments must respect each other. As my staff grew, and I assumed a greater leadership role, I staked out the middle ground.

In the classic, *The E-Myth Revisited: Why Most Small Businesses Don't Work and What to Do About It*, Michael Gerber emphasizes the importance of operations to entrepreneurial success. He tells entrepreneurs that they should be working on their business rather than in it.

Entrepreneurs need to continually create and refine systems for sales, accounting, production, marketing, hiring, and training. Systems require defining work flow, describing tasks, training employees, and getting feedback for ongoing improvement.

When I started, I did everything — all the work of the business, from creating and editing the newsletter to tracking subscriptions to marketing to mailing the newsletter. Without systems, I was always re-inventing the wheel for every customer call, marketing piece, magazine issue, employee interview, and product shipment.

Gerber writes of the importance of creating an organization chart, especially for a one-person business. Doing so provides clarity about the functions of the business, the people to hire, and their tasks. Typically, any business can be broken down into three parts: operations, marketing, and accounting. The expanded chart of the various roles in our business in January 1986, a month after the first issue of *The Portable Paper*, was remarkably complicated, even before any full-time staff or buying and selling HP Portables.

As my business systems evolved, there was less disorder and burnout. We became a place that employees, customers, and suppliers could count on.

As a small company, our success came from partnerships with larger companies. HP, Microsoft, and Apple customers became our customers. Eventually, a huge printing company printed and mailed our issues. We used the largest physical and digital newsstand distributors to promote and sell our magazines. Many of UsedHandhelds' sales today come from eBay and Amazon.

The entrepreneur is always selling. In the beginning, I convinced HP to provide me with registration cards, HP Portable users to subscribe, and readers to write for us for free. I later sold space to advertisers, jobs to potential employees, and dependability to used equipment customers.

I was enthusiastic and confident because I always believed the other would benefit. If I didn't think the person or company would be better off, I wasn't interested in the partnership.

"Luck"

Most people think that to have a successful business requires luck — bumping into the right person at the right time, getting a large customer out of the blue, catching a wave in a market trend. And that, conversely, without luck a business fails. But good fortune is not just fate.

Entrepreneurs create their own "luck" by actively generating and then pouncing on opportunities. They encourage good fortune through commitment, service, and meditation.

Johann Goethe wrote, "At the moment of commitment the entire universe conspires to assist you." Rita and I committed to Maharishi's vision of material and spiritual abundance when we left prestigious, well-paying Bay Area jobs and moved to Iowa. Then we committed to publishing a newsletter even though we had no idea how to do it.

Call it karma, right action, or service. Helping others, independent of personal gain, gets rewarded. In our case, we provided readers free technical support, assisted employees in need, and donated to the university and community.

Maharishi explained that during TM, meditators experience the "home of all the laws of nature." Then, in activity, they gain "support of the laws of nature." Stated differently, regular TM practice develops intuition. Most business decisions are based on incomplete information. Consequently, finely tuned intuition often proves more valuable than detailed analysis.

Money

Money is the lifeblood of business, and entrepreneurs must continually increase their understanding and respect for it.

From the start, Rita and I avoided debt. Savings and pre-paid subscriptions funded the company. We worked out of our home and hired only when we could afford it.

After starting The Portable Equipment Exchange, Rita and I moved our home and business into a larger house, which we quickly outgrew.

Over the next five years, we purchased three adjacent buildings on the Fairfield town square, paying them off as quickly as we could. Rents from the business and upstairs apartments came in handy during down times.

On the other hand, a pay-as-you-go strategy can limit growth. Many businesspeople prefer using other people's money to finance the equipment, marketing, and employees required for fast growth. But banks and investors supply capital in exchange for control and ownership, neither of which we were willing to give up.

We worked in the volatile technology and publishing industries. Without deep pockets or backers, we built a series of financial buffers that contributed to our longevity.

First, we evolved somewhat independent income streams. On the magazine side, revenue came from subscriptions, advertisement, and newsstand sales. In the UsedHandhelds business, we received income from equipment sales, fast turnover from great buys, and repairs. We sold proprietary software and accessories through both the magazine and UsedHandhelds.com.

Second, if things got problematic, we would loan my salary back to the business.

Third, since Rita and I were the landlords, we could let the rent slide until business picked up.

Fourth, employees earned modest salaries accompanied by a generous but arbitrary bonus program. I promised nothing but gave as much as four months' bonus in a good year.

Fifth, we maintained no long-term debt, which meant no lender could close us down for our assets.

I preferred to sell higher-priced, high-value products with little competition. That way my focus could be on making terrific products rather than operations efficiency. We started by charging $55 per year for our newsletter. Then, through the years, we created a number of high-margin, low-volume products. We sold software packages and hardware repair and upgrades with 60% to 90% margins and $30 to $300 profit per sale.

My greatest weakness as an entrepreneur was not having robust accounting and data analysis systems. At best, I would have an accurate cash flow statement showing cash, payables, and receivables. That report would give me a good idea of our position over the next several months.

At any given time, I might not know the basics, such as subscription numbers, newsstand sales, and renewal rates. It wasn't that I didn't think key business data was important — I tried to create proper systems. The problem was that inevitably I would underestimate the time required to specify my needs, hire the right personnel, and analyze the results. I preferred instead to work on the next new opportunity.

My new partners put a lot of attention on accurate and actionable data, which was one of their most important improvements of the business.

Shortly after college, I read Catherine Ponder's, *The Dynamic Laws of Prosperity*. In it, she referenced the Old Testament prescription for farmers to leave an unharvested portion of their fields for the poor. Rita and I both resonated with her premise that regular donation not only does good but would help us prosper. I have donated monthly for 40 years and believe this habit has played a fundamental role in my success.

Here's why donation works: First, just as we naturally want to give back to people who unconditionally give to us, the universe naturally wants to reward us when we are generous. "As you sow, so shall you reap." Second, regular donation helps dissolve our attachment and aversion toward money. That is, both needing money and not liking money creates resistance to attracting money.

Almost everyone associates money with survival. No money means no food or shelter. No money means business failure. To counter our attachment to money, Rita and I decide our monthly donations at the beginning of each year. Then, no matter what, like any other bill, our accountant makes the monthly payments. As we donate, our fear and desire to hold onto money diminishes. In business, that translates into the clarity to make decisions about money, free of fear, greed, and regret.

Regular donation also diminishes aversion to money. When I began the business, I still had the idea that money was somehow bad. That notion dropped as we started using some of our profit for causes that we believed bettered the world. The more we made in the business, the more we could donate.

Two important caveats. First, prosperity comes from giving from a pure heart, from a genuine desire to make a difference. Donating only because it increases prosperity produces limited results. Second, I began donating in the 1970s when my income was quite limited. I recommend starting with a small monthly donation when it is most challenging.

Success comes in different flavors

My entrepreneurial venture brought me success in various ways.

We made our stakeholders happy. My wife and children lived comfortably. Customers enjoyed and became more proficient with their devices. They also had a place to buy and sell older technology. Employees grew professionally as they supported their families. HP, Microsoft, and Apple had more knowledgeable and enthusiastic customers. Suppliers appreciated being paid promptly. Fairfield benefited economically. The TM organization had more meditators to take part in the world peace project. Donation recipients were better funded.

I consider doing what I loved and getting paid for it a great success. I enjoyed playing with the latest gadgets vendors would send me. I grew as a leader and a manager and kept learning in the ever-evolving technology and publishing industries. Learning, growing, and creating fit well with my desire for personal development. Rita and I were able to travel all around the world promoting our magazines.

Another measure of my success was our ongoing commitment to our 1991 vision of a creative, model company where employees functioned in an enjoyable, knowledge-based, and ethical workspace.

After investing so much of myself in the business, it was a great success to pass the business on to local, capable young people, who shared my values, continued my vision, and had the savvy and drive to make the business continue to succeed in the digital age.

The final measure of my success came from a profound learning. When I started, I often fooled myself into thinking that some big product sale, some partnership, or some other business achievement would make me happy. I was so driven that I seldom paused to celebrate even major accomplishments. As soon as I completed one goal, I was on to the next. I fooled myself again and again, acting as though achieving the next goal would bring me the satisfaction I craved.

Over time, with more years of meditation and more witnessing of the whole process, I realized that satisfaction comes first. When I brought inner happiness to work, I enjoyed my activities more, the ups became more satisfying, and the downs didn't feel so catastrophic. Over time, our company celebrations increased.

SPIRIT: Uplift others

Assisting, teaching, and inspiring others has always motivated me and given my life meaning and purpose. In my 20s, I helped people by counseling as a social worker and by teaching the TM technique. Then in my 30s, I worked as a software engineer at Hewlett Packard — a prestigious, well-paying position that I didn't enjoy. It just wasn't who I was or wanted to be.

Motivated in part by the desire to better the world, I moved to Fairfield. There, I launched a company which helped others get the most of their portable devices.

As CEO, the wellbeing of my employees played a major role in how I structured the company. For our customers, I was always trying to pack more information into our magazines and to make our product offerings more useful. I retired by giving an opportunity to talented young employees and keeping jobs in Fairfield.

After retirement, I asked other local entrepreneurs to join me in teaching undergrads at Maharishi University of Management what it takes to be a successful entrepreneur. From that experience this book emerged with its mission to inspire spiritually-inclined entrepreneurs.

I consider all this "doing good" as selfish. I believe I always got more out of giving than the people on the other end. I find it fulfilling to make a difference in someone else's life whether it be materially, emotionally, or spiritually.

A businessperson must keep his attention on the bottom line — making sure more money comes in then goes out. That being said, I recommend creating a business that makes others' lives better. That commitment to improve the lot of customers, employees, and suppliers brings success and satisfaction in so many more ways than just trying to maximize income.

Hal Goldstein's twelve tweets

1. A business expresses the collective consciousness of its owners, employees, customers, investors, suppliers, and community. That business develops its own character, survival mechanisms, and propensity to find purpose.

2. You must do three things to make a successful business: 1) Create a "Wow" product; 2) Know your customer; 3) Connect the product and the customer cost-effectively.

3. Start with the goal and make an unshakable commitment to achieve it. Goethe wrote, "At the moment of commitment the entire universe conspires to assist you."

4. Generosity served our business well. I always wanted my customer, employee, lender, partner, or supplier to get more out of a transaction than I did.

5. If you have a good product, want what's best for the customer, and don't make your wellbeing dependent on the sale, selling is easy.

6. In the daily grind, I often fooled myself into thinking that some sale, some partnership, or some other business achievement would make me happy. When I brought my happiness into work, the ups were more

satisfying, and the downs weren't so catastrophic.

7. Taking one full day a week off away from the business was the smartest thing I did for the business, my sanity, and my marriage.

8. Keeping your word is the cornerstone of success and builds self-confidence and trust. Customers must believe your product promise; employees must trust your word; partners, suppliers, and lenders must know they will get paid. If you always keep small promises, eventually you will be able to manifest anything you commit to.

9. Reaching the goal requires resting, letting go, and trusting unseen forces.

10. Both needing money and not liking money creates resistance to the manifestation of money. Regular donation attracts money by diminishing neediness and the desire to hold onto money, and by nourishing the desire to use the money for good.

11. TM develops intuition. A quieter mind is more in sync with the rhythm of the marketplace. Given the incomplete information available for most business decisions, finely tuned intuition is often more important than analysis.

12. The culture, the character, and purpose of a business are rooted in the entrepreneur's underlying vision. That vision sustains, inspires, and empowers the business, giving it meaning and direction.

Ponder

1. To prevent misuse, HP did not give out contact information of its support customers. Do you think Hal and Rita's decision to burn the 9,000 support names was misguided? What do you think you would do if you were in their situation?

2. Have you ever worked for an unreasonable, demanding boss? What kind of boss will you be when launching and running your business?

3. When you think about money, do negative emotions like fear, greed,

and disdain come up? How will those feelings affect your business?

4. What is your relationship like with friends and family who don't keep their word? Compare that with those who do keep their word. What percentage of the time is your word good?

5. Would you say your strengths are more in marketing and sales or operations and accounting? How do you plan to make the secondary side stronger?

6. Hal said that when things weren't going well, he was embarrassed to look at the ideals of his vision statement on the wall — "Creating a model heaven-on-earth business," "Be happy, Learn, Do right." What would you say to Hal?

Hal Goldstein and wife Rita at a 2004 Las Vegas press event

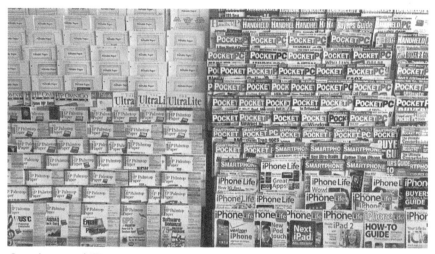

Complete set of 179 magazines on mobile computing published by Hal Goldstein

1999 Handheld PC Magazine team celebration. Hal on right with hands on shoulders of wife and partner Rita.

Hal and Rita Goldstein in front of Personalized Software Building, 1989

Hal (without ugly XMAS sweater) with iPhone Life team in 2017

PART SIX

Saving the Planet

Francis Thicke

Troy and Amy Van Beek

Francis Thicke
SOIL SCIENTIST, ORGANIC DAIRY FARMER, POLITICIAN

Francis Thicke and wife, Susan, own and operate a 90-cow, grass-based, organic dairy farm near Fairfield, Iowa. They run their farm as an ongoing experiment, applying what they learn from nature.

Francis has a Ph.D. in soil fertility. He worked as National Program Leader for Soil Science for the USDA-Extension Service in Washington, D.C.

Highly sought after in the fields of organic agriculture and sustainability, Francis has served on the Iowa Environmental Protection Commission, the Iowa Food Policy Council, USDA State Technical Committee, Iowa State University (ISU) Extension Advisory Committee, and National Organic Standards Board (NOSB). His many awards in sustainable agriculture and organic farming include those from Practical Farmers of Iowa, Leopold Center, Sierra Club Steward of Land, and ISU Extension.

In 2010, Francis ran as a Democrat for Secretary of Agriculture of Iowa. To educate the populace, he published *A New Vision for Iowa Food and Agriculture — Sustainable Agriculture for the 21st Century*.

For videos of the campaign and the farm, search for Francis on YouTube.

My son, Solomon, has worked for Francis and Susan for a number of years milking, processing, bottling, and delivering.

JOURNEY: Modeling organic, sustainable farming

EARLY YEARS

Born in 1950, I grew up with eight brothers and sisters on a small farm in southeastern Minnesota. We grew hay, oats, and corn, which we fed to our dairy cows, hogs, chickens, sheep, and horses. The farm took care of our family's food needs with the meat of butchered animals and with garden-grown fruits and vegetables that we canned and froze.

In the 1960s, the farm became a dedicated dairy farm with hogs and chickens raised on the side. In high school, my brothers and I would get up at 4:00 AM to milk the cows and be on time for the school bus.

In 1972, I graduated from Winona State College in Minnesota with a BA in music and philosophy. I continued studying trumpet at a Texas graduate school but soon returned to work the family farm. And in 1975, I married Susan Noll.

That summer, one of my jobs was to spray herbicides to protect the corn from weeds. Without telling anyone, I decided not to spray one of three strips of corn on the same hillside. The field remained almost weed free.

My brothers and I got excited. Over my father's objections, we converted the entire farm to organic. Our friends and neighbors thought that we were kooks.

It turned out we had been quite lucky with my first experiment. A number of agronomic and climatic conditions had come together to make it a year without many weeds. Our trial-and-error approach later led to some disasters, including weeds taking over our fields. We learned about timely weed control methods and after a few years, fine-tuned the operations.

In 1982, I returned to graduate school, first at the University of Minnesota and then at the University of Illinois where I completed a Ph.D. in soil fertility in 1988. I worked as a Soils Specialist with the U.S. Department of Agriculture's Extension Service in Washington, D.C.

and was promoted to the National Program Leader for Soil Science to head new initiatives.

To avoid colleagues ostracizing me at work, I didn't tell anybody I had been an organic farmer. Talking about sustainable agriculture already put me on the fringes.

Finally, in 1992, I decided to go back to farming. My colleagues thought it strange that someone at the USDA would want to farm. They didn't think I would last.

Raw milk and the origin of Radiance Dairy

A couple of Fairfield families got together in 1980 and started Radiance Dairy as a co-op. Meditating entrepreneur, Jim Schaefer, bought their first two cows from a dairy near my farm in Minnesota. (Jim also founded a successful soil technology company.)

The co-op, which sold raw milk, soon added more cows and a milking machine. The Iowa milk law says that if you own your cow, you can drink raw milk. Each customer owned a portion of the co-op, so each owned part of a cow. Eventually, the state of Iowa Department of Agriculture said no more — the dairy could only sell pasteurized milk products.

When Radiance Dairy could no longer sell raw milk, it purchased equipment and became the only dairy farm in Iowa with its own processing plant. Other farms store milk in a bulk tank, from where it is trucked to central processing.

When Susan and I took over the dairy in 1992, it had about 20 milking cows. An economist colleague at the USDA discouraged me. He didn't think I could make a living running a small organic dairy farm, but Fairfield is such a unique community that I just knew it would work. Plus, I thought it would be fun.

When we moved from Washington D.C. to Fairfield, we had a $30,000 student loan debt and no cash. We bought the cows with $20,000 borrowed from my brother. Jim Schaefer gave us a year before we had to pay for the equipment, and we rented the land for the dairy.

That first year, we were able to keep the farm going by bootstrapping as we went. Within a year, we established a relationship with the local bank and got a loan to pay off the equipment. We worked full speed from morning until night. I didn't mind, as I had been cooped up in Washington D.C. for four years. Money remained tight. I remember having very sore elbows from building fences with a sledgehammer since I didn't want to spend $18 for a post driver.

In 1996, with increased product demand and a bank loan, we bought an old, beat up, 176-acre farmstead. For many years, the farm had grown only corn and soybeans. Erosion had caused the loss of much of the topsoil. On some of the hillsides, all of the original topsoil was gone. The farm had no buildings ready to use.

The realtor who showed us the land grew up two miles from the farm. He later told us he had seen a lot of farmsteads disappear, but ours was the first he'd seen resurrected.

We built facilities for milking the cows and processing the milk on the new land. Susan and I lived above the processing plant in a storage room we had converted into an apartment while building our home ourselves with help from the farm workers. It would be four years before we could move in.

From the start, the goal of the farm has not been about maximizing profit. We run Radiance Dairy to provide healthy food to the community at a reasonable price, experiment to advance our ecological agriculture system, earn enough income to support ourselves and our employees, create a model of organic, sustainable agriculture for others to emulate, and have fun.

Using nature as the model for the farm

12,000 years ago, when the last glacier receded, northern Iowa was a geological wasteland without soil. Over time, a grassland ecology developed. Bison grazed the prairie grasses and helped create deep, black soil. The organizing power of nature's ecology developed the rich, productive soils of Iowa.

We decided to develop the farm by mimicking nature as best we could. To create the diversity of a prairie, we repaired the gullies and planted a diverse mix of grasses and clovers.

We fenced in small, two-acre pastures (paddocks) of grass and clover. Twice a day (after each milking) we moved the cows to a new paddock. As the cows rotated around the paddocks, each grazed paddock had time to regrow for the next round of grazing. The effect of that grazing system is similar to the soil building that originally occurred as the bison roamed the prairie. And, like the bison, grazing cows spread their own manure and fertilize the vegetation.

Over the years, we purchased several parcels of land that border us. We now have 730 acres, which allows us to grow our herd and produce organic crops for sale.

We added more products — skim milk, cream, yogurt, paneer, cheese. As the market expanded, we increased our herd 5% to 10% each year. In 2018, four employees, Susan, and I produced dairy products from about 90 cows to meet the demand from local restaurants, grocery stores, and the Maharishi University of Management.

Contented cows

Most modern dairy farms confine cows in what is called a Concentrated Animal Feeding Operation — CAFO. We let our cows graze, which has ecological, economic, and ethical benefits.

The farmer with a confinement system must harvest feed, store it, and feed the animals daily. Then the farmer must collect the manure, store it, and haul it back into the pasture. These activities require a lot of fossil fuels. Furthermore, many consider such confinement of animals inhumane.

When cows stand in confinement and eat a lot of corn, they produce about twice as much milk as our grass-fed Jersey cows. However, those confined cows don't live nearly as long as our cows and average only about 30 months of milk production.

Cows that graze are more contented and produce milk with a healthier nutrient profile. That means healthier animals and healthier people. At Radiance Dairy all feeds are certified organic. The breeding stock must come from certified organic animals. We have no animals treated with antibiotics or other synthetics. The cows graze in pastures and their living conditions support health and natural behavior.

We don't need the big equipment that confinement systems require. The cows do the work. At milking time, we open the paddock gate. The cows follow us to the milking barn where they get what seems a treat, a small amount of grain. After milking, we lead them to the next paddock and close the gate. They know that the new pasture will have fresh grass, so they're anxious to get there.

We make the grazing season last as long as possible. We start grazing the cows when the grass takes off in early April. We rotate the cows through 60 paddocks, allowing the grass to regrow after each time it is grazed. In August, we select certain areas of the farm to let the grass grow to reserve it for grazing after the growing season ends. Then in October and November, we let the cows graze there.

At first, we wintered the cows in and near the barn, where we kept adding bedding. However, by spring, we had three to four feet of bedding-packed manure to break up for composting. That took a lot of energy. Now, we winter the cows outside, which they prefer. We select an area of the pastures where we want to build up the fertility and feed the hay bales there. Each time we bring new hay bales for them to eat, we place the bales in a different place. That way the cows spread their manure uniformly on the pasture. They bed on residual hay and added bedding. By spring they've done the fertilizing work — the manure is where it needs to be. When it's very cold or windy, we keep them inside or in a paddock in a valley shielded from the wind.

We have Jersey cows, a small breed of dairy cows that are friendlier than most other breeds. Jerseys produce rich, flavorful milk with a lot of protein, butterfat, and other solids. A big cream line rises to the top of our milk.

The milk fat content of whole milk is normally standardized to 3.25% by removing some of the butterfat. Our whole milk is over 5%

butterfat, just as it comes from the cows. Vitamins are mostly in the milk fat. Even with the fat removed, our skim milk has body and flavor because of the higher level of protein and milk sugars. People who drink our skim milk say other skim milk tastes like water.

Cows gestate for nine months and start giving birth at two years old. With their first calf, cows start lactating and making milk. Each year, at about the same time, they have another calf. We milk them for approximately 10 months and then let them rest in pasture for two months. Cows that are at least 10 years old when they stop producing milk are retired. They live out their remaining years on pasture.

The female calves stay with their mothers for three months before we wean them. At about three months, they turn into "juvenile delinquents" anyway, so it works out well.

As new female offspring grow up into the herd, we sometimes have too many cows for our market demand. Rather than sending them to slaughter, we try to sell them at a reasonable price to families living on country acreage. These cows at the bottom tier of our herd still produce more than enough milk for a family. It gives the cows a second lease on life. Many such family cows live out their lives as family pets.

We keep a few bull calves to raise for breeding. We cannot keep all the bulls, or they would drink all the milk and be too expensive to maintain. Often kids from the country want to raise our bull calves for 4-H projects and to show them at fairs. However, eventually, the bulls are likely to end up in someone's freezer.

After over 40 years working with cows, I seldom need a vet as I have learned to take care of most health issues. I did once use a chiropractor to reset the back of a cow that had been injured and couldn't stand up. She was able to stand up and walk immediately after the treatment. We also use Reiki on cows with health problems.

We tattoo each cow's four-digit identification number in its right ear. For example, 1708 refers to the eighth calf born in 2017. The name tag on their collar has their name and approximate age.

We have the Maharishi University of Management, Gandharva Veda Music® radio station on in the milking parlor during the milking process. The music is said to produce harmony within the physiology.

We have a swing-style milking parlor that allows eight cows to stand on each side of a pit where the person milking the cows stands between them. Eight milking machines swing from one side to the other, for fast and efficient milking. The milk comes from the cow at 101 degrees Fahrenheit and then gets cooled immediately to about 34 degrees. On processing days, we use pipes and pump the milk through the wall into pasteurizing vats in the processing plant.

We pasteurize the milk in the vats by heating the milk longer at a lower temperature than is commonly done at central processing plants. This lower temperature removes unwanted bacteria but still preserves enzymes found in cow milk. We bottle milk twice a week.

Renewable energy

Harvesting wind and solar power has reduced our farm energy costs. By using alternative energy, I can combine a variety of systems and not be as dependent on externally supplied energy.

We use six solar, 125-watt, photovoltaic panels to pump water from a pond into a 6,500-gallon tank on the highest point on the farm. The water flows from this tank to small tanks accessible from all the 60 paddocks. The water traverses through one-inch polypropylene pipe buried eight inches underground. This system is used from spring through fall. During the winter, we have two cow watering tanks that are filled by gravity from ponds and are warmed by geothermal heat.

We use a lot of hot water for washing equipment in the on-farm milk processing plant. We pre-heat the water with solar panels on the barn roof, which heat water in storage tanks that feed into the hot water heater. We also use the heat released from cooling the milk to heat the milk house and processing plant in the winter.

We have a geothermal system for our house that keeps the house warm in winter and cools it in summer by exchanging heat from the water in a nearby pond. In the summer, we open windows in the cupola on the roof and first floor of the house, which creates a strong cooling draft and eliminates the need for air conditioning, except on the hottest days.

We also have a 40k wind turbine. Now, the wind that blows over the farm helps power the farm, producing about half of the farm's electricity needs annually. We intend to install additional solar photovoltaic panels soon.

Running for Iowa Secretary of Agriculture

In 2006, an organic farmer friend ran for Secretary of Agriculture in Iowa. Two weeks before the election, she was 14 points ahead in the polls. Then the farm industry lobbyists panicked and in a short time raised $250,000. They blasted her with a terrible, last minute, negative ad campaign and she narrowly lost.

In 2010, I decided to run as a Democrat for Secretary of Agriculture. I had been involved in Iowa politics previously, serving on the Iowa Environmental Protection Commission (EPC). The EPC oversees the Department of Natural Resources. The EPC and industrial agriculture advocates sometimes battled when I was on the Commission, particularly over hog confinement buildings.

I hoped, as Secretary of Agriculture, to shine a light on Iowa agriculture's major challenges and its great opportunities. And I wanted a public forum to discuss key issues such as soil erosion, water quality, animal confinement systems, ill-health, obesity, corporate farming, and dependency on fossil fuels. To get the word out I wrote a book, *A New Vision for Iowa Food and Agriculture: Sustainable Agriculture for the 21st Century.*

My friends in politics said, "Don't write a book, they'll attack you on everything you write."

I said, "That's what I want."

Ironically, the industrial agriculture advocates did not attack me for what I wrote in the book and did not want to engage in debate. A Republican year, the polls weren't close. The entrenched Republican and corporate establishment did their best to ignore me. I'd write an op-ed piece in the Des Moines Register, expect to get blasted, and there would be little response.

I learned that it takes lots of money to run for office and get the word out. The Governor and U.S. Senate races hogged both the free airways and the advertising venues.

Even so, we did plant seeds for future action. When I traveled around and spoke, especially in urban areas, people were quite interested in my message. They were open to learning about energy self-sufficiency, sustainable agriculture principles, and local foods. I also learned after the election that the book I had written was assigned reading in at least a dozen college classes.

The Iowa Secretary of Agriculture has a platform to speak about the issues but doesn't have much statutory power. Even if I had been elected, I am not sure I could have made much of a difference because the agriculture status quo would have done their best to marginalize me.

The industrial agriculture lobby holds great power. They have quite a bit of control over the Iowa Legislature, targeting legislators who don't do what they want for defeat in the next election.

The political race set Susan and me back financially, but I don't regret it. I enjoyed campaigning and raising critical issues. I probably will not run again, but I'm still speaking and writing on the issues, which is more fun anyway.

Here was my message on the campaign trail:

"Iowa has a long, proud tradition of being a leader in agriculture. Our prairies gave us some of the deepest, richest soils in the world. In our temperate climate, hardworking people farm the land. All this has made Iowa an agricultural powerhouse — a shining jewel among agricultural states.

Now in a time of flux, Iowa agriculture needs to change to continue to thrive.

Unfortunately, many of Iowa's challenges are not discussed or even acknowledged. For example, Iowa has some major water quality problems, and the response of the agriculture status quo has been denial.

Also, we have some exceptional opportunities that could allow us to surmount the challenges we face.

Meeting the challenges of the 21st Century requires new vision and new leadership. Iowa agriculture could lead Iowa and the nation to a new economy based on sustainable renewable energy, environmentally sound farming systems, and thriving rural communities.

Continuing the status quo will not get us there. The Iowa Secretary of Agriculture should be a watchdog for Iowa farmers, not a lapdog for corporate interests.

The position requires a clear vision of the future, creative planning and policy making, commitment to research and development of appropriate technologies, and firm resolve to carry us through. The Iowa Secretary of Agriculture should provide that vision and leadership."

Singer-songwriter, Arthur Lee Land visited me at Radiance Dairy. He wrote *Happy Cow* - © Arthur Lee Land, arthurleeland.com/custom-songs/ to support my campaign and to reach younger voters. As part of the campaign, supporters created music videos which can be found on YouTube (search, "lee land happy cow").

Land's playful lyrics include the word, "ticky," the pronunciation of my name.

Happy Cow

What's it gonna take
To see the writing on the wall?
What's it gonna take
to feel like the planet we inhabit is very small?
What's it gonna take
to know we're gonna reap what we sow on the farms?
What's it gonna take
to hear Mother Nature, she's rung her alarm?

I'm just a happy cow
Living in the here and now

Grazing in this field of green
But it seems like time is moving faster if you know what I mean
The clock is ticking…Ticky-tock
The clock is ticking…Ticky-tock

What's it gonna take
To see what's happening right in front of your face?
What's it gonna take
To spend your dollars in a way that'll change the marketplace?
What's it gonna take
To spread the word about a better way?
What's it gonna take
To be the change we want in the world today?

I'm just a happy cow
Living in the here and now
Grazing in this field of green
But it seems like time is moving faster if you know what I mean
The clock is ticking…Ticky-tock
The clock is ticking…Ticky-tock

We're just the happy cows
Living in the here and now
Grazing in these fields of green
But it seems like time is moving faster if you know what I mean
The clock is ticking …Ticky-tock
The clock is ticking…Ticky-tock
The clock is ticking…Ticky-tock
The clock is ticking.…Ticky-tock

WISDOM: Learn from nature, then experiment

ECOLOGICAL VERSES INDUSTRIAL FARMING

In today's industrial era, farms powered by inexpensive fossil fuels have focused on profit and efficiency. The ideal farm today is a well-ordered machine — a "Factory farm."

Because of cheap energy, energy-intensive technological solutions seem more effective than natural biological systems. In industrialized agriculture, for example, animals are not viewed as living, feeling beings. They are cogs in a mechanized process that efficiently produces meat and dairy, often with little consideration of environmental consequences. Similarly, corn and soybeans are planted to maximize yield, without enough regard for soil erosion or water pollution.

As cheap fossil fuels disappear and the unhealthy consequences for the planet and humans become more apparent, we must change paradigms. We must fundamentally redesign our agricultural systems, not simply invent new technologies to bolster our current industrial system.

Industrial agriculture is monoculture. And it relies on the intensive use of nonrenewable and hard-to-renew resources — soil, pest-control chemicals, fresh water, and fossil fuels. Due to lack of biodiversity in industrial agriculture, nutrients and pesticides leak into the water table and our surface waters, causing water pollution around the state. The environment and society then absorb the costs of resultant waste and pollution. In contrast, ecological agriculture is biodiverse and self-sufficient and conserves and recycles.

Agriculture is a biological and ecological enterprise. Accordingly, we should design and manage farms in ways that are ecologically sound. We should make use of the energy, efficiency, and organizing power of nature's ecology.

It took many years for Iowa's agriculture to reach today's pinnacle of industrial production and fossil fuel dependency. We cannot expect it to change abruptly. The important thing is to recognize the need for change and begin the process. Radiance Dairy is one of a growing number of innovative examples of ecological agriculture that serve as a model for the future of Iowa agriculture.

Problems of our current industrial agriculture system

Soil erosion and soil depletion

In Iowa in general, the more we farm, the more we compromise our natural resource base. Since farming began in Iowa, we've lost about half our topsoil to erosion and 60% of our black organic matter to oxidation. Such farming is not sustainable.

When growing corn and soybeans, Iowa farms lose soil at 10 times the rate that soil regenerates. Extreme weather events can greatly increase soil erosion and water quality degradation.

Our soil loss is not sustainable.

- Soils forms at rate of 0.5 ton/acre per year, but the soil erosion rate for corn and soybeans in Midwest averages 5.7 tons/acre per year

- Half of Iowa's topsoil has been lost or eroded from its original site.

- For every gallon of ethanol made from corn, two gallons of soil are lost to erosion

Water quality

Ninety-three percent of the nitrogen pollution to Iowa's water bodies comes from agriculture, predominately from corn and soybean production. Reverse osmosis to screen out nitrogen from the drinking water costs the Des Moines Water Works about $7,000 a day when nitrate levels exceed allowable levels.

The Des Moines Water Works has spent over 20 years trying to work with agriculture groups. In 2015 it brought a lawsuit against three agriculture-heavy Iowa counties. The suit holds these counties accountable for harmful nitrate contamination in the Raccoon River water supply.

In 2017, a federal judge dismissed Des Moines Water Works' lawsuit determining that Iowa's water quality problems are an issue for the Iowa legislature to resolve. He stated that the Des Moines Water Works "may well have suffered an injury," but the drainage districts have no power to address them.

CAFOs

The nature of cows is to move and the nature of grass to stand still. On modern conventional dairy farms, we reverse that. We make cows stand in one place and bring the grass to the cows, and then have to haul the manure back to the fields.

These Concentrated Animal Feeding Operations (CAFOs) are a source of great divisiveness in rural Iowa. They compromise air and water quality, property values, quality of life, and the health of Iowa citizens. CAFO animals spend their entire lives in cramped conditions, living on concrete often in their own excrement with no access to pasture, fresh air, or natural light. To accelerate growth rates and keep animals alive until slaughter, some animals are routinely fed antibiotics.

Monopolistic corporate agriculture usurps the profits of local farmers

Agribusiness corporations monopolize agricultural markets, usurping profits from local farmers. And, increasingly, concentrated agriculture sends profits, previously circulated in local communities, out of state.

According to economists when four or fewer corporations control 40% or more of a market, that market begins to act like a monopoly. Four pork corporations and four beef processing corporations respectively control 66% and 84% of the market. That means small Iowa farmers can have difficulty finding markets to sell their pork and beef products, and the prices they get are not competitive.

In dairy processing, one corporation controls 40% of the market. Dairy farmers suffer from low prices and losses while corporate processors enjoy record profits.

Agribusiness can afford lobbyists, who help legislators write favorable laws for Agribusiness. Large contributions help defeat dissenting legislators.

Genetic engineering

Genetic engineering (GE) is the process of manipulating an organism's genetic material — including combining genes from other species — to produce desired traits such as pest resistance or resistance of crops to herbicides. The long-term and epidemiological consequences of GE are unknown.

The GE industry has used its formidable marketing and lobbying resources to ensure its products dominate the seed marketplace and to perpetuate the industrial methods those products are designed to support.

Health problems and obesity

We have a crisis of obesity and diet-related health problems related to the food we consume. Industrialized production of crops and animals focus on quantity to the exclusion of other goals. These "cheap food" processes and policies have exacerbated the negative impacts of industrialized agriculture on human health.

There are outbreaks of foodborne illness, food contamination scares, volatile food prices, "food deserts," and an abundance of nutritionally deficient foods. Also, water shortages, water contamination, soil depletion, climate change, and fishery collapse impact nutrition and health.

Dependency on cheap fossil fuels

Today's agriculture depends on cheap fossil fuels. Without cheap oil, our current agriculture and food system will become imperiled and could fail.

Ethanol

The original idea behind biofuels was good: create a farmer-owned industry to produce home-grown fuels for the farm. Ironically, we now make ethanol for cars on highways but have done nothing for on-farm usage. Few ethanol plants have local ownership.

The expectation was that over time feedstocks (raw material for fuel) would transition from erosive and nutrient-leaky corn and soybeans to more sustainable perennial cropping systems. That hasn't happened. Corn ethanol production has become an extractive industry: extracting wealth from local communities while degrading our soil and water resource base.

Solutions from ecological agriculture

We now have a deeper knowledge of the ecology of crops, soils, weeds, insects, and other pathogens. That knowledge positions us to design and manage crop and livestock systems that mimic the functions of natural ecologies.

By using ecology as a model, we can strategically use crop rotations, beneficial insects, cover crops, nitrogen-fixing crops, managed grazing, and other practices to circumvent the need for herbicides, pesticides, fertilizers, and fossil-fuel energy. This ecology-based approach to agriculture will help us protect and improve soil quality, water quality, air quality, and wildlife habitat.

We are trending in the right direction, and I am optimistic long-term. Organic was considered "weird" when we started farming organically in the 70s, and sustainable agriculture was considered "off the reservation" for scientists when I worked at the USDA in 1988.

Now thousands of organic farmers share innovative ways of doing things. They attend conferences from organizations like the Midwest Organic Farming Conference (MOSES) and the Practical Farmers of Iowa. Such organizations are on the cutting edge of making agriculture sustainable.

Clean water with perennial and cover crops

The science about the causes of and solutions for our water quality problems is good, but little is being done to implement those solutions.

Leaky cropping systems can be improved by using deep-rooted cover crops and perennials that scavenge nitrate before it leaches into the rivers.

However, it costs money to put the cover crops in, and there is a learning curve. Virtually all farms in Iowa have a soil conservation plan that they must have to be eligible for federal programs. We could do the same thing for water quality. Farmers could choose farming practices that protect water quality and that are adapted to their own farms.

University research

At universities there's a dual mindset. Research and support for conventional industrial agriculture is strong. At the same time, at Iowa State University, there are about a dozen dedicated sustainable agriculture researchers and teachers.

It's exciting to see change coming. Most young students, unless already indoctrinated by industrial agriculture, are a whole different breed from when I attended college.

Integration of livestock and land

A managed grazing system of rotating cows among many paddocks means good quality grass for the cows while building the soil. Grasses, with their deep root systems, add organic matter to the soil, create richer soil and protect it from erosion, while protecting our water resources from nutrient pollution.

Wind, solar, and biofuel

Without cheap oil, we could not farm the way we do today. Renewable energy, like wind and solar, provide alternative energy solutions.

We can use the endless supply of wind that blows across farms to power farms. Using small to mid-sized wind turbines, farmers could keep profits of any excess energy generated. However, the rapid development and adoption of solar photovoltaic technology has greatly decreased prices for solar installations, making solar a better investment than wind energy at the farm level. Also, there have been a lot of fly-by-night companies trying to sell questionable wind systems to farmers. I recommend investing in solar energy systems rather than wind systems at this time.

At Radiance Dairy, we use solar energy to heat and pump water, to electrify fences, and to cool and heat our home and barn.

New technology being developed today could allow biofuel production for on-farm use from ecologically sound, perennial crops like prairie grasses. If processed on the farm, more profits would stay with the farmers.

Breaking up agribusiness monopolies to restore competition

Farm markets aren't working, in part because they're not functioning as free markets. We need to end predatory practices of corporate monopolies that take profits from farmers. We need Teddy Roosevelt-style trust-busting to break up those monopolies.

Local control of CAFOs

Local residents need more protection from the effects of concentrated animal feeding operations. The agribusiness lobby has influenced the Iowa legislature to take all CAFO zoning and regulation control away from local governments.

We should allow county governments to have control over siting of these operations and give residents opportunity to have input into their own destiny.

Increase local food production

Once again farmers are producing food for local communities. We should encourage that trend.

We could grow 80-90% of the eight billion dollars worth of food imported to Iowa. That way we would consume fresher, healthier, and safer food. It would also mean more money for the farmers, which helps stimulate rural economies.

The business of Radiance Dairy

When I left the USDA in Washington, my colleagues took bets on how long my dairy would last. My economist friend cautioned me that everyone was getting out of on-farm processing.

Eventually, I realized that the reason on-farm processing had fallen by the wayside was because farmers were selling in the commodity market. As industrial farming and commodity producers got bigger (large dairy processors have huge volumes and many semi-trucks delivering products), the small farmer could no longer compete.

Yet, today we see a resurgence in on-farm processing. In the same way that small stores can be successful in a Walmart town, farmers selling locally must differentiate their offerings from the commodity product. They must add unique value, so they no longer must compete solely on price.

Radiance Dairy is unique in a number of ways:

- We're organic.
- Our cows feed mostly on grass, not grain.
- We don't homogenize the milk, so cream rises to the top.
- Our milk comes only from Jersey cows and contains higher solids and more flavor.
- The milk is produced locally, which people relate to, and which cuts transportation costs.
- We pasteurize our milk in vats at low temperature.
- We leave all of the Jersey butterfat in our cheese, giving it a buttery flavor.

We couldn't afford to produce milk and cheese if we had to sell at commodity prices. People will pay more for a richer, healthier product.

Susan and I work full-time on the farm. Susan does all the accounting plus the paperwork required to run the business. We have a good crew of two full-time and two part-time people.

We price our products to make a living and pay our bills. Our products generally sell at a price similar to other organic dairy products. We could probably charge more, but we want to keep prices as affordable as possible for our friends and neighbors.

When I speak around the country, people are surprised that we don't advertise or spend for retail product placement. One reason is that Fairfield, our particular community of 10,000, has interest in local foods, alternative energy, organic farming, and alternative building systems.

Radiance Dairy has grown through word of mouth from its two-cow, 1980 beginnings. Local venues who appreciate our products sell them. We advertise only when asked to sponsor a publication or a cause. If we have a new product in a store, we often provide samples, so people can become familiar with it.

We have been fortunate to be able to expand the farm at an affordable price. Early on, we were able to add 60 acres. More recently several opportunities allowed us to add an adjacent 220 acres, which means we have carried as much as 1.6 million dollars in debt. To pay down the loan, we are growing and selling some organic crops in addition to our dairy operation.

Growing our own organic grain helps us become more self-sufficient. We have a diversity of crops, including hay, wheat, barley, oats, sorghum, corn, soybeans, pumpkins, and many species of grasses and legumes in our pastures. That diversity is our crop insurance. If one crop fails, other crops usually make it.

We have gotten more field equipment for growing our grain crops, but I like to keep it simple. Unlike cows, equipment does not multiply. A cow has offspring, but you never go outside in the morning and see a big tractor giving birth to a little tractor.

Running for office in 2010, and the droughts of 2012 and 2013, set us back financially. Now, with more land and a diversity of crops we are more resilient.

I probably spend half my time educating others by speaking, showing visitors around the farm, and writing articles on the internet. I talk to classes and conferences in Iowa and throughout the U.S.

Folks applying for a job tell us, "I want to work with cows." Sometimes they have the romantic idea that they're going to be turned into Henry David Thoreau, but dairy farming is a lot of work. Once a cow kicks them, most are gone. You really must want to do farm work. You can't go at it half-heartedly. You must be committed.

Susan and I do not have children, and someone will need to take over from us in the future. I want to be sure that they share our values — we run a service for the community. It would be easier to find someone to take over the farm with local roots than a meditator. At the same time, a local person may not necessarily have the same commitment to organic, ecologically based agriculture.

SPIRIT: Listen to your intuition
FARMING IN THE MOMENT

I call what I do "farming in the moment," which means learning from the land and listening to my intuition. I try to allow the universe to work through me and help me figure out what to do.

Nature has a game plan. My role is to recognize it. I solve problems co-creatively with nature by combining my intelligence with nature's intelligence. I sense right action from within. I let go of being in my head and leave room for intuition.

Prescriptive industrial agriculture takes the opposite approach. You plant, then you spray. You set goals, then you plan the entire year. When you want to do something, you pull out the goal sheet and make sure the action fits your goals. You try to overpower nature.

At Radiance Dairy, we try to mimic the efficiency of nature. Cow manure is not a waste to be disposed of. Rather it fertilizes our pastures, improves soil fertility, and makes grasses more nutritious. On our farm, cow manure is a resource that increases the health of the soil, the landscape, the cows, and the people who consume the milk.

When farmers follow the principles of nature's ecology, they solve both economic and ecological problems.

Improvise and innovate

An industrial farm requires following a recipe. Our farm, with all its diversity, requires creativity and artistry.

We enjoy improvising and innovating, watching for changes within the ecological system. For example, cows aren't made to eat grains. Cows naturally eat grasses, which make cows healthier. When we implemented our grazing system, I carefully watched how the grass grew and how the cows performed and then worked to adapt the system to the cows.

There are so many facets that we can work on: energy innovations, crop management, food production. There's no end to innovation. Each year I fine tune parts of the operation, watching and learning from nature.

I've seen a lot of farmers try the organic method as if it were another specialty crop. That reductionist approach will generally fail. Rather, a farmer must look at the big picture and approach the organic farm as a holistic ecological system. Otherwise, it won't be successful.

Once the current unsustainable agricultural system starts to fall off the cliff, we will need examples of farms that work. Radiance Dairy and other ecologically based agriculture farms can serve as models.

Francis Thicke's twelve tweets

The Business of Farming

1. Like small stores successful in a Walmart town, farmers selling locally must differentiate their offerings from commodity products. They must add unique value, so they don't have to compete solely on price. People will pay more for a richer, healthier product.

2. Our goal isn't to maximize profit but to provide healthy food, advance ecological agriculture, make a living, and have fun.

3. You really must want to do farm work. You must be committed. You

can't go at it half-heartedly. Folks apply, telling us, "I want to work with cows." They have a romantic idea, but it's a lot of work. Once a cow kicks them, they are gone.

4. We have gotten more field equipment, but I like to keep it simple. Unlike cows, equipment does not multiply. You never go out in morning to see a big tractor giving birth to a little tractor.

The ecology of farming

5. Nature has a game plan. My role is to recognize it. I solve problems co-creatively with nature by combining my intelligence with nature's intelligence.

6. An industrial farm requires following a recipe. Our farm, with all its diversity, requires creativity and artistry. We enjoy improvising and innovating, watching for changes within the ecological system.

7. As inexpensive, non-renewable energy disappears and unhealthy consequences for the planet and humans become apparent, we must change paradigms. Radiance Dairy and other ecologically-based farms will serve as models when the current unsustainable agricultural system falls off the cliff.

8. The Secretary of Agriculture should be a watchdog for farmers, not a lapdog for corporate interests.

9. Farming in the moment means learning from the land and listening to intuition, allowing the universe to inform us what to do. When farmers do what nature intends, they solve both economic and ecological problems.

10. Diversity is our crop insurance. We have hay, wheat, barley, sorghum, corn, soybeans, pumpkins. If a crop fails, others usually make it.

11. Industrial agriculture relies on nonrenewable and hard-to-renew resources. It depends on society to absorb the environmental costs. The alternative is to use the endless supply of sun and wind to power farms.

12. We lose connection to our food when the food travels great distances to get to our dinner plate. In Iowa, we could grow 80-90% of the eight billion dollars' worth of food imported to Iowa. Doing so would stimulate local economies and provide Iowans with fresher, healthier, and safer food.

Ponder

1. What do you think of Francis's concept of "farming in the moment"? Can you apply it to your own business or passion?

2. Is it realistic to think that industrial agriculture can be transformed into ecological agriculture in the foreseeable future?

3. With all its faults, industrial agriculture is efficient. Could ecological agriculture really feed the billions on the planet? Could (or should) Francis's model be scaled up to feed more people healthy dairy products?

4. What do you think Francis should do about passing on his farm and philosophy to the next generation? What succession plans do you have for your business?

Francis and Susan Thicke

Joe Biden with Francis and Becky Schmitz, Jefferson County Supervisor

Francis Thicke's book
(bonus for readers of this book)

A grass-fed dairy saves energy, protects the environment and provides a healthy habitat for the cows

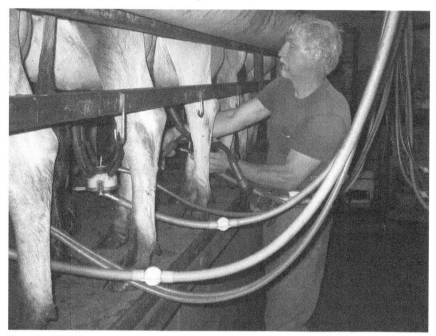

Francis milking

Most dairy cows on today's farms live in confined quarters

Radiance Dairy milk sold at local store, Everybody's Whole Foods

Aerial photo of Radiance Dairy farm

Amy Van Beek
THE ART AND BUSINESS OF SUSTAINABILITY

Second generation Fairfield meditating entrepreneur Amy Van Beek graduated from Maharishi University of Management in 2004 with a fine arts degree. She began her career as a children's book illustrator.

Soon after, she began working with her father, Doug Greenfield, who develops commercial and residential properties in Fairfield. Amy and Doug co-founded Greenfield Properties which focused on sustainable practices, non-toxic materials, and renewable energy. Along with Amy's sister Katie, they built residential developments using high-performance building design, non-toxic materials, and renewable energy systems. They also helped develop and grow the Abundance EcoVillage, an off-grid subdivision of homes powered by solar and wind energy. During her building career, Amy earned a reputation as a top Iowan green building expert and has been featured across the Midwestern news and media outlets.

In 2009, Amy and her husband-to-be, former Navy SEAL Troy Van Beek, founded Ideal Energy, which has become a leading Midwestern solar installation company. Together they run Ideal Energy where Amy serves as the Chief Marketing Officer. Amy brings the success stories of Ideal Energy clients to life through video, photography, and the written word. She uses those stories to educate Iowans about the benefits of solar energy, and ultimately, grow the company's client base.

JOURNEY: Using an art background to design sustainable buildings and market solar energy

GETTING STARTED AS AN ENTREPRENEUR

My father, Doug Greenfield, developed real estate, and as a child I spent a lot of time on construction sites. Throughout his career, my father worked with Maharishi Mahesh Yogi to help adapt Maharishi Vedic® Architecture (Vastu) to the Western world. A Vastu home or community uses natural law-based construction principles to promote health, harmony, and abundance. My father's primary business was in energy, through the oil brokerage firm Danaher Oil, which exposed me to energy issues.

I studied fine art in school and never thought of myself as an entrepreneur.

Upon graduation from MUM in 2004, I began working in children's book illustration. I soon realized that I didn't enjoy the long hours of solitary confinement in a studio. On the side, I had started working with my father part-time in real estate, where he was coaching me in all aspects of construction, from running spreadsheets and selecting contractors to reading blueprints.

In order to be taken seriously as a young woman on a construction site, I started reading everything I could find on all aspects of the business. I began falling in love with the building process and with the evolving dynamism of seeing design take form in three dimensions.

Although I wanted to leave Fairfield, my dad convinced me to stay as a partner in a new residential development. We formed a corporation together, and under his guidance, I ran the construction project from start to finish, managing the tasks, taking the design work to completion, and shepherding the houses through the sales process. I became enthralled with the process.

After the first successful development, my father and I continued growing Greenfield Properties, designing and constructing homes around Fairfield. We used sustainable practices, non-toxic materials, and renewable energy technology whenever possible.

One of the early projects required demolishing a building for an estimated $100,000, with the remains sent to a landfill. Instead, we recruited 20 local Amish to manually dismantle the structure in exchange for the materials. When finished, we only had to pay $10,000 to remove the concrete in the ground.

My research about sustainable building materials and energy efficiency techniques led me just north of the MUM campus to the Abundance EcoVillage, a project of visionary MUM Professor, Lonnie Gamble, and Michael Havelka. The village consisted of a field with a wind turbine, solar panels, and a few Vastu-designed homes with eco-minded residents.

At this point, my sister, Katie, had joined the family business and we began working together on the EcoVillage project. Katie and I spent the first year getting the permits to turn the village into a legal subdivision and for the village's unique renewable energy systems and constructed wetlands, which were uncommon in the Midwest in the mid 2000s.

I loved working with sustainable technologies, and we were getting excellent press, including a feature on Oprah when she filmed a special about Fairfield. I thought my career would continue in architecture, construction, and design, but life tends to rearrange itself.

When the economy crashed in 2008, we had 13 houses for sale, all with outstanding loans. Luckily, we were able to maintain everything as rentals, but I realized I would have to reinvent my career path.

I had met my future husband, Troy. Previously, Troy had served as a U.S. Navy SEAL. Post military, he became part of elite security details in Africa and the Middle East. At a certain point, he had started to feel that peace could not be made at gunpoint and wanted to explore alternatives to conflict resolution.

That change of heart led him to Fairfield to learn the TM technique and study sustainability. As CEO of Ideal Energy, Troy continues his personal mission in working to create an abundant world, where wars to secure resources are unnecessary.

How Ideal Energy began

In my construction days, we often had visitors coming to the Eco-Village asking if we could help them with solar and other eco-friendly building projects. Troy had served on the Fairfield Go Green commission initiated in 2008 by Mayor Ed Malloy, where he helped write the strategic sustainability plan for the city of Fairfield. Participating in this taskforce inspired him to start Ideal Energy, which would help implement emerging technologies like energy-efficient lighting and solar energy.

The city and local businesses were committed to the plan, but there was no Iowa-based company offering this type of work. Seeing the opportunity in Fairfield, with a community excited about sustainability, we started Ideal Energy. Even if the market wasn't there yet, we wanted to open a business and position ourselves to grow the industry.

Troy and I are dreamers. I don't remember even having a business plan, but Troy has reminded me that we did. At the start, Ideal Energy did a variety of projects, in which Troy and I did every job the business required. We began with a demonstration project in Alaska and with contract work from the City of Fairfield. The Fairfield Go Green commission had us conduct a carbon emission baseline report, which was used to set the city's milestones for energy efficiency, renewable energy, and lowering its carbon footprint. The City of Fairfield also hired us to make content for the Go Green website and to write a user guide that the city mailed to every Fairfield household. It was groundbreaking in 2009 for a town of 10,000 to send its citizens educational materials on best practices for energy conservation and recycling.

We formed Ideal Energy to educate Iowans about renewable energy and energy efficiency. While renewable energy is highly attractive because it's so visible, energy efficiency remains our foundation. We install solar only after we conduct a detailed energy audit. As we try to zero out the client's utility bills, we might start our work by changing the lighting, recommending efficient appliances, and upgrading the insulation. We have reduced energy requirements for clients as much as 30% before installing solar.

As incentive programs kicked in for Iowa, solar became economically viable for residents, businesses and communities. With incentives, a business could have a five- to seven-year payback on solar, something any intelligent entrepreneur would be interested in.

We also looked at wind, but wind has lots of problems with warranty issues and maintenance. Moving parts break. High winds mean turbines need maintenance at least once a year. Every few years, the blades must come off and be rebuilt.

As it happened, my father was one of our first solar clients, and he actually installed the first commercial solar installation in the state of Iowa. The project was inspired by one of his tenants, Genetic ID, who wanted their business to be powered by clean energy and was willing to renew a long-term lease with this differentiator.

We are fortunate to have our business based in the progressive, open-minded community of Fairfield. Clients knew my family background in construction and respected Troy for his military training. Our first big year in solar was entirely for early-adopter businesses and community centers in Fairfield.

To sell our projects, we created a 25-page, investment-grade proposal for clients that anyone with a financial background could understand. We were very clear about how the project cash flowed, how incentives could be used, and what returns could be expected going 25 years forward. This helped build confidence with our clients.

In our early days, I did the bookkeeping. Fortunately, we were able to recruit my sister Katie as the Ideal Energy Chief Financial Officer (CFO). In Los Angeles for seven years, Katie had worked as a small business financier, planner, and manager, consulting for dozens of different companies. Katie applied her experience and expertise to growing our business in both finance and operations. With a shortage of electricians in the state, Katie helped us set up the first state-certified apprenticeship program through a solar company to train our own electricians. She recently left us to grow Jefferson County Ciderworks, her own Fairfield entrepreneurial venture.

We have our own engineering teams, construction teams, and electricians. Doing everything we possibly can in-house differentiates us from our competitors. By doing tasks in-house, we gain expertise that we build on. Our crew continually comes up with new and better ways to do things.

We pride ourselves as leaders in the Iowa solar industry. We developed resources to help the public, business, and government understand the industry better. We educate Iowa legislators about the many benefits to renewable energy, best practices for electrical code, and solar tax incentives. We train local fire departments on safety protocol with solar-powered buildings.

As the first active Iowa solar company, we were able to catch an aggressive wave of solar growth. Often we doubled the number of installations from the previous year, reinvesting the revenue into the business. We're now pioneering the battery energy storage market in Iowa, which will be a game changer for our state's energy future. Working with the Iowa Economic Development Authority and the Fairfield Economic Development Association, we've created a state research grant to study emerging energy storage technology and it's many applications in our state.

Marketing Ideal Energy through the stories of our customers

Who are our ideal customers? How do we reach them? What do we want them to know about us? When prospective clients discover Ideal Energy, what do they see and how do they feel? Sales and marketing is the lifeline of any company and, as the Chief Marketing Officer, I am responsible to answer those questions.

As a part of a new industry, we have to build trust in our customers. We want our marketing to convey our dedication and professionalism in creating the best possible solar solution for each customer. Storytelling is the heart of our marketing strategy. We use the success of our clients to build momentum with a variety of media including print, online, and video. My department brings consistency by standardizing our branding and our messaging.

Rather than selling ourselves, we sell the success of our customers with their unique and captivating stories of how solar is benefiting their companies, employees, customers, and communities. We use video, photography, and the written word to make the stories as real, vivid, and vibrant as possible.

Our customer success stories span manufacturing, educational institutions, government, residential, and agricultural operations. We tell the stories in one-page information sheets, brochures, and videos that we feature on our website. When our sales team presents to a client, they refer to customer stories relevant to the client's industry, community, and demographics.

The first thing we want these stories to do is to change the thinking of customers from "I must pay utility bills each month" to "I can pay for energy upfront and, in the case of a large electric user, potentially save millions of dollars."

For example, we have written about, photographed, and created a video about Steffensmeier Welding & Manufacturing, the first manu-facturing business in Iowa to go 100% solar. A touching story, Jenny Steffensmeier inherited the business when her husband passed away. She had five kids and had been a nurse and radiologist assistant. Men who had worked for her husband for 20 years made up the welding operation.

Shortly after taking over, she installed a solar field. Our installation team heard employee grumblings: "It won't work. We're never going to see anything from this." We were there the day that Jenny got her first utility bills after she fully switched to solar. Her bills went from $9,000 to $13 a month.

With the projected savings of $100,000 a year, attitudes quickly changed. Jenny added dental and vision to her employees' health care plan, enrolled three men in advanced training, and introduced another equipment line.

Given greater public awareness about climate issues, companies can use their solar installation as part of their value proposition. For example, a university might publicize their solar energy installation to attract a particular kind of student. My team helps companies make solar part of their brand. During the selling process, we determine if the customer will benefit from a video and other publicity.

Our video storytelling focuses on the client and their success with using solar energy. Video is a captivating medium because people love to share good stories. Our customers share their videos with their colleagues and community and often place the video prominently on their website, which ultimately helps us earn referrals.

We place a lot of attention on getting earned media coverage for Ideal Energy. A story printed by a trusted media outlet about a manufacturing company using solar and saving $100,000 a year creates more genuine interest than a paid Ideal Energy ad. We're always looking for new outlets in the media.

We also look for award opportunities as part of our marketing. We received several awards for a Fort Madison project, including the 2016 Project of the Year Award from a national publication, *Solar Builder*.

Companies like Jenny Steffensmeier's are proactive in using their solar installation for PR. We've had Iowa Governors, Terry Branstad and Kim Reynolds, and President Obama's Secretary of Agriculture, Tom Vilsack, give speeches at solar installations.

I work to keep our messaging consistent across all media. I believe that a small discrepancy can cast doubt in the mind of a potential customer. I'm very particular about our branding, including the fonts, the colors, and the language we use as a company. I never want the consumer to see something misaligned and take that as a subtle cue that something is not right. I want everything we produce to be clean and clear and represent light and sunshine. We chose a color palette of orange and blue to stand for the boldness and vibrancy of solar energy. We use a clean, utilitarian font with a youthful edge as we compete with 100-year-old utility companies.

We approach our employees as we do our customers, communicating with them professionally, clearly, and consistently. When new employees start at Ideal Energy, we educate them on professional communication. As a non-partisan company, we do not align with a political party because we believe that solar is the way forward for everyone. Every day, we're servicing customers with a variety of beliefs and political backgrounds. We view renewable energy as a technology that can bring humanity together and shouldn't drive us apart.

I believe visual communication to be most effective, and maybe that's from my background in the arts. I believe in "show rather than tell," so we put a lot of work into our photography and company visuals. I look for vibrancy and consistency, nothing too dark. We take most of our pictures in the mid to late fall, when the light is naturally very warm, especially around sunset. In our photography we show employees wearing Ideal Energy gear, and clients in their natural environment, which makes images look personal rather than stock.

We have an ever-growing library of brochures and educational pieces at Ideal Energy, which we update often. We use a Statement of Qualifications for our utility clients and government entities, with dedicated brochures for educational institutions, commercial operations, and residential customers. We use real case studies in all of our work to emphasize how solar and battery energy storage technology is positively impacting the lives of our clients.

The sales process

Our primary customer base is large electric users, with a focus on the manufacturing industry. Most of these customers aren't aware that they can benefit from solar energy. With our outreach programs, potential clients come from our website, magazine articles, referrals, word of mouth, and white papers.

When we began, we were one of two or three Iowa-based solar companies. Today, with 45 solar companies in Iowa we might bid on a job in competition with a half dozen others, but, as a result of our seniority and ongoing efforts, we are one of the the largest solar providers in Iowa and implement some of the most innovative installations in the Midwest. We focus on quality, which is why we're not the low-priced leader, and not afraid of our higher price tags.

I work with the sales team to create scripting and visuals for their sales presentations. When we bring on a new salesperson, they perform many practice runs. We train salespeople to keep things positive and not use fear or pressure-based selling.

Our sales process starts with a complementary consultation where we analyze a customer's utility bills, tax appetite, and available incentives, and then produce a one-page estimate of costs and payback. We usually get within five percent of the number we quote.

If those numbers work for the client, we offer an engineering study. The study costs start at $1,000 and go upward from there, depending on the project scope. In the engineering study, we carefully examine every detail of the client's energy profile, which is especially important for large electric users. For these customers, we might need to understand the cycling of their equipment, their manufacturing schedule, the times of large demand loads, seasonal changes, the number of shifts, break times, work avoidance on hot days, expansion plans, and so on. The savings estimate takes into account generators, batteries, and other technology we will install to help the client avoid costly demand charges with the utility. No other company in the state measures energy consumption and equipment cycling with the detail we do.

Projects for large electrical users involve millions of dollars in costs and benefits, so customers feel more comfortable with every detail scrutinized. We close 95% of the prospects that move to engineering studies, and the rate of clients opting for engineering studies is increasing.

We have staff dedicated to operations and maintenance in our office whose job is to routinely monitor the several hundred systems we've installed. We do annual physical inspections onsite as well. Everything we install comes with a strong manufacturer five-year warranty that covers parts and labor. After the Ideal Energy five-year warranty expires, we offer an operations and maintenance program, a continuation of our monitoring service, to keep production high. We describe the program at the initial sale, which gives customers confidence that they will be taken care of for the life of the system.

Politics and a challenging 2017

At the end of 2016, we had large projects ready to go that had been in the pipeline for over a year. By early 2017, changes from the state and federal government were causing uncertainty. Businesses put on hold their million-dollar energy installations, which made 2017 a challenging year for sales. Bombarded by local legislative battles, we also faced an environmentally regressive Trump administration that threatened trade tariffs that could double solar panel and steel prices. The Iowa legislature even considered applying extra fees for solar installations already grandfathered into current rates.

Entrepreneuring gets real when faced with these types of problems. Regardless of the challenges, our team persevered, showing up each day with solutions.

When we started Ideal Energy, we knew that we couldn't just sit back and wait for the government or regulators to move the industry forward, and we maintain a high degree of political involvement. During the legislative season, Troy, myself, or a company representative will go to the state capital in Des Moines almost weekly to meet with legislators. From early on in our company, we talked to politicians, worked on legislation, invited legislators to tour our installations, and made sure they understood the benefits of our state's growing solar industry.

Our non-partisan political solar work and Troy's elite military background have helped magnify our involvement. We have been invited to the White House a number of times to meet with senior energy staff, and also participated in the United Nations COP21 in Paris, France.

We developed a good relationship with our Iowa Governor, Kim Reynolds, who has visited several of our projects, and has helped fight to protect solar policy.

Iowa's growing solar industry often lacks a well-funded lobbying organization to defend it. That means lobbying efforts fall on the shoulders of business owners and a few small organizations who must continuously monitor proposals that could negatively impact our industry.

MUM's one megawatt solar array

From our inception, installing a large-scale solar array for MUM had been our fantasy project. Starting in 2015, we began conceptual designs for a megawatt installation. With the generous support and guidance from Trustee Tom Factor, we completed an installation in late fall of 2018. The 1.1 megawatt Maharishi University of Management Solar Power Plant is the first solar installation to combine active tracking technology and vanadium-flow battery energy storage in the U.S. The system uses an intelligent tracker control system that allows each individual row to move independently to compensate for shading, weather conditions, and the topography of the site in real time. Robust vanadium-flow battery technology is high-performing and does not degrade over time. Installed in 2018, this is one of the most technologically advanced solar installations in the nation.

The new solar and storage power plant brings the University's renewable energy share to around 43%. By combining active tracking technology with battery energy storage MUM will cut its utility costs by a projected 30%.

The future

Iowa has some of the least expensive electrical rates in the country for general users like homeowners and small businesses. However, we also have some of the country's highest demand charge rates for large electric users. A recent report from the National Renewable Energy Lab (NREL) estimates that there are 23,000 large electric users in Iowa alone that can benefit from peak demand reduction with the use of battery energy storage.

The report ranks Iowa among the top 10 states in the nation to benefit from combining large-scale solar and battery storage for demand reduction and peak shaving. This has been a big area of growth for our company in the past year.

WISDOM: Integrate your values into the company culture

WE POSTED OUR VALUES

After some years doing the business, Troy and I took some quiet time to clarify our values. We posted them on our website for our customers and employees to see. We consciously integrate those values into Ideal Energy operations to help shape the company culture.

Our Values

At Ideal Energy, we look beyond profitability. We measure our success through our customer's satisfaction, the impact we have on the environment, our ability to work as a team, and our contribution to our local community.

Teamwork

We view our team as family and work together to meet our goals.

We celebrate our successes and take responsibility for our mistakes. We're always learning.

We believe in the creative potential of each team member, and we encourage creative problem solving.

We focus on building strong relationships both internally as a team and externally with our customers and vendors.

We believe that achieving sustainability is a group effort that involves working with vendors, customers, communities, utility companies, and government officials to find solutions.

Exceeding Customer Expectations

Our goal is to exceed our customers' expectations every step of the way.

We strive to communicate clearly with our clients and respond promptly to customer service needs.

Our customers are our family. We look after their property as if it were our own.

Creating Affordable Solar Solutions

Our goal is to make clean energy accessible and affordable.

We're eternal students, always studying cutting-edge technologies and methods, streamlining our processes, and increasing efficiency.

We educate ourselves on upcoming incentives and financial opportunities that will improve our customers' return on investment (ROI).

We work hard at becoming more efficient and keeping costs down. We never build extra costs into installations.

Safety and Quality Workmanship

We take great pride in the quality of our work and we stand behind our products and installations.

We engineer our systems to the highest standards, accounting for harsh weather conditions like hail and high winds.

We invest in the training and education of our team so that we can continue to offer industry-leading products and service.

We install tier-one products, which boast the best system performance and durability. Our products have the longest lifecycles and warranties available in the solar industry today.

We Are Creative Thinkers & Embrace Change

We're a team of trailblazers. We're not afraid to challenge the status quo.

We embrace change and rise to the occasion with creative solutions.

We resolve to learn, grow, and improve our process every day.

We're Doing Our Part

Making the world a better place is our business, and we're passionate about what we do.

We contribute financially and volunteer our time to complete projects that make our local community more vibrant and economically resilient.

We believe in the power of clean energy. We're here for the long haul.

Community Involvement

We're dedicated to transforming our homebase community of Fairfield, IA into a thriving, sustainable urban habitat through job creation and sustainability efforts. Ideal Energy serves on the Mayor's Go Green Commission for the City of Fairfield, and helped author the Strategic Go Green Plan for the City of Fairfield.

We continually participate in a range of our city's projects, and help fund clean energy initiatives such as solarizing our local public library.

Operating as a team

As a husband and wife team, Troy and I make sure we communicate with each other clearly, openly, and honestly. We talk things out in real time, never harboring grudges. We always strive to respect and support each other, even if we don't always agree.

We strive for excellence as a company, and often use the saying "Good enough is not good enough."

There's a big difference between just installing solar at somebody's business and building a lasting relationship with the customer. This requires our team to offer seamless customer service on a continuous basis. Solar is incredibly complex, and is a high-touch sales process. Our company is a team comprised of sales personnel, finance experts, tax equity experts, designers and engineers, project managers, electricians, installers, and field technicians. We all work to provide a consistant, quality experience to our customers.

Creativity, profits, and new product launches make entrepreneurship fun. Yet, it's not always glamorous, and it's mostly hard work. Perseverance is key.

Our company has learned how to deal with pressure. Often, we are under rigid deadlines. Other times we have taken on a new type of project that challenges everyone to meet our self-imposed high standards.

We strive to take excellent care of our hardworking employees, and provide a good quality of life. We recently switched to a four-day work week for our office staff.

Family, the Fairfield community, and TM

My parents moved to Fairfield with big dreams. My father built his success from the ground up, and has been generous with sharing his lessons in entrepreneuring with my sister, myself, and Troy. We've spent many years mulling over thoughts about construction, contracts, and other business matters together.

Coming from a family business, I would find it strange not to be close to the people I work with. Yes, family can bring difficult issues; family also brings loyalty, security, and trust.

We would not be what we are today without the Fairfield entrepreneurial community. I have found that our talented local entrepreneurs love helping a growing business. Fairfield's many successful entrepreneurs, like Chappel Studio's Joe Mandarino, Global ID's Ken Ross, and Skyfactory's Bill Witherspoon, have contributed to our foundational, employee-oriented Ideal Energy infrastructure.

The people who ascend to top management positions at Ideal Energy have a high degree of emotional intelligence. When situations arise, they slow down and avoid reacting emotionally. They are able to go to the calm, centered place within and find the best solution. I value this in my life as well, and always use my morning Transcendental Meditation practice as a time to begin the day centered.

SPIRIT: Find meaning in your work

I'm lucky that I have creative flexibility in the work that I do. As an entrepreneur, I also do all sorts of things that I don't prefer, such as looking at spreadsheets, paying bills, and solving human resource problems. But it is so worth it. I love telling customer stories. I report how their lives changed, and I see how those changes impact our employees.

At our company, I am responsible for every customer touchpoint, and I love designing and refining our customer experience. I've transformed my days as a studio artist into something more dynamic, more functional. I am motivated to continually find new ways to engage and excite our customers around our changing energy paradigm, and excited about what the future will bring.

Amy Van Beek's twelve tweets

1. We post our company's values on our website and integrate those values into Ideal Energy operations to help shape the company culture.

2. We use mistakes as opportunities to grow and learn. As a team, we discuss lessons learned and how to continually improve our operations.

3. Switching to a four-day work week has allowed our employees to enjoy greater quality of life and achieve a better work-life balance.

4. Good enough is not good enough. We always strive for the highest level of quality.

5. We measure our success through our customer's satisfaction, the impact we have on the environment, our ability to work as a team, and our contribution to our local community.

6. Perseverance is key. When challenges are great, we remind ourselves of the big vision, why we started the company.

7. People who ascend to top management have a high degree of emotional intelligence. When situations arise, they slow down and avoid reacting emotionally.

8. We use vivid storytelling to bring our client's journey to life.

9. We are passionate about creating the world that we want to reside in. We talk to politicians, work on legislation, invite legislators to tour our installations, and make sure they understand the benefits of solar energy.

10. In our proposals, we provide customers our most conservative projections. We prefer to surprise and delight our customers when their installations are performing better than projected.

11. By doing everything we possibly can in-house, we gain expertise that we build on. We are always coming up with new and better ways of doing things.

12. I love the dynamism and creativity of building things, of seeing design take form in three dimensions. The art I do is functional and serves a purpose. It allows me to incorporate my passion for sustainability to make a difference.

Ponder

1. Amy posted the company's values on their website. Ideal Energy uses them as standards for their internal operations and for working with customers. What are your values? How important are they to you? Would you be willing to make them explicit, so your customers, employees, and suppliers can see them?

2. Amy describes the slogan, "good enough is not good enough," as a standard for Ideal Energy. How do you relate to the idea? Is good enough sometimes good enough?

3. One of the company's values measures success not by profit but by customer satisfaction, environmental impact, teamwork, and contribution to Fairfield. How do you measure success?

4. Family atmosphere and family business is a theme in Amy's story. Amy says Troy thinks big, while she likes to focus on details. Could you, would you, go into business with your loved ones? What are the pros and cons? Could you make the natural differences work for you?

Tom Kimbus, Executive VP Solar Energy Industries Association; Jenny Steffensmeier, Steffensmeier Welding and Manufacturing; *Iowa Governor Kim Reynolds*; Troy Van Beek; Amy Van Beek; Iowa Lt. Governor Gregg; and Mary Sundblad, Stuff Etc. Quality Consignment

Award-winning transformation of ready-for-landfill schoolhouse into solar-powered apartments, Madison, Iowa

Troy and Amy Van Beek at 1.1 Meg MUM inauguration, Dr. John Hagelin behind Troy

Indoor portion of inaguration ceremony for MUM 1.1 Megawatt solar panel and storage array. On stage from left to right: U.S. Congressman Dave Loebsack; Fairfield Mayor Ed Malloy, Troy and Amy Van Beek; Benefactor and MUM Trustee Tom Factor. Off camera and speaking, MUM President Dr. John Hagelin.

Troy Van Beek
FROM NAVY SEAL TO SOLAR ENERGY CEO

Troy Van Beek spent over 12 years working elite security details in Asia, Africa, and the Middle East. After a successful Navy SEAL Team career he co-founded a high-risk personal protection company and was the lead sniper for a detail protecting Hamid Karzai, the president of Afghanistan. Over time, Troy became aware of the humanitarian and environmental problems surrounding carbon-based energy sources. He also realized that pointing guns at people didn't bring positive, peaceful change.

Troy returned to the States and enrolled in Maharishi University of Management, where he began practicing the Transcendental Meditation technique. At MUM, he pursued a degree in Sustainability Studies and learned about energy alternatives that could increase global security and create a healthier planet.

Troy and his wife-to-be, Amy, saw the opportunity to bring solar technology to the forefront and help build the solar industry from the ground up. Together, they founded Ideal Energy in 2009, one of the first dedicated solar energy firms in Iowa.

During the Obama administration, Troy spoke to the Energy Department at the White House and participated in the climate talks in Paris. By 2018, Ideal Energy was the leading Iowa solar company, having installed hundreds of systems for homeowners, businesses, the government, and educational institutions. Ideal Energy estimates that their solar installations have prevented hundreds of thousands of metric tons of CO_2 from entering the atmosphere and saved customers tens of millions of dollars.

JOURNEY: Keeping the world safe as a Navy SEAL warrior and a solar power entrepreneur

NAVY SEAL SNIPER

I joined the Navy SEAL Teams, the elite United States Navy "Sea, Air, and Land Teams," to evolve as a person and make a difference.

After nine years as a SEAL, I served as the lead sniper on a high-risk, personal protection detail for Hamid Karzai, the president of Afghanistan. Over 40 people on our team helped keep safe one of the most wanted-dead individuals on the planet. Around the clock, we dealt with car bombs and the possibility of people walking into restaurants with explosives. We lived 90-miles-an-hour with our hair on fire.

One day we were driving through a crowded market area in Afghanistan, too populated and too confined for comfort. As our armored vehicles squeezed through, a radio call told us that one of our vehicles had been separated. Pulling out of the motorcade, I got out to assess the situation. I saw a police officer on his radio looking right at us. In front of me, heavily armed militia were stepping off their vehicles.

I realized the cops were not on our side and we were about to be on the wrong end of a shooting gallery. An accompanying government agent panicked. Our team leader took command. I secured my weapon.

Time stood still.

I suddenly found myself at an earlier moment in the day. We had been driving at high speeds to a recon site when a little girl, about four years old, stepped out in front of our vehicle. I recoiled in anticipation of the sound of a thud off the vehicle's front reinforced bumper.

I looked behind and saw her standing on the far side of our vehicle, having just missed the Humvee behind us. I couldn't understand how she survived. I felt as if she had passed right though me. Grabbing the driver, I said, "Did you see that?" The driver shrugged, not comprehending what I was saying.

I tried to shake off the memory. I felt hollowed out by the experience.

As I lifted my gun, an idea hit me: that little girl was a message from beyond the veil. Death was very close. My heart dropped as this realization took hold. In the nanosecond it took to realize this I also knew I would not go down without a fight. I slipped my finger onto the trigger ready to take down the first person.

I made eye contact with one of the militia pointing an RPG at me. He had one shot. He looked at me and I at him. He stepped back, knowing I was about to shoot. I split my attention between him and the high-power machine gun that was my second highest threat.

Then, out of the corner of my eye, I saw an Afghan general storming toward me from the vehicle left behind. He slapped down my muzzle. The general was screaming in Afghani, "Big mistake, big mistake, big mistake!" The militia thought we had been coming for their leader, and they came to execute us. The general managed to calm everyone down, and we narrowly made it out with our lives.

Later, after nine years in the SEALs, I moved to Africa where I helped found Ridgeback, a company specializing in high-risk personal protection. There, we also trained VIPs and UN officials on security issues.

One day in Africa on my way to a business meeting, wearing a suit and carrying a lot of money, I was stopped in traffic. A man stuck his mud-filled hand in the car window holding a glass bottle. He said he would break it on my face if I didn't give him 50 shillings (12 cents).

I said, "OK," and reached into my pocket, feeling the big wad of cash I was carrying. I didn't want to miss my meeting and wondered how I was going to get out of the situation. Having taught hand-to-hand combat in the military, I felt I could easily take him. I knew whoever this was, I would be faster and I could knock him backwards before he even knew what happened. But then I caught the smell. It wasn't mud, but feces in his hand. And when I looked at his face I saw the most depraved image of a man I had ever seen. His eyes were completely bloodshot. There was literally foam coming out of his mouth. If I were to break the skin on my hand hitting him I might die of whatever was killing him.

I found a 50 and told him, "Here you go."

Having seen the wad, he said, "No, give me a thousand."

At that moment the traffic opened up. I floored the gas pedal. Boom. He spun off my car and was gone.

That incident changed me forever.

In Afghanistan and Africa, I wanted to make a difference. I did so by holding a gun, which didn't always settle well. Seeing the destruction of war and destitute people caused me to look in other directions. As my perspective broadened, I started considering different ways to impact world security.

I had spent all that time in Afghanistan and now was building this company in Africa. I saw the separation. I thought we could fix this and started talking with my business partner: "Is there anything we can do? How can we get involved?"

My partner replied that we were there to start a security company, not save the world. He needed me to work on the company. But I kept finding ways to bring up living conditions. Finally, my partner said, "Troy whatever you do, you'll be great at it." Badly needing to hear that, I dropped everything and transitioned back to the States.

To become a better person, I had chosen the SEALs, the most rigorous entry-level branch of the military. To evolve further, I started focusing on my spiritual side and ended up in Fairfield, meditating and working on sustainability.

MUM, TM, and sustainability

My transition brought me to the States, something within drawing me to investigate my spiritual side. While in Africa, I had googled "enlightenment," and Fairfield appeared. Further, Fairfield's Maharishi University of Management (MUM) had the first four-year degree in sustainability.

In 2006, on a trip to see family in Michigan, I detoured south to Fairfield to visit MUM. I found Fairfield amazing. People everywhere were discussing spirituality and their personal evolution. I soon enrolled at MUM in its sustainability program. To this day, the influx of people coming to MUM to better themselves and the world inspires me.

My interest in sustainability came from noticing that most problems in the Middle East had to do with conflict around scarce, non-renewable resources. When I told my friends and parents about getting a degree in sustainability, nobody knew what I was talking about. Even the university was not fully committed.

As a soldier, I had fought for others' freedom and safety to make the world a better place. I came to realize that for positive peaceful change I had to start with me. At MUM, I meditated with the TM technique, deepening my spirituality while immersing myself in sustainability studies. I saw sustainability as an expression of my spirituality.

Compared to the previous 12 years, being at MUM was like walking on the moon. Slowly, I acclimated to the peaceful MUM campus. The grip of the past began to ease. MUM gave me the ability to defragment my brain and body and take in a whole new world of possibilities. I dove into the MUM curriculum and its understanding of how consciousness connects me with everything.

The university was just starting to invest in its own sustainability, and I realized that it wasn't living up to its talk. I decided to drop out of school but didn't want to leave the field of sustainability. From my military training I realized that if I didn't see leadership I had to lead.

The Sustainable Living Department wanted students to develop their educational track. MUM had put the department in an old science wing. A buddy from class, Robbie Gongwer, and I became general contractors for the school. We started implementing projects we had been working on. And I appreciated how the university supported me as my ideas evolved.

We installed a student-built wind turbine that powered a classroom. I built a bio-diesel processor that created revenue for the university. We installed skylights in all the science wing classrooms and offices, reducing lighting costs by 95%. We put in a garage door and created a micro-enterprise center in an old science classroom. We now had a pretty cool Sustainable Living Department.

After six months, I returned to school. MUM gave me degree credit for some of the contract work, and I graduated in three years.

Amy and the Abundance EcoVillage

In Fairfield, I met Amy Greenfield, a Maharishi University of Management graduate. Amy was working with others to create one of the country's most innovative green communities, an off-the-grid sustainable community in the countryside near the campus. I picked up on Amy's passion for sustainable technologies and Maharishi Vastu Architecture. Amy's passion matched my interests and aspirations.

We married in Bali in 2012 and then lived in a cottage in Fairfield's thriving sustainability community, Abundance EcoVillage. Still maintaining a small environmental footprint, the village uses sustainable materials. Two wind turbines and 88 solar panels provide almost all the electricity needed by Amy, me, and our 27 neighbors.

A brief history of Ideal Energy

I grew up in a town of 1,225 people and left right after high school. Before becoming a SEAL, I fished king crabs in Alaska, worked at a ski resort in Colorado, and drove a motorcycle across the country. As a civilian and later, as a soldier, I was always traveling with my bags packed.

Fast forward to my work implementing MUM campus sustainability projects. Fairfield Mayor Ed Malloy approached Professor Lonnie Gamble and me to take part in the 2008 Go Green strategic plan, a commission to implement sustainability for Fairfield.

I'm all about team, yet never realized what being part of a community meant. Fairfield and the university had already embraced me. The commission gave me the opportunity to meet Fairfield citizens and learn how Fairfield functioned. By helping make changes in Fairfield, I joined the community and became part of one large team.

We interviewed local business leaders asking if they would participate in sustainability plans that made business sense. If they said yes, they signed a pledge stating they would participate.

We came up with many possibilities. Unfortunately, there was no local business or government agency outside of the commission we were in to make them happen.

Back on campus, Lonnie Gamble inspired students with his ideas. He'd tell us, "That's worth a million dollars. Who's going to run with it?" One day he said, "Energy efficiency is the cornerstone of sustainability."

Taking the idea to Amy, I said, "Let's start an energy company."

Fairfield had a need and we could address it. In 2009, at the height of the recession, Amy and I started Ideal Energy to bring wind and solar power technology to homeowners, businesses, and the government so they could use clean energy and save money.

A professor helped us write a business plan. We calculated that in order to be profitable we had to bring in one million dollars of revenue the first year — which we did. I laughed thinking about Lonnie's one million dollar ideas.

I educated myself in energy efficiency, construction, building maintenance, and how it all worked together. I did energy audits for Fairfield homes and businesses until I was almost broke.

We recognized early on that solar was a good way to grow the business. Solar panels show immediate impact, passively producing energy with almost no maintenance.

I knew that the amount of solar energy reaching the Earth's surface in one year is about twice as much as what could be generated by all the Earth's non-renewable resources — coal, oil, natural gas, and mined uranium. An hour of solar energy could power the world for a year. We just have to learn to pick up the sunlight that falls onto the Earth more efficiently.

Extracting non-renewable resources from the Earth is costly to the consumer and to the environment. In contrast, once installed, consuming solar energy does not degrade the environment and costs nothing.

While taking classes at MUM, a group of Native Americans visited. They were looking for energy solutions for the 500 people of Angoon,

Alaska, a remote island about two hours from Juno. Much of the oil that the U.S. consumes comes from Alaska, but oil from the pipeline bypasses the southeast region of the state. Instead, diesel fuel gets shipped back to the state on barges with the ever-present danger of oil spills. Angoon residents could pay up to 10 times what we paid in Iowa for electricity. And with average monthly electric bills that reached $1,000 or more, they could no longer afford to live there, even with subsidies. Now, the government was contemplating relocation of these people who had lived on their island for 5,000 years.

After I graduated, we helped the Angoon group get a grant. They used the grant money to hire Ideal Energy to do an energy efficiency trial on one Angoon home.

Lonnie Gamble provided the knowledge and encouragement to test different approaches. Ideal Energy's first project, we weatherized the house, installed solar panels, created a solar hot water system, put up a wind turbine, and used more efficient appliances and lighting. Not taking weatherizing into account, we projected that $95,910 would be saved over the 25-year life of the system, and no diesel exhaust would poison the environment. A documentary of the Angoon experiment can be found on YouTube.

Back in Fairfield, we made presentations to local businesses. At the time, solar energy equipment was expensive, but with government incentives a customer could enjoy a five- to seven-year payoff due to lower utility bills.

We told prospective customers that we lived in the EcoVillage and that solar and wind entirely powered our home. We gave tours to show them the technology. "It's the middle of winter, and our lights are on."

The numbers made sense, and many meditating business owners were ready to move forward. I sold and installed all the solar systems. Amy did the marketing, website, and the other backend duties. I would work 24 hours straight. During the day, I would put on my hard hat and overalls in the dead of winter and install the arrays. At night I worked on proposals for the next jobs. Finally, Amy said, "Troy, stop."

I heeded Amy's advice. At any one time, I would focus either on installations or sales. While putting systems in, I wouldn't sell. We called this up and down cycle, the "solarcoaster." That first year of business, Ideal Energy installed solar panels producing 150 kilowatts of energy.

Here are some of Ideal Energy's achievements during the first ten years:

In 2012, Ideal Energy completed a breakthrough project, installing a 54,000-watt solar panel at Fairfield's Sky Factory, a producer of virtual skylights. In the summer, with higher sun and longer days, the company overproduced electricity, which it uploaded to the grid to earn credit. In the winter, with less sun, it drew off that credit. Annually, 100% of their energy needs were met. With incentives, they had a five- to six-year payback. It was the first light manufacturing plant in the state to be net-zero — no utility expense — when calculated annually. It woke people up that this could happen.

In 2013, Ideal Energy worked with a Fort Madison developer, converting an old high school into 38 energy efficient apartments, installing over 300 kilowatts of solar panels. The city initially wanted to demolish the building, which would cost about a half-million dollars. We helped the developer write grants that featured solar. That job allowed us to take on more employees, many of whom are still with us today. The installation demonstrated that the solar industry was taking hold in Iowa.

In 2015, we completed construction for Steffensmeier Welding & Manufacturing, which became the first entirely solar-powered manufacturing and fabrication business in Iowa. From this installation, over a 25-year period 9,000 metric tons of CO_2 will not be expelled into the atmosphere. That equates to 230,000 trees planted. Each year, the company will save $92,000. That's 2.3 million dollars over the 25 years of operation.

In 2016, we installed a half-megawatt solar field array for Schaus-Vorhies Manufacturing in Fairfield. They have become the largest privately owned industrial solar installation in Iowa. The $1.2 million project would pay for itself within 5-6 years and cover 100% of the company's electrical needs on a net-annual basis.

Returning to our MUM roots, in 2018 we installed a 1.1-megawatt array on five acres of land adjacent to campus. The project included a one megawatt-hour-battery energy storage system. It is the most advanced operation of its kind in the Midwest.

The solar array generates enough power to meet one-third of MUM's annual electricity needs. In addition to those savings, the battery energy storage system decreases the demand surcharge tariff portion of MUM's utility bill by reducing electricity consumption during peak usage times such as hot summer days. Between 30% and 70% of the utility bill comes typically from these demand surcharges.

The sophisticated active tracking system follows the sun's path across the sky, yielding 20-25% more energy than a fixed tilt array. The MUM array is the first system in the Midwest to combine active tracking and battery energy storage on a large scale.

As the first solar installer in Iowa, we have received much recognition. From day one, we leveraged each victory and turned it into future projects. We document our work with videos, which we place on our website. The videos serve as PR for our clients, publicizing their success and their environmental stewardship.

I've been asked to the White House several times to speak to the Department of Energy. Amy and I were invited to go to Paris, France for climate talks where 196 countries came together to discuss solutions for our planet and our species.

We use the renown to accomplish bigger projects. We now tell prospective customers of our record and that we have been solving Iowa's energy problems for years. Ideal Energy has evolved into a premier Midwestern installation firm for renewable energies, mainly solar. We've installed about 95% of the solar systems in Fairfield and have expanded throughout Iowa and into Missouri, Illinois, and Minnesota.

We now target larger, commercial entities, since one large installation is more efficient with less paperwork than 100 smaller ones. We are always looking for special projects that sing. Our largest customers are environmentally responsible. Some require their suppliers to be the same way. These companies show courage and leadership, educating their industry and local residents. Working with such companies multiplies our effect of lowering utility bills and caring for the environment — and that brings us much satisfaction.

In the midst of its successes, Ideal Energy has spent much of its time on the solarcoaster with dramatic ups and downs. Government incentives come and go; the price of solar panels decreases and battery technology improves; entrenched utility companies lobby against our interests; moving from the Obama to the Trump era, the U.S. signs the climate change agreement and then pulls out; we grow so fast our systems break and are short on cash; we are on the verge of a huge success; we are waiting for complete collapse.

Even riding the solarcoaster, we see renewable energy as the future. Energy independence means a better economy, more jobs, and more opportunities. Renewable energy offers the peace and freedom that I fought for as a Navy SEAL.

How Ideal Energy works

When we started, Amy and I did everything — the marketing, analysis, proposals, sales, system design, and installation. As the business grew and became more complex, we added people and created business systems. Our standards of excellence and customer-centricity propelled the expansion.

As CEO of Ideal Energy, I oversee our operations, which centers around turnkey solutions for our customers. The customer signs a few documents and then watches us build a solar array that takes care of utility costs for the next 25 to 40 years.

Amy, originally an art major, heads marketing. She makes sure that any representation of Ideal Energy a customer sees is consistent, professional, and polished. Her purview includes the website, brochures, color and font choices, videos, slides, written proposals, and what we look like when we enter a room.

We were fortunate to recruit Amy's sister, Katie, who moved from Los Angeles to become Chief Financial Officer (CFO). Good CFOs are worth their weight in gold. Our CFO takes charge of our bookkeeping, keeps track of where we're spending money, shows how the business is growing, makes projections, and creates spreadsheet templates for customer presentations. The CFO's forecasts allow us to plan for cash flow shortages.

Customers start with a down payment and pay for their projects as we install them. Still, cash flow can be difficult. To grow we must hire, buy equipment, purchase vehicles, pay vendors, build internal infrastructure, and survive our mistakes. At times, Amy and I have used our real estate and other income to float the company.

It's a labor of love. I can't say that we're getting rich although that's always possible. We've grown our assets with a 30,000-square-foot building, lots of vehicles, inventory, and electrical equipment, but it's never easy. Whenever we get things well-tuned, the next curve ball comes. A climate-change-denying administration gets elected; the utility company wants to change the rules about the credit for energy put back on the grid; the threat of a larger solar company moving into our market looms in the background.

We don't like wasting anything. Yet, growing fast means holes in our pockets, deficiencies in our systems, and hard decisions under fire. As we progress, we've put better systems in place. We always invest in training employees so our teams can do top quality work.

We often commit to work that we haven't done before. And we always keep our promises, which means we can find ourselves throwing money at a project and straining cash reserves. One time, we promised to complete a job by the end of the year so the customer could earn a tax credit. The installation turned out to be a nightmare. The combination of mud, severe weather, and the problematic electrical interconnection made it grueling to complete the 430-kilowatt system on time. We hired extra people. I stayed on the job, working hard, cracking the whip.

We have a disciplined, well-trained sales staff that understands the issues. Amy's team develops the documents, slides, and the language that the sales staff use. Presentations reference my U.S. Navy SEAL background, which adds to company credibility.

A salesperson must explain the investment opportunity to the client clearly and concisely. Currently, the customer pays the energy bill without any return. We offer a return by moving the utility bill expenditure into something that has a payoff. In around five years for a business and 10 years for a resident, savings from lower utility bills pay off the investment. The client's significant initial investment can yield as high as a 20% to 30% or more internal rate of return.

A customer can call Ideal Energy and get a free evaluation to see if there's an opportunity. On the first contact, we describe our services, explain the technology, and answer questions. With 12 months of utility bills and the last 30 years of weather data, we can predict energy usage. From energy usage, we calculate how much roof and ground space we need for solar panels to cut utility costs. We can design a project using online satellite imagery without having to go onsite.

For clients ready to move forward, we have a team of designers who do all the specifications and 3-D renderings of the system. We give investment-grade presentations and a professional-looking 25-page agreement that the customer can show to the bank for financing. The document includes the design, the amount of power the system will generate, and a return on investment spreadsheet. We describe the videos and brochures we will create that document the industry and community leadership of the client.

To reassure larger clients, we hired one of the most reputable Iowa CPA firms. The firm examines the assumptions and the numbers in our agreements. We relay the CPA's conclusions during our presentation.

Finding a good contractor in small rural communities can be hard. For Ideal Energy to build respect, we decided to be the best contractor possible. We make the entire process, from presentation to implementation, as easy as possible for the client, taking away the headaches of an arduous process. We do all the design, permits, interconnection agreements, installation, and ongoing maintenance. With hundreds of thousands of dollars involved, we carefully negotiate the complexities with the utility company before the final design and installation.

We train everyone to be professional and represent the company well so customers can talk to anyone from Ideal Energy. Each of us can access the customer database, which we update with each contact. The project manager coordinates meetings between customers and our salespeople, electricians, engineers, designers, and installers.

We try to hire slowly and fire quickly. We vet prospective employees, collecting information and interviewing them individually and as a team. We've been lucky in getting quality people, which is not always easy. Exceptional people who like being part of a company that works for good gravitate towards us.

We have hired many MUM alumni and employ marketers, writers, designers, project managers, salespeople, engineers, building performance specialists, security professionals, social change experts, renewable energy consultants, architects, electricians, and installers. Our teams are ready to install vast arrays of solar panels.

We built a foundation for Ideal Energy in which creative people with drive can function. I love the creativity that many of the MUM graduates bring.

I ask our employees to double themselves. I tell them to make things easier for everyone and never be worried about working themselves out of a job. We're always looking for good people who can organize, communicate, and adapt. I also need detail-oriented people who get things done without much concern with the big picture.

We want people who understand technology and are willing to do whatever we need. Everyone must understand the financial opportunity for the customer. The more well-rounded, trained and experienced the employee, the better job he will do.

I might hire someone in finance and have her work in the field for the first few months. That gives her a more in-depth experience of how the company works. She might later become a sales manager, well-positioned to update the sales process. With different work experiences, employees are strong team members who appreciate others' responsibilities. Further, well-rounded employees communicate effectively with customers. Our employees want to make Ideal Energy successful and have taken ownership over their areas. I no longer have to shoulder all the responsibility.

I bring intensity, commitment, and the life and death experiences of a Navy SEAL to being the CEO of Ideal Energy. I seldom look back. I enjoy being present and in the flow. My work exhilarates me.

The sun can power everything, and we are proud of our contribution.

WISDOM: Lead

LEADERSHIP AND TEAM BUILDING

I have a passion for leadership. I'm hungry for it. Even the word empowers me.

Leadership means putting my heart and soul into what I do. I frequently ask myself: "Is what I am doing inspiring me? Am I a role model? Do I empower others to lead? Do I love my community as I love my home? Am I inspired to be a community leader?"

Leadership for me is about first finding the passion within and then cultivating it in those around me, getting them fired up, getting them to fully participate in what we are doing. Then we drive that passion out into the community, the city, the state, and into the world.

The work at Ideal Energy is hard. Yet, I wouldn't do anything else. Ideal Energy is where I'm meant to be. I love it. I am driven by it. My passion energizes me and makes the process flow. I can make decisions on the fly all day long. I love being in control and being able to relinquish control. I am okay with failure and learning from it.

Amy and I work day and night, non-stop. When we are at home, we promise not to talk about the business, but we do anyway. Often I wake up in the middle of the night to process something. On vacation, I am on the phone. So yes, life balance is a good thing, but it's not easy.

I credit my team building and leadership skills to the military. The SEALs beat "team" into me.

In basic training, I learned how to take care of myself, how to step in line, how to take orders. As I progressed through the military ranks, I learned how to give orders. I learned that giving away too much authority too soon can be detrimental. Too many cooks in the kitchen and too many people with ownership can bring disaster.

I learned that to lead, I must first take charge of my mind.

During one SEAL Teams training session, I sat at attention on the edge of a pool to make sure no one drowned. The instructors swarmed like sharks, creating tortuous situations for team members. One trainee at the end of a brutal interaction tried swimming towards me.

We locked eyes, and I didn't think he would make it. Rather than helping, an instructor gave him a rubberized brick and the man sunk to the bottom. The instructor turned to me, "You think he's coming back up?"

I looked at the water and saw an air bubble break the surface. "No, he's not coming up."

The instructor grabbed my mask and went for him. It seemed like forever. I helped the instructor get the man onto dry concrete. I thought, *There's nothing left in him; he's dead.* But the instructor revived him.

The first thing out of his mouth, the soldier says, "I'm not quitting!"

What willpower. He ingrained in his mind, "I'm not quitting." Leadership over his mind allowed him to come back from the blackness. His words remain with me and carry me through Ideal Energy's many challenges.

As a SEAL, I taught hand-to-hand combat and physically beat people. A mistake by the student meant harsh feedback. In civilian life, I have had to adjust my skills. Beating people down physically or emotionally doesn't work.

Amy and I couldn't do it all ourselves. We built a team that has become second only to my experience on the SEAL Teams. Our belief in the Ideal Energy mission drives us and drives our communication. By bringing our customers' utility bills to zero, we make a difference in the world. We use our passion for the mission to inspire employees and customers to join us.

A foreman and his team leaders take charge of installations. We avoid contracting out any of the work. That way, we control the quality of the project, and our solar expertise grows. We take on ambitious projects and break new ground. As we discover creative solutions, we help grow the industry.

We want to create a great company that brings wealth to our customers and our employees. We want to give employees security, knowing that we're doing it together. We are always evaluating business models that let employees feel more ownership in the company. It's a process.

Politics and the Climate Accord

The politics of solar and the energy paradigm shift play an essential role in our business. We joined the American Sustainable Business Council and Environmental Entrepreneurs. Both organizations focus on a healthy planet and healthy economics and allow us to be involved in politics without giving up all our time.

The organizations asked us to go to Paris, France, for the historic 2015 United Nations, 196-country climate change negotiations. Enthusiastically accepting, we represented Iowa-based renewable energy businesses by writing op-eds, participating in press conferences, and doing whatever to support the cause.

We have the opportunity to liberate everyone on the planet with inexpensive renewable energy. The change is coming, even though the old power structure is clawing at the walls. The old guard has pulled out of the climate agreement and is trashing environmental regulations. The utility companies want to eliminate some of the credit for energy that solar installations upload to the grid.

As citizens, we must stand up for ourselves and recognize that together we can move things in the right direction.

We're a PR company

We're not just a solar company, and the name "Ideal Energy" does not pigeonhole us. Given the evolving energy paradigm, we think in terms of selling a black box that takes care of all the energy needs of the customer.

We tell potential clients that we're not only a leading solar design and installation company, but also a premier PR and marketing company.

We say, "We look forward to you evaluating us and our proposal. Since we will do publicity for both our companies, we also need to make sure you are a good fit for us, especially given our busy schedule." Often the prospect starts selling us on what they can do for us. We consider this switch of roles "Ideal" selling.

Working with Amy

I love working with my wife. We're close and get along well. We understand and care for each other, knowing when to guide and when to nurture.

Amy plays a big part in our success. As a marketer, her detail-orientation and fantastic eye shape the Ideal Energy brand. Amy's team puts together the videos, the website, everything we show to the outside world.

We moved to a house across the street from the 30,000 square foot office headquarters, which means we're never separate from work. Our relationship evolves through our work together.

Amy and her family have been involved in construction for many years. Amy, her sister, her mom, and her dad worked in concert in their business. Amy is an amazing team player, who brings that strong family dynamic to our entire company.

I understand team. Amy brings maternal energy that makes for a nice balance. We care about our people and create a family environment. We supply hand warmers and extra gear for our workers in the field. Employees make breakfast in our stocked kitchen. Amy brings cooked treats, and we take people out for meals.

People respond to Amy, who cares for everyone. They like that Amy asks them to take pictures of their job locations for our website. Given our mission and family atmosphere, people take pride in working for Ideal Energy, and our reputation attracts strong people.

Amy is super smart and always there. She puts me in check and brings me back to earth. I respect and listen to her. When I say let's think big on this matter, Amy listens and respects me. It's a good balance.

Internal supercomputer

As CEO of Ideal Energy, I'm under constant pressure. The SEAL Teams gave me a background for living with stress. Transcendental Meditation practice gives me a way to manage and eliminate stress.

I run my business knowing that everything will change — the technology, the political environment, the competition, the market, my team — and I must consider the many variables that change brings. Should we branch out? Should we adopt a new technology? How do we deal with the political environment? Should I hire more people? How does it all fit together? I deal with change by starting the day with meditation.

During my TM practice, I digest the many variables that change brings. After the quiet of meditation, I watch the pieces arrange themselves. It's like having a supercomputer inside. I give it directions, and let the parts come together.

I think big — big about the planet, big about making the largest possible deal. Amy and I think globally and act locally. I credit much of my big-picture, detail-oriented capacity to quieting my mind in meditation.

The future

Our company operates in the challenging marketplace of evolving technologies and entrenched interests. To survive and prosper, we are always studying the market and planning our next move. With so many opportunities coming together quickly, we have to be smart and stay informed.

The energy transition is happening throughout the world. We have the expertise, the systems, the manuals, and the training to open up offices anywhere. While we might expand to asset-rich Iowa City, we also have a potential partner in Dubai, which has invested over 50 billion dollars into solar energy.

I make sure we diversify. When we are slow in solar, our team of electrical contractors serves the community in other ways. We are also looking at LED lighting, not just solar. Diversification will help us weather any storm.

Even though the solar industry employs more people than all the fossil fuel industries combined, I anticipate it will be rough for a while. I don't take anything for granted. We're ready for a fight but prefer to move forward and create as much low-cost energy as we can. Covering our bases, we even consider exit strategies if entrenched, powerful corporate and political interests come after us too aggressively.

The high cost of utilities in major coastal cities gave big solar companies their start. As of 2018, we believe that larger companies like Solar City will find a way to come to the Midwest — the last frontier.

When they come to smaller rural communities, they will muscle out the little guys. That's why I work so hard to build up our company. We must be a force to be reckoned with, or the competition will marginalize us. When Solar City does come, I understand that I might have to sell the company, and I'm okay with that.

With solar starting to cost less than fossil fuel, the utility companies want to work with us. We are always negotiating with utility companies, partnering on big installations. Those partnerships will make us more formidable when Solar City arrives.

We like staying ahead of the pack, but we're cautious. Each year, Ideal Energy employees go to solar power conventions. We analyze the latest technology and see how it is evolving. We listen to claims that this or that will revolutionize everything, but we use off-the-shelf products with strong warranties.

Three significant changes are coming that will help liberate humankind: free energy, automation including 3-D printing, and blockchain technology. (With blockchain, financial transactions between two parties can take place securely without a bank or other intermediaries.)

Robot-made, solar-powered vehicles will be built without significant energy or labor costs, dramatically reducing transportation costs. With abundant energy, robotic manufacturing, and free transportation, the cost of production decreases exponentially.

Computers will be able to 3-D print new types of substances that will store energy. Instead of solar panels, a home's siding and roofing will be made out of a material that absorbs the sun's energy. Cars won't have to have batteries since their frames will store energy.

Storing energy cost-effectively will be a game changer. We will use large-capacity, lithium batteries in our vehicles, homes, and businesses. (Lithium is abundant and comes out of the ocean.) With technological advances in batteries and the grid, homeowners and businesses will be able to use Bitcoin and other blockchain-based crypto-currencies to seamlessly transfer energy from solar installations to any location in the world. Blockchain payments and free energy allow businesses to offer their services throughout the planet for near zero marginal cost.

Much of the planet is arid desert. With abundant free energy, we can create channels and bring water anywhere on Earth.

Instead of an attitude of "let's build a wall and protect what we have," let's figure out how to provide for everyone. We are close.

SPIRIT: Make war no more

Having served in the military, gun in hand, I am driven to eliminate the need for war. In Afghanistan, it became clear to me that scarcity leads to conflict. Whether it's oil or some other resource, when someone lacks something, they will fight for it. Once solar panels are inexpensive and widely available, solar energy will have a dramatic effect in the Middle East where factions fight wars to control non-renewable energy resources.

Although many people think it impossible, I believe humankind will eliminate war. Everything changes when we harness the unlimited supply of energy from the sun. Automated factories running on free energy will produce goods that cost almost nothing to produce and transport.

Now, we are divided into the haves and the have-nots including the impoverished. The people in the top 10% consume most of the resources, which they want to hold onto. When abundance is available for everyone, there will be nothing to fight for. Having seen the ravages of war, the mission to eliminate war consumes me. I can work tirelessly, filled with passion and vigor for Ideal Energy.

In coming to Fairfield from the Navy SEALs, I found a pathway to peace by meditating every day and through harnessing the sun's energy for everyone on the planet.

Troy Van Beek's twelve tweets

1. I have a passion for leadership. I'm hungry for it. Leading means taking charge of my mind, putting my heart and soul into what inspires me, and never giving up.

2. Our belief in the Ideal Energy mission of eliminating war by bringing abundant energy into the world drives us and drives our communication with employees and customers.

3. As CEO of Ideal Energy, I'm under constant pressure. The SEAL Teams gave me a background for living with stress. Practicing Transcendental Meditation gives me a way to manage and eliminate stress.

4. During my TM practice, I digest the many variables that constant change brings to Ideal Energy. After the quiet of meditation, the pieces arrange themselves. It's like having a supercomputer inside. I give it directions and watch the parts come together.

5. We must be a force to be reckoned with or a larger entity will move in and marginalize us.

6. To make me to a better person I chose the SEALs, the most rigorous entry-level branch of the military. To evolve further, I started focusing on my spiritual side and ended up in Fairfield, meditating, and working on sustainability.

7. The amount of solar energy that reaches the Earth in one year is twice what could be generated by all the Earth's non-renewable resources — coal, oil, natural gas, and mined uranium. An hour of total solar energy could power the world for a year. We must learn to pick up the sunlight more efficiently.

8. We never want to waste anything. Yet, since we always keep our promises, we can end up throwing money at a project. Growing fast means holes in our pockets and deficiencies in our systems.

9. We avoid contracting out work. Self-sufficiency allows us to build our solar expertise and to control the quality of the project.

10. Giving away too much authority too soon can be detrimental. Too many cooks in the kitchen and too many people with ownership can bring disaster.

11. Exceptional people who like being part of a company that works for good gravitate towards us. Folks approach us fired up and willing to do whatever we need.

12. The more well-rounded, trained, and experienced the employee, the better job they do in their teams and communicating with customers.

Ponder

1. During Navy SEALS training, the first words of a soldier who almost drowned were, "I'm not quitting." How strong is your intention to not give up and make your business successful?

2. Troy says that in civilian life it doesn't work to beat people down physically or emotionally. When employees or suppliers make mistakes, how do you treat them?

3. Troy explains that his mission to end war through inexpensive energy inspires employees and customers. Do you have a mission? Do you use it to inspire others?

4. Most companies outsource jobs that are not core competencies and that others can do more efficiently. Troy chooses not to outsource because he wants to own the whole process and build internal skills. Where do you stand?

5. Troy says he has a passion for leadership. Do you? How do your feelings about leadership affect your business?

Above left: Seeing ravages of war was a major motivating factor for Troy Van Beek in starting Ideal Energy

Above right: Troy Van Beek: "War is a matter of scarcity. As energy becomes abundent, we will eliminate scarcity and eliminate the need for war. That is my mission."

Left: Troy joined the Navy SEAL Teams to help protect people

1.1 megawatt, five-acre, 3150 solar-panel Maharishi University of Management solar power plant. White encased battery storage in middle

Conclusion:
Inner Peace, Outer Abundance
WHAT EACH ENTREPRENEUR TAUGHT US

The 15 featured meditating entrepreneurs shared what they learned launching their businesses, selling their products, and structuring their operations. Like colors of the rainbow and flavors of fruit, the businesses, personalities, and main messages of the entrepreneurs differ.

Fred tells us that hard work is a fraud — the secret to success is to have fun. (Play for success.)

Janet teaches that we can live a purposeful life by following our dreams and choosing in favor of our passions. (Follow your passion.)

Ed demonstrates how disparate factions can work together on common goals to create a great community. (Unite with a shared vision.)

Betsy explains that with clear intention, we can manifest our vision. (Create through thought.)

George makes a business of his art by putting service ahead of ego. (Be of service.)

Ron maintains a community of artists tasked with bringing celestial art to the world. (Bring Heaven to Earth.)

Jim pleases people by photographing their greatest accomplishments. (Make people happy.)

Steven bypasses emotions and goes deep within to create success. (Stamp your intentions on the infinite.)

Monica provides the structure, organization, and persistence required to turn big ideas into big business. (Create structure.)

Peter shows the importance of people-centricity in business. (Put people first.)

Eva applies her writing skills and lifelong learning habit to create an internet-based teaching business. (Be a pro.)

In my publishing company, I demonstrate the power of integrity and wanting to improve the lot of others. (Uplift others.)

Francis turns his dairy farm into one large science experiment to help make food production life-sustaining. (Experiment with life.)

Amy taps into her artist's nature to communicate stories of solar energy success. (Use customer victories to market.)

Troy applies his Navy Seal training to become a warrior for abundant solar energy and world peace. (Lead for greatness.)

Common threads emerge through their stories:

- Fred and Janet implore us to follow our bliss.

- Betsy and Steven teach us to get clear on what we want and then commit to it.

- Monica and Eva remind us to do the necessary foundational work.

- George, Jim, Peter, and I invite us to serve others.

- Ron, Francis, and Amy inspire us with the power of the big idea.

- Ed and Troy demonstrate that accomplishing anything great requires a team, leadership, and a common purpose.

By combining all these messages, we learn that successful entrepreneurs lead by living their passion, mastering the basics, creating with intention, serving others, and thinking big.

WHAT THE ENTREPRENEURS HAD IN COMMON

In addition to the passion, will, and desire to serve, we practiced the Transcendental Meditation technique. Several thousand of us each day experienced pure consciousness — the stillness within.

Maharishi explained that pure consciousness is the field of all possibilities, the unified field, the fundamental essence from which all thought and matter emerge. We brought the experience of that quiet, non-disturbed peace to the frenetic activity of our businesses.

We were confident, motivated, flexible, and fortunate to live in a community of comradery, trust, and common purpose.

Confidence

During daily TM practice, we transcended the doubt and turbulence of our minds and the outer world and experienced peace and silence. After meditating, we believed that we could accomplish anything we set our minds to and that we could surmount any obstacle.

Many of us in our 20s spent months in long meditation and watching videos of Maharishi. Our confidence grew as we went out and taught the TM program, which meant lecturing to groups, educating CEOs and high-level government officials about TM, and creating independent self-sustaining *TM* Centers. By the time we moved to Fairfield, we were used to stretching our comfort zones and entering new arenas without prerequisite knowledge or experience.

Motivation

Motivation shows up as passion and persistence, the two required traits for any kind of success. In Fairfield, we were motivated by the need to earn a living, by our desire for self-realization and to create an influence of peace, and by wanting to share our passion through our business.

The TM technique nourished our enthusiasm from the inside. Meditating is like pulling the arrow back, deep within our minds, and becoming familiar with the most powerful levels of thinking where creation arises. After meditation, we aimed the arrow at our target, applying our creative potential to our businesses.

Flexibility

Fairfield meditating entrepreneurs demonstrated great flexibility — the ability to turn the challenges of fast, always-changing marketplaces into opportunities. We adapted so that operating from isolated, small-town, pre-internet Iowa became an advantage with its low-cost housing, inexpensive labor force, and community of meditators.

Practicing the TM technique expanded our awareness, allowing us to see the big picture. That larger perspective allowed us to be flexible and see possibilities.

Community

Business is a communal process where people work together, pooling their talents, efforts, and skills. In need, we could call a meditating lawyer, accountant, or plumber. In addition, farm and manufacturing-based Iowa provided a hard-working, well-educated, and honest workforce.

Good fortune

No business can succeed without good fortune. We were able to create the foundation for luck through an attitude of service, generous spirits, strong commitment, and regular TM practice.

10 WAYS TO DEVELOP YOUR ENTREPRENEURIAL MUSCLES

How can you apply what you learned from the stories of these 15 entrepreneurs? Can confidence, motivation, flexibility, community, and luck be developed and nourished?

Here are suggestions:

1. Every day, transcend your thinking mind, your business, and the world. Regenerate by tapping into the source of your energy and intelligence with the TM technique.

2. Reread the stories of the entrepreneurs you resonate with.

3. Review a meditating entrepreneur tweet each day. Spend the time to write out how you will apply it in your business. (Visit meditatinge.com/goodies for many extras including this book's 180 tweets along with other meditating entrepreneur's tweets.)

4. Take a personal inventory. Of confidence, motivation, flexibility, community, and luck, which is the strongest? Which needs the most development? Ride your strength and shore up your weakness.

5. Develop confidence: Stretch.

- Keep pushing the boundaries of your comfort zone in different areas of business life (writing, public speaking, selling, organizing, accounting).

- Practice keeping your word. Know that what you promise will come to be.

- Double down on what you enjoy. Notice what is easy and natural for you that others might find a struggle.

6. Develop motivation: Do what you love.

- Find what you love to do by trying things out, talking with friends, and journaling.

- Develop plans to monetize what you love doing.

- Make a list of the things you most want in life. Set specific goals. Write out why you want each thing. Take action. When stuck, recharge by rereading the why.

7. Be flexible: See opportunities, not problems.

- Notice difficulties in businesses you interact with. Examine challenges in your life. Discover the opportunity in each problem.

- Embrace change. Read about fast-growth technologies like Artificial Intelligence, robotics, sensors, biotech, inexpensive renewable energy, and blockchain that are dramatically changing the world. Think how you might apply one or more of them to a subject that you are passionate about.

- Make a list of your strongly held beliefs. Argue the other side.

8. Be part of a community: Join a mastermind.

- Surround yourself with people you trust.

- Form a mastermind, a group of people who will support you, brainstorm with you, and hold you accountable.

- Find your tribe locally and online — engage with people who share your passions.

9. Create the ground for luck: Go all-in.

   - When you make a decision, don't hold back, go all in. Nature supports commitment.

   - As you sow, so shall you reap. Be generous with your employees, customers, and community. Only do what you believe to be right.

   - Play the long-game. Continue to nourish the foundation of your enterprise, even if the results aren't immediate. Plant enough seeds in rich soil and some will come up.

10. Don't create your business to be happy. First be happy. Then create your business from happiness.

   - Nothing outside yourself can bring you the happiness and fulfillment you seek.

   - At best, achieving a business milestone will make you temporarily happy. Then its move on to the next challenge.

   - Practice the TM technique and each day experience the vast reservoir of happiness and peace within until happiness and peace becomes a permanent part of your every day life.

INNER PEACE, OUTER ABUNDANCE

The opposite of a great truth is also true. — Zen Koan and favorite of Nobel Prize winning quantum theory physicist, Niels Bohr.

The Fairfield meditating entrepreneurs pursued what seemed like opposite life paths: be/do; inner silence/outer dynamism; self-realization/material abundance. Yet, deep rest each day made our activity more dynamic. Equanimity and self-knowledge helped us make better business decisions which led to material success.

Our story is the story of inner freedom and outer achievement working together — silence and dynamism as part of the same reality.

We created inner peace and outer abundance in the same way — by being ourselves (big "S" and small "s"). What could be simpler and easier than being who we really are on the inside and the outside. Not being ourselves takes effort and causes strain, unhappiness, and suffering.

The TM technique is the process of doing less and less and less until we are just consciousness, aware of itself, without objects of perception, the simplest form of awareness, the Self alone by its Self. We meditate, and we just are.

We come out of our TM practice refreshed, full of energy, and in touch with our deepest aspirations. We listen to our intuition, pursue what we love, and serve others. Even if we don't create an abundance of money, we are creating an abundance of joy for ourselves and others.

We trusted our intuition and moved to Fairfield. Then we let our inner voice, enthusiasm, and generosity guide us through the ups and downs of our business journeys to live authentic, dynamic, abundant lives. We are all most grateful.

Maharishi describes it as living 200% of life:

> THE PURPOSE OF MAN'S LIFE IS TO LIVE A STATE OF UNLIMITED ENERGY, INTELLIGENCE, POWER, CREATIVITY, AND BLISS OF ABSOLUTE BEING ... MAN IS BORN TO PROJECT THE ABUNDANCE OF THE ABSOLUTE STATE OF LIFE INTO THE WORLD OF REL-ATIVE EXISTENCE ... TO BE A BRIDGE OF ABUNDANCE BETWEEN DIVINE INTELLIGENCE AND THE WHOLE CREATION.

About the Author

Hal Goldstein spent his first 35 years traveling, earning three masters degrees, and working as a social worker, software engineer, and teacher of the Transcendental Meditation technique.

In 1984, Hal and his wife Rita moved from Palo Alto, California to Fairfield, Iowa to practice the TM technique in large groups for personal development and to create an influence of peace in the world.

In Fairfield, Hal and Rita started Thaddeus Computing, which supported mobile computing users with magazines, apps, and refurbished devices. The company created magazines for HP, Microsoft, and Apple mobile computer users.

Hal semi-retired in 2011. Today the company publishes internationally distributed *iPhone Life* magazine and hosts the popular iPhoneLife.com website.

Hal teaches entrepreneurship at Maharishi University of Management where guest Fairfield entrepreneurs share their stories and wisdom. Hal based *Meditating Entrepreneurs* and the MeditatingEntrepreneur.com website on talks from the course.

Appendix A — Fairfield Entrepreneurs

Fifteen of hundreds of Fairfield meditating entrepreneurs were selected for this book. I could have easily selected a different 15 — and 15 again and 15 again and then others. Future volumes will include other Fairfield meditating entrepreneurs and their stories and wisdom.

Below are the names, companies, and websites of the 15 featured entrepreneurs along with the other meditating entrepreneurs mentioned in their stories.

Fred Gratzon	Great Midwestern, Telegroup gratzon.com/fred
Cliff Reese	Telegroup
Lawrence Sheaff	Artistabsoluteimage.net
Janet Atwood	Passion Test thepassiontest.com
Chris Attwood	The Beyul thebeyul.co
Earl Kaplan	Books are Fun booksarefun.com
Debra Poneman	Yes to Success yestosuccess.com
Marci Schimoff	Happy for no Reason happyfornoreason.com
Ed Malloy	Danaher Oild anaheroil.com
Fairfield, Iowa	cityoffairfieldiowa.com
Jim Danaher	Danaher Oil danaheroil.com
Betsy Howland	Revelationsfacebook.com
John Dey	Everybody's Whole Foods everybodyswholefoods.com
Paul Praither	Everybody's Whole Foods everybodyswholefoods.com
Jennifer Howland	Acupuncturist
Joan Allen	Revelationsfacebook.com
Julie Stephens	Art52artfiftytwo.com
Dale Stephens	Art52artfiftytwo.com
George Foster	Foster Covers fostercovers.com
Ron Flora	Word/Form Corporation

John Kremer	Book Marketing bookmarket.com
Ron Bovard	Bovard Studio bovardstudio.com
John Kremer	Book Marketing bookmarket.com
Jim Davis	Jim Davis Images jimdavisimages.com
Jim Belilove	Creative Edge creativeedgemastershop.com
Joe Mandarino	Chappell Studio
John Narducii	Chappell Studio
Brenda Narducii	Chappell Studio
Steven Winn	Seminar Crowds seminarcrowds.com
Ed Beckley	The Beckley Group
Mark Delott	Seminar Crowds seminarcrowds.com
Don Schmidt	Angel Graphics
Tim Hawthorne	Hawthorne Direct hawthornedirect.com
Monica Hadley	Aeron Lifestyle Technology aeronlifetech.com
Fairfield Accounting Services fairaccounting.com	
SEO Design Solutions seodesignsolutions.com	
Country Fresh	countryfreshinc.com
Writer's Voices	writersvoices.com
DriveTime	Fragranceraerondrivetime.com
Bryan Herr	Country Freshcountryfreshinc.com
Patrick Kosar	Aeron Lifestyle Technologyaeronlifetech.com
James Moore	KRUUwww.kruufm.com
Jeffrey Smith	SEO Designsseodesignsolutions.com
Nick Wolfe	Accounting
Margie Wood	Fairfield Accountingfairaccounting.com
Peter Huggins	Phoenix Energy, Inc. phoenixenergyinc.com
Earl Kaplan	Books are Fun booksarefun.com
Ken Seawall	Economist, Investor
Ted McLaughlin	Books are Fun, CFO

Eva Smith	Yoga University Online yogauonline.com
Tim Hawthorne	Hawthorne Direct hawthornedirect.com
Terry Smith	Body worker, Yoga therapyyogauonline.com
Hal Goldstein	Thaddeus Computing meditatingentrepreneur.com
Ron Flora	Word/Form Corporation
Susan Flora	Word/Form Corporation
David Averbach	Mango Life Media iphonelife.com
Raphael Burnes	Mango Life Media iphonelife.com
Alex Cequea	Mango Life Media iphonelife.com
Noah Siemsen	Mango Life Media iphonelife.com
Donna Cleveland	Mango Life Media iphonelife.com
Francis Thicke	Radiance Dairy facebook.com
Jim Schaefer	Soil Technologies soiltechcorp.com
Troy and	
Amy Van Beek	Ideal Energy idealenergysolar.com
Tom Factor	Maharishi University Trustee mum.edu
Doug Greenfeld	Greenfield Properties greenfieldproperties.com
Katie Greenfeld	Jefferson County Ciderworks cider.work
Ed Malloy	Danaher Oil, May Fairfield danaheroil.com
Michael Havelka	Abundance EcoVilliage abundanceecovillage.com
Ken Ross	Global ID foodchainid.com
Bill Witherspoon	Skyfactory skyfactory.com
Lonnie Gamble	Abundance EcoVilliage abundanceecovillage.com
Joe Mandarino	Chappell Studio

Appendix B —
The *Transcendental Meditation* program

The material in this appendix is reprinted by permission from the informational websites and publications of various non-profit educational organizations that teach with the TM technique and its related programs. The first section is reprinted by permission from *The TM Technique: The Transcendental Meditation® Technique: The Technique for Inner Peace and Wellness*, a 2018 informational brochure published by Maharishi Foundation, the non-profit educational organization responsible for teaching the TM program in the United States.

"The potential of every human brain is unbounded, infinite. Everyone is equipped with the physical machinery in his brain physiology to experience, through Transcendental Meditation, that level of intelligence which is the ocean of all knowledge, the ocean of all energy, intelligence, and bliss."

— Maharishi Mahesh Yogi, Founder of the Transcendental
  Meditation technique

MUM president, physicist John Hagelin answers questions about TM

John Hagelin, Ph.D., is a world-renowned quantum physicist, educator, author, and a leading researcher on the benefits of the Transcendental Meditation technique for the individual and society. Dr. Hagelin is President of Maharishi University of Management and International Director of the Global Union of Scientists for Peace. Here he answers questions about the TM technique.

What is *Transcendental Meditation?*

The Transcendental Meditation® (TM®) technique is a simple, effortless method for improving all areas of life. The technique is easily learned and is practiced sitting comfortably in a chair with the eyes closed for 15 to 20 minutes twice a day.

What happens when you meditate with the *TM* technique?

During TM practice, the active thinking mind settles down naturally to a state of "pure consciousness," where the mind is silent yet fully alert. At the same time, the body gains a profound state of rest and relaxation.

What are the benefits of this experience?

This unique state of "restful alertness" enhances brain functioning and eliminates accumulated stress and fatigue. This experience is the basis for the increased creativity and intelligence and improved health reported by people who practice the TM technique.

Is there any scientific evidence to show that the technique works?

Yes, more than 675 scientific studies on the benefits of the Transcendental Meditation technique have been conducted at 250 independent universities and research institutions, including Harvard Medical School, Cornell Medical School, University of Michigan Medical School, and UCLA Medical School.

Has the research been published?

Yes, 406 studies have been published in leading, peer-reviewed scientific and medical journals, including *Scientific American*, *Science*, the American Heart Association's *Hypertension and Stroke*, and the American Medical Association's *Archives of Internal Medicine*. Moreover, during the past 18 years, the National Institutes of Health has awarded over $24 million to study the beneficial effects of the TM technique on heart disease, hypertension, and stroke.

To practice the *TM* technique do I have to change my diet or adopt a particular lifestyle or religion?

No, the Transcendental Meditation technique does not require a change in lifestyle. Introduced by Maharishi Mahesh Yogi more than 60 years ago, the TM technique has now been learned by over five million people of all ages, nationalities, and religions. TM meditators report that the reduced stress and increased clarity of mind resulting from Transcendental Meditation practice have helped them to appreciate life more fully — and, for religious people, to follow their religions more faithfully.

Is it correct to say that all meditation techniques produce similar results?

No, there are striking physiological and neurophysiological differences between various meditation techniques. For example, EEG and brain imaging technologies clearly distinguish the TM technique from all other practices, showing enhanced EEG coherence and marked improvements in the all-important prefrontal cortex (the "CEO" of the brain), which governs such key executive functions as planning, decision making, problem solving, and judgment.

Do other meditation techniques produce similar health benefits?

Many comprehensive meta-analyses of published studies on meditation and stress-reduction techniques clearly show that the Transcendental Meditation technique produces highly beneficial effects for health that are not produced by other techniques. These include marked reductions in high blood pressure, anxiety, depression, insomnia, and other stress-related disorders.

I am a skeptic.

Being skeptical is fine. Fortunately, no belief or change in beliefs is required to learn and practice the TM technique — and to gain all the benefits. In fact, you can be 100% skeptical and the TM technique will work just work.

Three Easy Steps to Learn *TM*

1. Attend a free introductory talk by a certified TM teacher. What you'll will learn:

   • Why TM practice is so effective for stress and anxiety

   • How TM practice improves brain function and memory

   • What happens during TM practice

   • Why anyone can practice the TM technique

   • Why the TM technique works from the start

2. Meet privately with a certified TM teacher. This free personal discussion normally takes place right after the introductory talk.

3. Take the TM course — four consecutive days plus follow-up sessions:

   • Day 1 — Personal instruction (1-2 hours): One-on-one instruction in the TM technique with a certified TM teacher. Note: The TM course fee is required at this step.

   • Days 2 to 4 — Small group sessions (60-90 minutes per day): Additional guidance and instruction based on your personal experience.

   • Follow-up sessions (1 hour each): A small group session with Q&A, and a one-on-one "tune-up" session to ensure your Transcendental Meditation practice is easy and correct, and you're gaining maximum benefit.

   • Group follow-up: About 10 days after personal instruction

   • A one-on-one "tune-up" session on or after the day of the group follow-up.

   • Life-time "tune-ups" and follow-up classes are available at any *TM* Center and included in the course fee.

To find a local *TM* Center and phone number throughout the world, visit www.tm.org. In the U.S., call 888-532-7686.

Research on the *TM* technique

For more information on the more than 400 peer-reviewed research studies on the TM technique, visit the summaries of research on the Marahishi University of Management website, at https://research.mmu.edu.

These studies demonstrate that practicing the TM technique results in:

- Frontal brain coherence
- Increased use of brain reserves
- Increased creativity
- Broader comprehension and improved ability to focus
- Increased self-development
- Increased calmness
- Increased strength of self-concept
- Decreased anxiety
- Decreased depression
- Deep rest
- Improved health in university students
- Reduced illness and medical expenditures
- Reduction of high blood pressure
- Increased job satisfaction
- Improved job performance

In addition, there has been some remarkable research on the effects of the Transcendental Meditation technique on society.

References and details can be found at https://research.mum.edu.

TM Organizations

To find a local TM center and phone number throughout the world, visit, www.tm.org. In the U.S., call 888-532-7686.

Maharishi University of Management

All the students, administration, and faculty at Maharishi University of Management (MUM) practice the TM technique. The information given here is drawn by permission from the MUM website (https://www.mum.edu/about-mum#education).

Through Consciousness-BasedSM Education at MUM, students study the subjects they are passionate about while embarking on a journey of self-discovery and inner growth. As awareness expands, the ability to absorb knowledge and see the big picture improves, and students connect what they're learning to their own lives.

MUM students enjoy the block system which brings more focus and less stress. In this system, students study one subject per month full-time for up to 10 months per year. This allows them to dive into each course with undivided attention, gaining deeper understanding of each subject. The professors really get to know the students. Students don't have to juggle four to five classes, each with homework, and then have to cram in each subject for finals week.

What defines the MUM experience?

- Focus on creating a better, more peaceful world
- Supportive environment
- Professors who care about their students
- Transcendental Meditation (TM)
- Healthy lifestyle
- Commitment to sustainability
- Organic, vegetarian meals
- Creative, sustainability-focused town
- Single rooms are standard
- Leadership

Many students transfer to Maharishi University of Management

(MUM) looking for a more meaningful and less stressful educational experience. With an open, diverse, and supportive campus community, Consciousness-Based education, the block system, and the Transcendental Meditation technique as part of the curriculum, MUM is often the alternative they are looking for.

MUM at a glance

- Accreditation: MUM is accredited by the Higher Learning Commission (HLC), the accrediting agency for universities and colleges in the North Central region of the US.

- Non-profit: MUM is a federally-recognized 501(c)(3) non-profit university.

- Founder: In 1971, Maharishi Mahesh Yogi founded the University (initially called Maharishi International University) and developed Consciousness-Based Education so students could gain deep self-knowledge while studying the academic field of their choosing.

- Campus: 370 acres and 45 buildings, including the net-positive Sustainable Living Center and a 60,000-square-foot recreation center.

- 2018 Enrollment: 1,733 total students (292 undergraduate and 1,441 graduate).

- Academic programs: MUM offers undergraduate and graduate degrees on campus and online. In addition, a variety of unique enrichment programs are available online.

- Pioneer: MUM is the first university in the US to offer degrees in Sustainable Living, Regenerative Organic Agriculture, Consciousness and Human Potential, Ayurveda Wellness, Ayurveda and Integrative Medicine, and Maharishi Vedic® Science.

- Grants received: MUM has received more than $32 million

in federal and other grants, including $26 million from the National Institutes of Health.

- Campus diversity: Students from 86 countries and a wide range of religions are welcomed on campus. MUM is an LGBTQ safe zone.

- 2013-2018 commencement speakers: US Senator Tom Harkin, US Congressman Tim Ryan, filmmaker David Lynch, former Prime Minister of Japan Dr. Yukio Hatoyama, former US Deputy Secretary of Veterans Affairs Scott Gould, actor Jim Carrey.

This book is based on a course on entrepreneurship taught in the undergraduate business school. Each day of the month-long course, the author of this book invites a local entrepreneur to share his or her journey and wisdom with the class.

People frequently ask: Is MUM real? It is. MUM invites prospective students to its monthly visitors' weekends.

To learn more, visit https://www.mum.edu/.

David Lynch Foundation

Since opening its doors in 2005, the non-profit David Lynch Foundation℠ (DLF) has helped to bring the stress-reducing Transcendental Meditation technique to more than 500,000 children and adults around the world. The DLF focuses its efforts on under-served inner-city students, veterans with PTSD and their families, and women and children who are survivors of violence and abuse. The information provided here is drawn from their website at https://www.davidlynch-foundation.org/.

The mission of the David Lynch Foundation is to help prevent and eradicate the all-pervasive epidemic of trauma and toxic stress among at-risk populations by promoting widespread implementation of the evidence-based Transcendental Meditation program in order to improve health, cognitive capabilities, and performance in life.

Working with an international network of specially trained TM instructors, the David Lynch Foundation has become a global catalyst for the adoption of the Transcendental Meditation program by:

- Establishing mainstream understanding of the effects of the Transcendental Meditation program among government, health, education, media, business leaders, and the general public.

- Raising funds to implement TM pilot programs in institutions that serve at-risk populations.

- Ensuring the institutional implementation of the TM program throughout the world.

- Funding independent research on the TM program to better understand the wide-ranging effects of the technique on the brain, health, and behavior.

Appendix C — *TM* Glossary

Some of the terminology used by the entrepreneurs in this book is based on the teachings of Maharishi Mahesh Yogi. Maharishi is the Founder of the Transcendental Meditation program and of Maharishi Vedic® Technologies including the TM-Sidhi® program, Maharishi Vastu® Architecture, and Maharishi Gandharva Veda Music®.

Enlightenment — "Inner calmness, the quiet state of least excitation, even when we are dynamically busy. We cleanse the awareness of all stresses and strains, leaving the conscious mind completely free in its pure value." — tm.org

"Being is never lost irrespective of our engagements during the day or restfulness in the night. It remains permanent." — Maharishi, 1968, lecture Lake Louise, Canada

Field of all possibilities — "Completely identified in transcendental consciousness with the full potential of natural law, the human mind is a field of all possibilities spontaneously functioning in harmony with all the laws of nature, and able to accomplish anything." — *Maharishi on Modern Science and Vedic Science*, mum.edu

Knowledge is different in different states of consciousness — "When the same object is cognized in different states of consciousness, its values are differently appreciated. Life is appreciated differently at each different level of consciousness. They are as different from one another as spectacles of different colors through which the same view looks different." — Maharishi, *Bhagavad-Gita: A New Translation and Commentary, Chapters 1-6.*

Knowledge is structured in consciousness (original motto of Maharishi International University) — "The process of education takes place in the field of consciousness. The prerequisite for gaining complete education, complete knowledge — the prerequisite for knowing everything, experiencing everything, and doing everything — is to bring the awareness to the level of pure intelligence, pure knowledge, self-referral intelligence, self-referral consciousness, Transcendental Consciousness." — globalgoodnews.com

Maharishi Effect — In 1960, Maharishi Mahesh Yogi predicted that 1% of a population practicing the Transcendental Meditation technique would produce measurable improvements in the quality of life for the whole population. This phenomenon was first noticed in 1974 and reported in a paper published in 1976. The finding was that when 1% of a community practiced the Transcendental Meditation program, the crime rate was reduced by 16% on average. The meaning of the Maharishi Effect was later extended to cover the influence generated by the group practice of the TM-Sidhi program. Generally, the Maharishi Effect may be defined as the influence of coherence and positivity in the social and natural environment generated by the practice of the TM and TM-Sidhi programs.

On the basis of analogies to physical systems, scientists estimated that the coherence generated by group practice of the TM-Sidhi program should be proportional to the square of the number of participants. Taking into account the "1% finding," it was predicted that a group with size equal to the square root of 1% of a population would have a measurable influence on the quality of life of that population. For example, a group of just over 1,800 people practicing the TM-Sidhi program together in the United States would be enough to influence the 326 million 2018 population. Several published studies tracked reduction of crime and other negative variable predictions made prior to large groups practicing the TM-Sidhi programs together. — research.mum.edu/maharishi-effect.

Maharishi Gandharva Veda Music — Proper sounds played at the proper time that enlivens the moment, leading to greater success — maharishi-gandharva.com

Maharishi International University (MIU) — The original name of Maharishi University of Management when it launched in 1971 in Santa Barbara, California.

Maharishi School — A preschool to grade 12, day and boarding school with college prep academics, located on the MUM campus. The understanding and experience of the TM technique is integrated into the curriculum. — maharishischool.org

Maharishi Vastu Architecture —A building or community that has nourishing influences on its occupants. A home that promotes health, family harmony, peace and abundance. It is based on ancient principles of design and orientation in accord with natural law. — maharishivastu.org

Meditation domes — Also known at the "Golden Domes of Pure Knowledge." Two large, gold-painted, geodesic meditation halls on the Maharishi University of Management campus where hundreds of students, faculty, administrators, and Fairfield residents practice the TM and TM-Sidhi programs together twice-daily to create an influence of peace in the world.

Pure consciousness — The state of Being, completely out of the field of relativity; there is no world of the senses or of objects, no trace of sensory activity, no trace of mental activity. In this state, experienced during the TM technique, there is no trinity of experiencer, process of experiencing and object of experience. — drfredtravis.com

Self-referral — In its "self-referral" or transcendental state, consciousness knows itself alone; as such, it is the knower of itself. By being the knower of itself, it is also the object of knowledge and the process of knowing. Thus, in its self-referral state, consciousness is the unified state of knower, knowing, and known. — mum.edu

Support of Nature — "When our activity is promoted from the level of self-referral consciousness or Transcendental Consciousness, which is the home of Natural Law, then our activity is upheld by the infinite organizing power of Natural Law. This is commonly known as Support of Nature, and it can be gained not only by the individual who experiences Transcendental Consciousness through the Transcendental Meditation technique, but can even be gained by national consciousness—the collective consciousness of the nation—through the collective practice of the Maharishi Transcendental Meditation and Transcendental Meditation Sidhi programs." — Maharishi, *Science of Being and Art of Living*

The purpose of life is the expansion of happiness — "Expansion of happiness is the purpose of life, and evolution is the process through which it is fulfilled. Life begins in a natural way, it evolves, and happiness expands. The expansion of happiness carries with it the expansion of intelligence, power, creativity, and everything that may be said to be of significance in life." — Maharishi, *Science of Being and Art of Living*

TM-Sidhi program — "Transcendental Meditation allows the mind to settle down naturally and effortlessly to experience one's own Self, pure consciousness, the silent inner reservoir of creativity and intelligence that underlies all our mental activity. The Transcendental Meditation Sidhi Program cultures the ability to think and act from this profound inner silence so that thoughts and actions are maximally effective." — motherdivine.org

"Research also found when the TM and TM-Sidhi program was practiced in groups that the positive effect on the surrounding was so greatly increased that it was predicted that as little as the square root of one percent of the population would be needed to create a powerful influence of coherence for the population." — tm.org

Transcendence — The state in which the mind has moved beyond everything other than itself. It has settled down in its own authority and intelligence. — tm.org

Transcendental Meditation — The Transcendental Meditation technique is a simple, effortless method for improving all areas of life. The technique is easily learned and is practiced sitting comfortably in a chair with the eyes closed for 15 to 20 minutes twice a day — tm.org

Unified Field — Maharishi University of Management is one of the leaders in making the connection between the unified field of physics and the self-referral state of pure consciousness. Einstein believed that there was an equation for a unified field that could explain the reason for everything in existence. With this knowledge, time, space, and even humanity's origin could be deeply understood. Quantum physics, the most successful predictive theory of the universe, contains many mysteries that our current understanding of reality seems unequipped to grasp.

Quantum Physicist and MUM president, Dr. John Hagelin, explains that the foundation of the Universe is a single universal field of intelligence. Particles of nature are understood to be One, a universal ocean of pure, vibrant consciousness in motion. We are just different ripples on a single ocean of existence at the basis of everything. — mum.edu

Unity Consciousness — Full awakening that keeps unfolding. Oneness, eternal and temporal, absolute and relative. Everything in terms of the Self, myself is the Self of all. There is only One. — tmhome.com

"I am That, Thou art That, all this is nothing but That." — Maharishi

Appendix D — Bonuses

Please visit meditatinge.com/goodies to find these bonuses and more:

- A PDF with all 180 tweets in this book

- Additional tweets from more than 40 other Fairfield entrepreneurs who spoke in my class

- Audios and videos of meditating entrepreneurs

- Links mentioned in this book

- A PDF of the photos in the book in color with bonus photos

- Free chapter from the next volume of *Meditating Entrepreneurs* as soon as it's available

- Bonuses from meditating entrepreneurs Janet Attwood of the Passion Test, Francis Thicke and agriculture for the 21st Century, Hal Goldstein of *iPhone Life* magazine, Jeffrey Hedquist audio-book producer of this book, and more.

Acknowledgements

A lot of people, mostly Fairfield TM practioners and community friends, helped make this book possible.

Late in 2011, shortly after I retired, I approached Vicki Herriott, the head of the Maharishi University of Management business department and now Dean of Faculty. I asked her about teaching a course on entrepreneurship to MUM students. I would invite entrepreneurs from the Fairfield TM meditating community to share their journey and wisdom. Vicki immediately said yes. Ever since, Vicki has been a huge supporter of the class, this book, and me personally.

One day in early 2014, walking from the campus meditation dome where a thousand of us practice the TM technique and the advanced TM-Sidhi program, my friend Ken Daley asked me how the class was going. I told him how inspiring it was for all of us to hear a new entrepreneur, day after day for three weeks. He said, "It sounds like a book, an online course, and a video series." The next day after watching some of the guest videos from class, I bought a website domain name and began the book.

I then turned to my good friend, George Foster (who created both the final cover and interior layout), to mock up a cover. I reasoned if I committed to the project and saw the cover each day, the book would be a given. I only had to fill in the blank pages. George has a great sense of humor and used Photoshop to create a cover with me floating over Iowa corn fields while meditating.

The book took almost five years to write because I could work on it only an hour at a time. I wrote, edited, and rewrote each chapter many times. The experience of transforming the transcriptions from the course videos into first-person narratives, getting inside the heads of my fellow entrepreneurs, was engrossing and exhilarating.

When the featured 15 entrepreneurs volunteered to speak for an hour to my class, they didn't know I would be writing their story and pestering them for feedback. Thank you, Fred Gratzon, Janet Attwood,

Ed Malloy, Betsy Howland, George Foster, Jim Davis, Ron Bovard, Steven Winn, Monica Hadley, Peter Huggins, Eva Norlyk Smith, Francis Thicke, and Amy and Troy Van Beek for your patience and tolerance as I assumed your voices.

Thank you to the hundred-plus students who have taken the class and to the 60 different entrepreneurs who came to my class to speak. Each presentation could form another chapter as each talk seemed more inspiring then the previous. I look forward to producing more volumes of *Meditating Entrepreneurs.*

Two former students, Dusty Moon and Gde Brawiswara Putra, met regularly with me, reviewing each chapter, helping with social media, creating graphics, and taking photos. Rebecca McDowell and Catherine Castle also read chapters as I completed them, providing me with feedback.

Social media expert, Phyllis Khare, who had worked for me at *iPhone Life* magazine, gave me sage advice. In fall of 2018, I asked what I should be doing to market the book. She said, "Don't worry about it now. Just finish the book," which took me months longer than expected. From the start, I regularly received encouragement from Steven Winn, George Foster, and close friend and meditating entrepreneur, Jonas Magram.

When it was time to look for an editor, I wanted someone who was not from our Fairfield Transcendental Meditation community. A good friend, David Fisher, who originally conceived of and helped launch the MUM Sustainable Living Center, read the entire manuscript and provided feedback. David recommended Amber Lea Starfire. Amber proved a perfect choice. She edited for readability without injecting her voice, provided critical feedback, and committed wholeheartedly to the project. She helped me ensure that the content would benefit people not familiar with the TM technique or Fairfield.

I got a nice confidence boost when the new CEO of the Fairfield chamber, Darien Sloat, asked to read a late draft. He read it all and told me, as a non-TM practioner, how helpful it was to him to read the fascinating meditator-related business history of Fairfield.

Darien put me in touch with meditating entrepreneur, musician and photographer, Werner Elmker, who takes beautiful photos of Fairfield. Jim Davis and I spent several blissful afternoons going through them to select the most relevant for the book. Jim and his daughter Eugenia also helped by photographing some of the entrepreneurs and improving the look of the photos.

Hannah Nichols joined me in early 2019 to help with marketing. She has assisted in a myriad of ways, including with the website, social media, and recording short videos of the entrepreneurs.

I contacted meditating entrepreneur Jeffrey Hedquist, an audio marketing leader in his field. He not only patiently worked with us to create the audiobook, he injected a number of helpful marketing ideas.

Sam Katz, along with colleague Harbour Hodder, provided important marketing advice and feedback about proper TM vocabulary usage.

My wife and business partner, Rita, played an unusual but definitive role in the publication of this book. Rita has always supported me, encouraging discipline and focus when I was ready to jump to the next new great idea. Rita contracted a rare progressive neurological disease. Taking care of Rita the past seven years has given my life much structure while expanding my heart. I love you, Rita.

Finally, I have only gratitude for Maharishi and his knowledge. He taught me to transcend my mind and go inside to find life's answers.

* * *